THE
REFERENCE
SHELF

THE UNITED NATIONS' ROLE

IN WORLD AFFAIRS

Edited by DONALD ALTSCHILLER

THE REFERENCE SHELF

Volume 65 Number 2

THE H. W. WILSON COMPANY

New York   1993

THE REFERENCE SHELF

The books in this series contain reprints of articles, excerpts from books, and addresses on current issues and social trends in the United States and other countries. There are six separately bound numbers in each volume, all of which are generally published in the same calendar year. One number is a collection of recent speeches; each of the others is devoted to a single subject and gives background information and discussion from various points of view, concluding with a comprehensive bibliography that contains books and pamphlets and abstracts of additional articles on the subject. Books in the series may be purchased individually or on subscription.

Library of Congress Cataloging-in-Publication Data

The United Nations' role in world affairs / edited by Donald Altschiller.
    p. cm. — (The Reference shelf : v. 65, no. 2)
  ISBN 0-8242-0841-2
  1. United Nations. 2. International relations. I. Altschiller, Donald. II. Series.
JX1977.U458 1993
341.23—dc20   93-21142
                                                CIP

Cover: General view of the U.N. Security Council during a vote.
Photo: AP/Wide World Photos

Printed in the United States of America

CONTENTS

IV. THE UNITED NATIONS AND ITS CRITICS

BIBLIOGRAPHY

PREFACE

The collapse of Communism and the end of the Cold War helped to usher in an era proclaimed by former President Bush as a new world order. Indeed, in 1991 the former President helped assemble an unprecedented alliance of European, Arab and Moslem countries to repel the Iraqi invasion of Kuwait.

Yet the formation of this remarkable alliance would not have been possible without the United Nations. In an impressive demonstration of its moral and legal authority, the U.N. declared the Iraqi invasion of Kuwait morally indefensible and passed several resolutions against Iraq in the General Assembly and Security Council, allowing the military action that culminated in the complete withdrawal of Iraqi troops.

The expanding involvement of the United Nations in world affairs can be traced to several major world developments. The breakup of the Soviet Union and the dissolution of the Warsaw Pact have helped eliminate the confrontational politics that marked U.N. debate and policy for decades. As a result, the U.N. has been able to broker peace agreements from El Salvador to Cambodia. In addition, the selection of Secretary General Boutros Boutros-Ghali—a moderate Egyptian Arab who had close ties with the late Anwar Sadat—and the 1991 repeal of the Zionism-is-racism resolution have helped demonstrate the peaceful intentions of most U.N. members.

Nevertheless, war and conflict persist in many places around the world, as evidenced in daily headlines from such places as Sarajevo, Lima, and Mogadishu. Since these conflicts are considered by many people to be internecine, rather than international, the calls for U.N. intervention raise both serious legal and moral questions.

Thus, as 1992 drew to a close, the United Nations found itself with a total of twelve peacekeeping missions involving over 50,000 soldiers in trouble spots such as the Balkans, El Salvador, the Middle East, Somalia, Cambodia, Angola and the Western Sahara. At the same time, working against the U.N.'s determination and ability to bring a successful conclusion to these missions were two powerful challenges, the intractable nature and severity of the conflicts, and the organization's lack of resources and consensus.

What, then, is the proper role of the United Nations in this new post-Cold War era? This compilation contains articles that discuss and analyze the renewed and redefined role of the U.N. in world affairs.

The first section offers an overview of the United Nations. Besides providing background information, the articles describe past activities of the U.N., analyze its current role, and speculate on future prospects of the world body. The United Nations is an unique world institution. Composed of 179 member nations as of January 1, 1993, the world body conducts its affairs in six official languages and employs a huge bureaucracy with offices in every continent.

The second section deals with efforts to reform the United Nations and the complex methods needed to finance this multi-national institution.

The third section presents different views of the United Nations expressed by various governments, including the United States, China, Russia and several African states.

Although approval of the U.N. has dramatically increased in recent years, critics have not remained silent. The final section focuses on ideological criticism of the organization and contains polemical pieces from both liberal and conservative journals.

The Editor wishes to thank the H. W. Wilson General Publications staff for its assistance and to the authors and the publishers who have granted permission to reprint their material in this compilation.

DONALD ALTSCHILLER

January 1993

I. OVERVIEW OF THE UNITED NATIONS

EDITOR'S INTRODUCTION

This section presents a historical survey as well as an analysis of the present activities of the United Nations. In the first article, former Assistant Secretary of State Harlan Cleveland assesses current political, social and economic developments around the world and suggests that new concepts of international governance are needed. The second article is a brief history of the United Nations Peacekeeping Forces from their first efforts in 1948 to 1991. The Peacekeeping Forces were awarded the Nobel Prize for Peace in 1988.

In the third essay, reprinted from *Foreign Affairs*, Yale Professors Bruce Russett and James S. Sutterlin examine the U.N.'s role in the Persian Gulf War and suggest how the organization might handle future world crises. In a complementary article that appeared in *Washington Quarterly*, Edward C. Luck and Toby Trister Gati argue that the U.S. must help forge a new collective security system based on the U.N. Charter.

The final article by James E. Goodby, also from *Washington Quarterly*, explores how the explosive conflict in the former Yugoslavia has been the first test of "Peacekeeping in the New Europe."

RETHINKING INTERNATIONAL GOVERNANCE[1]

Knowledge has always been power. The wide spread of knowledge produced much progress for the growing educated fraction of the human race. But its thoughtless exercise also produced

[1]Article by Harlan Cleveland, former Assistant Secretary of State and U.S. Ambassador to NATO. *Futurist* 25:20–27 My–Je '91. Copyright © 1991 by the World Future Society. Reprinted with permission.

dirty air and water, more and more powerful weapons, and a rising backlash of second thoughts about the waste, danger, and unfairness that seemed to be the handmaidens of this progress.

The current cacophony of change—the "democracy movement" in Eastern Europe and the Soviet Union, the "greening" of politics and business, the debating of settled assumptions, and the pushiness of people wanting a voice in their own destiny—is the natural consequence of getting hundreds of millions of people educated to think for themselves and to learn to use modern information technologies.

The opportunities are enormous for what the United Nations Charter calls "peace and security" and "better standards of life in larger freedom." There are also plenty of age-old miseries to tackle afresh: shocking contrasts of poverty and affluence, human hunger in the face of technological plenty, and injustice and bigotry.

Forces for Change

Knowledge brings with it a number of forces for change in world affairs:

• **Explosive power**. A generation of mutual deterrence taught the two major nuclear powers that their "ultimate weapons" were ultimately unusable. Nuclear strategy became an information game, with deployment, arms negotiations, and crisis management among the counters in the game. The spread of nuclear weapons now creates a need for multilateral deterrence. And the speed and complexity of crisis information systems, shortening reaction time and greatly expanding the number of options available, heightens the danger of suicidal acts by political leaders.

• **Biotechnology**. A world economy built more around bio-resources could be a fairer world. Much of the world's supply of biomass and life-giving radiation from the sun are located in the tropical and subtropical lands where most of the world's poorer people live. Their poverty is not of physical resources but of knowing how to use them. Developing countries could shift comparative advantage in their favor by educating their citizens to help them understand their biotechnological potentials.

• **Communication**. The miracles of information technology could be used to reinforce control by the few and technological unemployment for the many. But they can also be used to provide new chances and choices. A society with better communications among citizens and between citizens and government will put a higher premium on early education and lifelong learning; its style of governance will be consultation and consensus, and its society will live by an ethic of dynamism and fairness rather than equilibrium and "fitting in."

• **Ecology**. The lesson of the mutual relations between organisms and their environment is basic and brutal: We interdepend or perish. Widening awareness of the dangers to global systems is creating a consensus that we had better protect and enhance the human environment we hold in common. The ecological ethic is not "limits to growth" but rather limits to thoughtlessness, waste, and neglect—which imply limits to poverty and affluence, limits to depletion and degradation of resources, and limits to the scale of armed conflicts about resources, religion, cultural identity, or anything else.

• **Fairness**. As information becomes the world's dominant resource, fairness increasingly depends on encouraging learning, permitting people to think for themselves, and rewarding brainwork about all. Fairness is a function of human rights and development. "International human rights" has become the first truly global political philosophy. But development—economic growth with fairness—is not universal. The basic fairness gap is between those who have access to modern knowledge and those who don't.

• **Cultural identity**. The desire to identify with a congenial "we" against a presumably hostile "they" is a primordial urge. The clashes of ancient religions and modern ambitions, of self-conscious ethnicity and professional solidarity, bear witness to the "inward pull of community." Far from melding the world's rich variety of cultures into a homogeneous lump, the global technologies that make us one world also help intensify a whirlwind of conflict among groups, peoples, and nations. The more congested the world, the more cultural diversity and identity must be provided for.

• **Participation**. The dominant metaphor of our time is "the right to choose." All around the world, people are breaking away from authoritarian rule because they observe that where political choice works, however messily, citizens seem to live better, with more chances to choose their personal futures. To accommodate the growing numbers of people who insist on participating in the decisions that affect them, leadership will have to be more consensual and future institutions of governance at every level will have to be loose and pluralistic.

World Problems Are Interconnected

The line between "domestic" and "international" is irretrievably blurred, and various forms of cross-border intervention—some uninvited and some by invitation—are required for reasons of security or humanity or both.

On human rights, agreed-upon worldwide norms are spelled out in much international law. But the main instrument of cross-border intervention has been information, mostly purveyed by courageous and persistent nongovernmental organizations.

Where there is a breakdown of governance (Lebanon and Cambodia are recent examples), outsiders especially concerned may need to intervene to restrain partisan violence, help build new frameworks for governance, and provide resources and technical help.

The main dangers to world security are likely to start with turbulence and terror in the poorer countries, driven by resentments about economic fairness and cultural conflict. In these conflicts, 85%–90% of the casualties are civilians, most of them children. World security requires that we organize to anticipate, deter, and mediate regional conflict, manage crises, mediate ancient quarrels where possible, isolate those that cannot yet be settled, stop wars when they break out, and restore peace after it is broken.

International terrorism—threatening or detaining or mistreating or murdering innocent bystanders for purposes of extortion—is of growing concern in international affairs. No government can even pretend to protect all its citizens wherever they are—especially if they insist on staying in a dangerous locale after warnings are given. But if governments refuse to be swayed by the plight of their kidnapped citizens, the hostages become less valuable, and travelers and workers outside their own countries are correspondingly safer.

The drug epidemic requires a major international effort on all three parts of the problem—demand, production, and trading. Bankers, educators, social agencies, and police forces—all key to attacking the drug epidemic—could organize internationally and thereby persuade their governments that this scourge needs to be taken more seriously.

There are almost as many international refugees (15 million) as there were just after World War II and an equal number of displaced persons chased from their homes inside their own countries. A permanent U.N. agency, along the lines of the U.N. High Commission on Refugees, should be set up to ensure the temporary care of people unable to return to their homes but not yet able to be resettled.

Coping with catastrophe is another cross-border function that needs more professional attention and international cooperation. Disasters will occur due to both natural causes (earthquakes, floods) and human inadvertence (Bhopal, Chernobyl). Disaster relief requires ready funding, forces and facilities in place, and the executive energy to deploy them in a hurry, in large operations in unknown places at unpredictable times.

Rethinking International Systems

We have learned much from what worked and what didn't work in this century's first two tries at "world order"—the League of Nations after 1919 and the United Nations after 1945. We have a chance now to revise the flawed assumptions on which the United Nations was built: that the world is truly a "community," that the major powers who won World War II would squash aggression by always working together, that the Western parliamentary model would apply (with nations substituted for individuals), and that the United Nations would be a way station to some kind of world government—which could too easily have become another form of oppressive authority.

The fruitful lessons of the United Nations' 46 years are found in bits and pieces, in its parcels of functional operations. Some of these are in highly political arenas, such as the codification of human rights or the unremitting pressure on South Africa to end apartheid. But most of the bright spots in international cooperation show up where new technologies make win-win situations possible—and restrain the temptation of political leaders to score debating points instead of deciding to do together what can only be done together.

Most of the daily news about international cooperation is its absence: distrust, suspicion, controversy, conflict, terrorism, and war. But many international systems—ranging from weather forecasting and international civil aviation to transnational investment and international health-care efforts—are working more or less the way they are supposed to work.

International cooperation works when there is a consensus on desired outcomes, when it's clear that no one loses, and when sovereignty is pooled rather than argued about. It takes special effort by national citizens willing to take the lead as international people.

In all the success stories, modern information technologies have been of the essence. Also, nongovernmental organizations have played key roles. Flexible, "uncentralized" management seems to work best, and the education of "local talent" is essential.

From a mix of world experience and universal aspirations, we can derive some guidelines for this "new try" at organizing international systems, the third in the twentieth century. For example, experience shows us that, under a workable system, no one country or individual is going to be "in charge." Experience has also shown us that nations, like people, can agree on next steps to be taken together if they can avoid arguments about *why* they are agreeing.

Some norms are already widely accepted, and violations are dramatic because they are rare. These include territorial integrity, the immunity of diplomatic missions and civilian aircraft and ships, and the obligation to help refugees. Slavery and colonial rule are effectively banned. Also on its way out, much more slowly, is overt official discrimination against people for being different. There is also a striking unanimity of agreement on avoiding a third world war, on protecting the air and the earth from further degradation, and on the ambition that no child should go to bed hungry.

Building New Institutions

In every part of the international system, what works best is a wide consensus on norms and standards, leaving to uncentralized systems the task of carrying ideas into action. "Consensus" doesn't mean unanimous consent. It means the acquiescence of those who care, supported by the apathy of those who don't. The lack of centralization means there is much more room for "coalitions of the willing" and for nongovernmental organizations of many kinds.

In building global institutions, we will have to get beyond the traditional U.N. formula—committees of sovereigns with a staff. Where an international capacity to act is of the essence, an extranational institution is more likely to be effective. It features a strong but collective executive that is able, from an international platform, to do policy analysis, negotiate consensus on norms and standards, keep a watchful eye on how markets and managers are carrying out agreed policies, and blow the whistle in public when such policies aren't carried out.

The finances of ongoing international functions—such as peacekeeping, development aid, and environmental protection—must be set free from the need for national legislatures to scratch their heads each year, pondering whether their international obligations should be funded. A stream of funds for such purposes should be created by international taxes on functions that crucially depend on the maintenance of a peaceful world: travel, transportation, communications, international transactions, and the use of the global commons (Earth's oceans, its atmosphere, Antarctica, and outer space).

The purposes and principles of the U.N. Charter are still a good guide for the third try at organizing international systems. But many of the Charter's procedures are outdated obstacles to cooperation and will have to be bypassed in the future of international governance. For example, U.N. peacekeeping is already done in ways not spelled out in the Charter yet consonant with its purposes. Nongovernmental organizations, largely ignored in the Charter, will play major roles in the policy analysis and consensus building that will guide most of the world's work: preventing armed conflict, regulating the world economy, and enhancing the human environment.

A Worldwide Crisis-Information Network

Managing crises now requires a worldwide crisis-information network. Space satellites, for observation and communication, can keep the world apprised of most military-related movements. Computer teleconferencing and satellite broadcasting can also play a role. But the key role will still be played by individuals who have to organize the data into information, integrate it into their knowledge base, use their intuition, and derive from all this the wisdom to foresee conflict and work to mediate and moderate it.

Conflict resolution usually needs a "third party" instantly available to talk frankly with and listen hard to both (or many) disputants. Heads of governments and U.N. secretaries general have done this, themselves or through personal representatives. There are also international courts and arbitrators. But what is needed is an international panel of conciliators, experienced people known for their independence of spirit and skill in human relations, designated ahead of time by the United Nations, who agree to drop immediately whatever else they may be doing and act for the community of nations in defusing or resolving an international conflict.

U.N. peacekeeping forces have already chalked up some notable successes. But training and funding have been left to ad hoc arrangements, different for each case as it comes up. It's high time that peacekeeping become an established part of the U.N. system, funded by the world community as a whole and recruiting and training military personnel from as many countries as possible.

A Nobody-in-Charge World

The movers and shakers in our unruly world will still be the political democracies and their market economies and the smaller countries that choose to associate with them. But their troubles at home bedevil the leaders' capabilities both to cooperate and to lead.

The United States is still first among equals: The Iraq crisis bears witness. But U.S. financial and industrial mismanagement have made it impossible for Americans to "lead with the purse." The most important thing Americans can do to create a world system that works is to get their own economic house in order.

The European Community is soon to become the world's largest single market—and potentially its greatest economic power. But Europe is a long way from having a "European" foreign and security policy; the continent is still a determined diversity of cultures and connections in search of a unified world view. But Europe is likely, in time, to act as one of several great powers in world affairs.

Japan is caught between its reluctance to lead and the world's assumption that Japan's wealth obliges it to step forward in dozens of contexts as a major partner in the United Nations, in peacekeeping coalitions, in international banks and funds, and in refugee relief and resettlement. Hard work and astute business strategies, the hallmarks of Japan's success, will sharpen these dilemmas, not cause them to go away.

The internal reforms anticipated to take place during the 1990s in the Soviet Union and Eastern Europe depend heavily on those nations' cooperation with industrial democracies and their knowledge-driven economies and on aid, loans, investment, and technical help from their more-dynamic world neighbors. Uncertainties about Western and Japanese relations with the Soviet Union will be further complicated by the wholesale revision of relations between the Kremlin and the newly feisty Soviet republics. That internal crisis makes unpredictable the pace of both conventional and nuclear disarmament and thus the Soviet role in the world security system.

China's aging leaders still don't believe the advice that Gorbachev gave them in 1989 (but didn't take seriously enough himself): You can't loosen up the economy without loosening up the political system, too. Until that lesson sinks in, with all it implies for change and reform, China will be marginal in the world economy and (except for its veto vote in the U.N. Security Council) in world politics as well.

Among the developing nations of Asia, Africa, and Latin America, no leading champion yet stands out. These countries will contain the great bulk of the world's population. Continued rapid growth of population in developing countries risks increasing their dependence on the industrial democracies—and also risks generating resentful behavior that threatens the delicate networks of the global knowledge economy.

The hope for healthy growth-with-fairness and for regional security arrangements lies not in the developing nations clubbing together to confront the world's richer minority, but in natural groupings of more-developed and less-developed countries. For example, the United States and Canada will be associated anew with Mexico, the Caribbean, northern South America, and the richer world of America south of the Amazon.

A "Club" of Democracies

As the Cold War fizzled out, all sorts of world-scale issues elbowed their way to center stage. Iraq's invasion of Kuwait, and the global coalition it brought into being, is the most dramatic of these. But many others were evident: eruptions of long-suppressed ambitions for cultural identity in Eastern Europe; the need for international machinery to anticipate, deter, and resolve conflicts around the world; the probability of vast, unprecedented migrations of people; and the need for education, which affects the behavior of whole populations.

Issues such as these become a collective responsibility. Our nobody-in-charge world system will now require a more consensual style of leadership, featuring less command and compliance and more consultation and compromise.

Each issue requires action by a different community of those concerned. A "club" of democracies is now becoming the gyroscope for world security, the world economy, and world development. It is a consultative grouping of those willing and able to act together, with a different mix of leadership for different issues. It was the core of resistance to Iraq's thrust to the south; it has been the core of U.N. peacekeeping; it is the main source of development aid; and it is the key factor in protecting Earth's environment. It is a center of initiative with a habit of consultation and an activist caucus within the United Nations and other international organizations—what Massachusetts Institute of Technology political science professor Lincoln Bloomfield calls a "coalition of the willing."

The "club," of course, is open-ended. A good many nations that were democracy's adversaries are trying now, in various ways, to chart paths to government by consent. Moreover, this informal "club" will consist more and more not only of governments, but also of nongovernmental organizations influential in world affairs.

By the beginning of the twenty-first century, it seems probable that the "club" of democracies will still provide most of the knowledge, imagination, energy, and resources required for international governance. But the broadening leadership of that informal grouping will likely make the global community, even more than it is today, a world with nobody in charge—and, therefore, with many elements of the world's breathtaking diversity partly in charge.

UNITED NATIONS PEACEKEEPING FORCES[2]

The United Nations (UN) peacekeeping forces originated in 1948 when the UN Security Council sent observers to monitor a

[2]Article from *Nobel Prize Winners, Supplement* 1987–1991. Copyright © 1992 by the H. W. Wilson Company.

truce between Israel and the surrounding Arab states. Since that time, the UN peacekeeping forces have been involved in eighteen operations around the world, helping to maintain or reestablish peace in areas that have been the scene of armed conflict. The forces consist of two distinct groups: unarmed observers, who are employed to gather information and monitor activities; and lightly armed military forces, who are employed to separate hostile parties and maintain security.

Many of the conflicts in which the UN peacekeeping forces have intervened are the direct result of the fall of the British empire. From the mid-nineteenth until the early twentieth century, Great Britain had been the world's greatest military and political power. Large parts of Africa, Asia, and the Middle East were under British control. After World War I, however, British influence in the world began to weaken, declining even further during the years of the Great Depression. In the two decades after the end of World War II, Britain granted independence to most of the nations in what had been its empire. The withdrawal of British control left power vacuums in many regions of the world, precipitating a number of regional conflicts that continue to the present day.

In 1922 the land of Palestine was placed under British control by the League of Nations, an international organization founded at the end of World War I. The League of Nations hoped that, under the guiding hand of Great Britain, Palestine would emerge as an independent, self-governing nation. Britain, however, found it impossible to settle the continuing conflict between Arabs and Jews, both of whom had historical claims to the land. The problem escalated after World War II, when Jewish immigration to Palestine increased drastically.

In 1947 the United Nations—successor to the League of Nations—proposed a partition plan by which the land of Palestine would be divided into an Arab state and a Jewish state. Despite protests from the Palestinian Arabs, this plan was implemented on May 14, 1948, when Great Britain withdrew from Palestine. Israel, the Jewish state, declared its independence and was almost immediately attacked by the armies of five surrounding Arab states: Lebanon, Syria, Iraq, Transjordan (now Jordan), and Egypt. After several weeks of fighting, the UN was able to persuade the disputing countries to declare a truce.

In order to make sure that the truce would hold, the UN Security Council sent a group of observers to the area. Originally, the observers consisted of a few soldiers and members of the UN Secretariat. The logistics of their operation were largely improvised and their ability to communicate with one another was limited. They were, however, able to provide reliable reports to the United Nations of any violations of the truce agreement. By 1949 this ad hoc group of observers had evolved into an official body called the United Nations Truce Supervision Organization (UNTSO). The UNTSO remains active today, with observers stationed in Israel, Egypt, Jordan, Lebanon, and Syria.

While Israel and its Arab neighbors were quarreling over the future of Palestine, India and Pakistan were fighting for control of the tiny province of Kashmir. India had been under British rule since the eighteenth century. On August 15, 1947, Great Britain withdrew from India, leaving behind two independent states: the Muslim state of Pakistan and the Hindu state of India. Kashmir, whose leadership was Hindu but whose population was primarily Muslim, was claimed by both countries. The armed conflict over Kashmir ended in July 1948, when the United Nations succeeded in arranging a cease-fire. In 1949, inspired by the success of its observer group in the Middle East, the UN Security Council sent a similar group—the United Nations Military Observer Group in India and Pakistan (UNMOGIP)—to monitor the cease-fire. The dispute remains unsettled, but the cease-fire holds and a small observer force remains in the area today.

Meanwhile, the troubles in the Middle East continued. The Suez Canal, controlled by Great Britain since 1875, was suddenly nationalized by Egypt in 1956. Britain, France, and Israel attacked Egypt in retaliation. Worldwide opinion condemned the invasion. The UN Security Council realized that unarmed military observers would not be able to handle this conflict, which had spiraled into a major international crisis. It therefore sent an armed peacekeeping force to separate the combatants. The new force, called the First United Nations Emergency Force (UNEF I) supervised the withdrawal of foreign troops from Egyptian territory. The force also served as a buffer along the Egyptian-Israeli border and in the Gaza strip (a narrow band of land situated between the two countries, bordering on the Mediterranean Sea). By the summer of 1957, UNEF I had proven its ability to maintain stability in the region.

The use of armed forces to make peace was an unprecedented step for the United Nations, and it was taken only after significant debate and reflection. In 1956 UN secretary-general DAG HAM-

MARSKJÖLD defined a set of principles to guide the use of peace-keeping forces—principles that are still followed today. Under Hammarskjöld's guidelines, a UN peacekeeping force may not intervene in a conflict without the permission of the disputing parties; it must achieve its goals by means of negotiation and persuasion rather than violence; it may take orders only from the UN Security Council; and it must be supported financially by all the member nations of the United Nations.

Since the time when Hammarskjöld first articulated these guidelines, UN peacekeeping forces—both observer groups and military troops—have played a significant role in ending conflicts and maintaining stability in trouble spots all over the world [among them Lebanon in 1958 and West Irian (New Guinea) in 1962]. In 1960, for example, when Belgium granted independence to the Congo (now Zaire), Belgians living in the former colony responded with violent protests. Belgium sent in troops to quell the uprisings, but the Congo government, seeking to preserve its independence, considered this an unwelcome invasion. A UN peacekeeping force (ONUC) was dispatched to supervise the withdrawal of Belgian forces and to prevent civil war in the country.

Also in 1960, the island of Cyprus, which had long been the object of disputes between Greece and Turkey, officially declared its independence. Although its new constitution was carefully designed to allow Greek Cypriots and Turkish Cypriots to share power equally, the country soon erupted into civil war. In 1964 a UN peacekeeping force (UNFICYP) was sent to Cyprus, where, for a decade, it prevented war between the ethnic groups.

In 1967, after the Six-Day War, which pitted Egypt, Syria, and Jordan against Israel, a UN peacekeeping force (UNEF II) was assigned to monitor the truce agreement between the countries. In 1974, after an attack on Israel by Egypt, Jordan, and Syria, another peacekeeping force (UNDOF) was installed in the Golan Heights, on the western border of Syria, to maintain a buffer zone between Israeli and Syrian forces.

In the 1970s the Palestine Liberation Organization (PLO)—a coalition of Palestinian groups whose goal is to liberate their homeland from what they view as an illegitimate Israeli occupation—began a series of terrorist acts against Israel. In 1978 Israel retaliated against a PLO raid by invading Lebanon, which was then a PLO stronghold. Following this invasion, the UN established the United Nations Interim Force in Lebanon

(UNIFIL), an unusually large peacekeeping force whose duties included monitoring Israeli troop withdrawal, maintaining peace among Lebanon's warring ethnic factions, and helping the Lebanese government reestablish its authority. UNIFIL did succeed in having the Israeli troops withdraw, although the conflicts continue.

In 1988, at the conclusion of an eight-year war between Iran and Iraq, the United Nations installed a peacekeeping force (UNIMOG) along the border between the two countries to observe the withdrawal of troops and to monitor any violations of the cease-fire agreement. [That same year a peacekeeping mission was sent to monitor the withdrawal of Soviet troops from Afghanistan and the return of refugees who had fled to Pakistan.]

Shortly thereafter, the UN peacekeeping forces received the 1988 Nobel Prize for Peace. In presenting the award, Egil Aarvik of the Norwegian Nobel Committee called the UN forces "a tangible expression of the world community's will to solve conflicts by peaceful means." He explained, "The technological development of weapons systems has resulted in the peaceful resolution of conflicts becoming the only realistic possibility. Nuclear weapons have made the concept of wielding total power an absurdity. In conflict situations it is therefore vitally necessary that there are openings where real negotiations can be initiated."

Aarvik pointed out that despite the acknowledged success of the UN peacekeeping forces, "confidence in the United Nations has otherwise been a variable factor. The United Nations has for many been seen as a body without power or effectiveness. . . . This year's peace prize is a recognition and homage to one organ of the United Nations. But it ought to be understood as a serious comment on the fact that we must, united and with our whole hearts, invest in the United Nations."

UN secretary-general Javier Pérez de Cuéllar accepted the prize on behalf of the peacekeeping forces. In his Nobel lecture, he pointed out that despite regional conflicts in many parts of the world—conflicts in which the United States and the Soviet Union, with their immense nuclear arsenals and broad political interests, might easily have become involved—the UN had played a significant role in preventing serious confrontations between East and West. At the time Pérez de Cuéllar accepted the award, there were already signs that the Soviet Union would abdicate its position as a world superpower, and the prospect of a third world war looked increasingly unlikely. Nevertheless, he said, "the community of nations . . . [is] now encountering a new generation of global problems which can only be faced effectively through an unprecedented degree of international cooperation." He suggested that the notion of peacekeeping—"the use of soldiers as a catalyst for peace rather than as the instruments of war"—may be the key to resolving international disputes in the future. To be successful, however, a peacekeeping operation "must have a workable and realistic mandate fully supported by the international community." He urged the countries of the world to support the UN peacekeeping activities both logistically and financially.

The annual cost for the UN peacekeeping operation continues to rise. In 1988, considering the imminent deployment of forces in other areas, such as southern Africa, the western Sahara, and Cambodia, Pérez de Cuéllar calculated that the cost could reach $1.5 billion a year. In a news conference in December 1988, he expressed his fear that the Nobel Prize might turn out to be "a posthumous award" for the UN peacekeeping forces unless governments show greater willingness to pay for them in the future. Financing the peacekeeping forces has been a longstanding problem for the UN, partly because member nations have tended to withhold portions of their annual dues for various political reasons. Also, despite Dag Hammarskjöld's directive that the cost of the peacekeeping forces be shared by all UN members, many governments have maintained that the forces should be paid for only by interested parties.

Today's UN peacekeeping forces, made up of military personnel from fifty-eight countries from every continent, are made available by the Security Council upon request. They are most often dispatched to areas where a cease-fire has been established but a formal peace treaty has not yet been drawn. They are generally placed in a buffer zone between the disputing parties so that if hostilities resume, the combatants will confront the UN troops first.

UN soldiers wear the military uniforms of their own nations, but they also wear distinctive blue caps or helmets that identify them as members of the peacekeeping force. They carry light defensive weapons, which they use only when necessary for self-protection. (Members of observer groups carry no weapons at all.) As of 1988, 764 soldiers had died while serving in the UN peacekeeping forces.

Since winning the Nobel Prize in 1988, the UN peacekeeping

forces have been involved in several additional operations. In December 1988 a force was sent to Angola (UNAVEM) to monitor the departure of occupying Cuban troops. In April 1989 another force was sent to Namibia to help the former South African colony make the transition to independence. In September 1989 a force (ONUCA) was sent to Central America to patrol the borders around Nicaragua, whose government—under the control of the left-wing Sandinista party—had been offering military assistance to leftist insurgents in neighboring El Salvador. By halting the flow of Nicaraguan guerrillas to El Salvador, and by disarming members of the contras (Nicaraguan rebels who opposed the Sandinista government), the UN force hoped to prevent further fighting in both countries.

Most recently, in April 1991, after a coalition of international military forces led by the United States compelled Iraq to withdraw from its violent annexation of Kuwait, a UN peacekeeping force (UNIKOM) was sent to the area to supervise troop withdrawal, monitor Iraq's adherence to the cease-fire agreement, and serve as a buffer along the Iraq-Kuwait border. [Since this article was written, UN peacekeeping forces have been sent to Cambodia, Yugoslavia, El Salvador and Somalia.]

THE U.N. IN A NEW WORLD ORDER[3]

The new world order envisioned by Presidents Bush and Gorbachev would be founded on the rule of law and on the principle of collective security. That principle necessarily entails the possibility of military enforcement measures by the United Nations. Twice in its history the Security Council has authorized such action. The first instance was in the Korean War in 1950; the second was in the Persian Gulf in 1990. More occasions are likely to follow.

The U.N. Charter gives the Security Council the authority "to

[3]Article by Bruce Russett, Professor of International Relations and Political Science at Yale University and James S. Sutterlin, former Director of the Executive Office of the U.N. Secretary General. From *Foreign Affairs* 70:69–83 Spring '91. Copyright © 1991 by the Council on Foreign Relations, Inc. Reprinted with permission.

maintain or restore international peace and security," and to enforce the will of the council on a state that has broken the peace. Use of military force by the council for these purposes was foreseen by the founders of the United Nations. Indeed it was seen almost half a century ago as an essential element in the world order that the United Nations was intended to establish. Should the need arise, countries would be protected from aggression by forces provided to the Security Council by member states, serving as a U.N. army at the council's will. Military forces, however, have not been available to the council on this basis and improvisation has therefore been required. The action taken by the Security Council in response to the Iraqi invasion of Kuwait amounted to just that—an improvisation to permit enforcement of the council's will without the specific means provided in the charter for that purpose.

Military force has much more frequently been used by the United Nations for the purpose of peacekeeping, something not foreseen in the charter at all. This improvisation was first devised in haste to facilitate an end to the 1956 hostilities in the Middle East. Since that beginning, which amply demonstrated the value of the technique, U.N. use of military and civilian personnel provided by member states for peacekeeping has become a well-established practice now supported by all the major powers.

The use of military force by the United Nations for both of these purposes—enforcement and peacekeeping—is surely essential to a world order in which international security is heavily dependent on the Security Council. The experience of the Gulf War and of the more distant past offers important lessons and raises trenchant questions as to how this can most effectively be done in the gulf (as action moves from military victory to the maintenance of peace in the region) and wherever else peace may be endangered.

II

Since the Suez crisis of 1956, the United Nations has developed a notable elasticity in using peacekeeping forces, to the point that it is now difficult to formulate a precise definition—or the limits—of what peacekeeping functions may be. The original role of standing between hostile forces has been expanded to encompass, among other functions, the maintenance of security or stability within a given area (as in southern Lebanon), the monitoring of elections (Namibia, Haiti), the provision of human-itarian assistance (Cyprus) and the disarmament of insurgents (Nicaragua). This flexibility greatly increases the value of peace-keeping forces as an instrument available to the Security Council in dealing with potential or existing conflicts. For example, the permanent members of the Security Council have recently devel-oped a plan to bring peace to Cambodia that would use peace-keeping forces—both military and civilian—for broad purposes of pacification, stabilization and administration.

Three limitations on the use of peacekeeping have been con-sistently honored: (1) peacekeeping has been interpreted, as orig-inally articulated by U.N. Secretary General Dag Hammarskjöld, as a provisional measure under the U.N. Charter, that is, as a measure undertaken without prejudice to the rights, claims or positions of the parties concerned; (2) peacekeeping operations have been undertaken only with the consent of all the parties concerned; (3) peacekeeping forces may use arms only in self-defense. Again in accordance with the original decision by Ham-marskjöld, U.S. and Soviet troops have never been included in peacekeeping forces.

In domestic conflicts the consent of all the parties is likely to remain a compelling requirement. It was clearly shown in non-U.N. peacekeeping undertakings, in Lebanon in 1983–84 and more recently in Liberia, that without the consent of the parties grave risks are involved and the results can be disastrous. This may not, however, be the case in interstate conflicts. When peace-keeping forces are deployed between hostile forces after a truce or ceasefire has been achieved, an essential purpose is to deter a renewal of hostilities. In this sense deterrence is already an ac-cepted function of peacekeeping. Yet in interstate conflicts a situ-ation could well arise in which peacekeeping forces are needed for deterrence purposes but the consent of one of the parties is not obtainable. This should not, a priori, preclude a Security Council decision to deploy them if the other characteristic limita-tions are maintained.

The situation in the gulf could present the council with pre-cisely such a need, as a long-term settlement of hostilities is sought. Some sort of convincing deterrent force will be needed to prevent renewed threats against Kuwait and, conceivably, to mon-itor any demilitarized zones that may be established. For the near term, further military adventures are unlikely. But in the long run, neither Iraqi motives and potential for revenge nor the ambitions of one or more of its neighbors can be ignored. Whatever misgivings some parties may have about the U.S.-led gulf operation, they have excellent reasons to converge on some sort of substantial U.N. presence in the gulf in the future. The emergence of the United Nations as an important institution for promoting international security can moderate any revival of Soviet-American tensions that might stem from disagreements regarding the gulf or other regions.

U.S. and Soviet forces could be usefully included in such an operation to ensure, through its size and composition, maximum credibility. But to be acceptable to the majority of U.N. members such a force must retain an indisputable U.N. identity and must not be dominated by one member state. In other border disputes—of which many exist—a comparable need for deterrence may arise, preferably under circumstances that would permit deployment of peacekeeping forces before hostilities actually occur. Indeed, if at the request of Kuwait a peacekeeping force had been deployed on its border with Iraq in August 1990, the Gulf War might have been avoided.

It is worth emphasizing that nothing in the charter prohibits the Security Council from deploying peacekeeping forces without the consent of all the parties, or from including troop contingents from the permanent members of the council in such forces where the need for deterrence arises. (U.S. and Soviet military personnel already serve in U.N. military observer missions.) Such action would still fall under the definition of a provisional measure to be taken by the council "to prevent an aggravation of the situation" before deciding on enforcement action as foreseen in Articles 41 and 42 of the U.N. Charter. The provision of troops by member states for such deterrence operations would remain voluntary, as in other peacekeeping missions, with financing determined on an ad hoc basis by the council, either through assessment of all members or through payment of the cost by the countries requesting the deployment, as could be the case in a situation like the gulf where wealthy states are involved as parties.

The command structure need be no different from other peacekeeping operations: a commander of the U.N. force is appointed by the secretary general after the peacekeeping operation has been authorized by the Security Council for a defined mission. Troop contingents provided by member states serve under their national officers—a battalion commander, for example—who in turn receives orders from the U.N. force commander. The U.N. force commander reports to the secretary general from whom he receives operational guidance. The secretary general reports to the Security Council and obtains its concurrence if any change in the mission of the peacekeeping force is contemplated.

One can question whether it will be logistically feasible for the United Nations to mount, and maintain over a period of time, peacekeeping operations of sufficient size to provide a credible deterrent. It can only be said that where the need for peacekeeping has been evident, as in Namibia, the magnitude of required support has not inhibited action.

A good number of countries might well oppose in principle the idea of deploying peacekeeping forces without the consent of all the parties concerned, fearing that it would open the way to action contrary to their own national interests. Unlike the United States and the other four permanent members of the Security Council, they would not enjoy the protection of the veto. When a similar idea was put forward some years ago, in the course of confidential consultations in the Security Council on how its effectiveness might be enhanced, there was little response. The Gulf War has served, however, to heighten interest in effective deterrence using multilateral means not under the domination of one or several U.N. members. There is certainly now a broad recognition that adequate means of deterrence will be essential to a peaceful world order.

III

The second broad purpose for the Security Council's use of military force falls largely under the heading of compellence, or coercion, rather than simply deterrence. In the context of the Security Council such action is best understood as enforcement action. Use of "air, sea or land forces" for enforcement is specifically foreseen in Chapter VII, Articles 39–46 of the U.N. Charter, in which all members undertake to make available to the Security Council "on its call and in accordance with a special agreement or agreements, armed forces, assistance and facilities, including rights of passage, necessary for the purpose of maintaining international peace and security."

Since no such special agreements have been concluded, no standing multilateral force has been available to the Security Council. Therefore the Security Council authorized the use of ad hoc forces to restore international peace in Korea and the Persian

Gulf. When the North Korean attacks on South Korea were formally brought to the Security Council's attention, the council's resolution of July 7, 1950—adopted in the temporary absence of the Soviet Union—called on member states to assist South Korea in resisting the North Korean aggression. It recommended "that all members providing military forces and other assistance pursuant to the aforesaid Security Council resolutions make such forces and other assistance available to a unified command under the United States." It requested further that the United States designate the commander of such forces. The same resolution authorized use of the U.N. flag.

Thus in the case of Korea the Security Council requested one member state to lead a combined effort on behalf of the United Nations to resist aggression. Notwithstanding his designation as commander of U.N. forces in Korea, General Douglas MacArthur, the commander named by the United States, never reported directly to the Security Council. (Routine, unclassified status reports were provided by the United States.) Neither the Military Staff Committee—a body composed of military representatives of the five permanent members intended to advise the council on military matters—nor the council itself had any role in directing military operations of the unified command. The General Assembly did, however, establish a three-nation ceasefire committee that sought a formula to end the war, and the secretary general suggested the procedure of direct talks between the military commanders that was ultimately followed and through which an armistice was achieved.

The advantages offered by this procedure were:

• Expeditious action to resist aggression. Only the United States had troops deployed in South Korea capable of taking quick military action.

• The unambiguous command structure needed for large-scale field operations.

• A practical way to meet the responsibilities of the United Nations under the charter in the absence of a multilateral force under the Security Council for which the necessary agreements with member states had not been reached.

• Validation of the concept of collective security, since states acted jointly in response to Security Council (and subsequently General Assembly) decisions.

The disadvantages of this procedure (which became more evident in the course of time) were:

• The United Nations lacked control or influence over the

course of military action or the precise purposes for which it was exercised (e.g., to repel and punish aggression, to reunify the country).

• The military operation became identified with the policy of the nation leading the effort rather than with the United Nations.

• Divisive forces within the United Nations were encouraged by the dominant role of one member state pursuing goals not universally shared.

• Opportunities were afforded the aggressor to identify the struggle with one country, the United States, rather than with the international community as a whole.

All of these disadvantages were intensified in the Korean case by the bitter disagreements that prevailed at the time between the Soviet Union and the United States. Under conditions of harmony among the permanent members of the Security Council, these various disadvantages could have considerably less force.

In the Persian Gulf crisis the Security Council authorized, albeit in oblique language, the use of force for enforcement in another interstate conflict. After imposing a comprehensive embargo in order to bring about Iraqi withdrawal from Kuwait and the restoration of its legitimate government, the council called upon "those member states cooperating with the government of Kuwait which are deploying maritime forces to the area to use such measures commensurate to the specific circumstances as may be necessary under the authority of the Security Council . . . to ensure strict implementation" of the provisions laid down in the resolution relating to economic sanctions. Then, in Resolution 678 of November 29, 1990, the Security Council authorized "member states cooperating with the government of Kuwait . . . to use all necessary means to uphold and implement Security Council Resolution 660 and all subsequent relevant resolutions and to restore international peace and security in the area." All states were requested to provide appropriate support for "the actions undertaken."

This action, with specific reference to Chapter VII of the charter, constituted a new approach to implementation of the collective security concept. As in the earlier enforcement action in Korea, when there was no reference to Chapter VII, a basis for the council to mobilize a U.N. force for military enforcement action did not exist. Therefore the council again turned to member states to act in its behalf through such measures as might be necessary. But this time no unified command was established, and the use of the U.N. flag was not authorized.

The gulf action became possible because the permanent members of the Security Council cooperated on a matter of peace and security in the way originally foreseen when the United Nations was founded. Representatives of the United States and the Soviet Union have repeatedly suggested that such action is an important element in a new world order; that is, a world in which nations will be secure because of the capacity of the United Nations to guarantee their security through collective measures. This fundamental goal of the United Nations is unquestionably brought closer through the sustained cooperation and a notably increased commonality of interests among the major powers, evident not only in the Gulf War but also in other conflicts such as Cambodia and Angola. Two questions nonetheless warrant careful examination: Is the approach that was taken to enforce the council's decisions with regard to the Iraq-Kuwait crisis necessarily a viable model for implementing collective security in the future? Is there a realistic alternative that would offer greater advantages?

IV

With regard to the first question, it is clear that the Security Council, in deciding on action to counter the Iraqi aggression, prescribed action for all member states. While it authorized individual states to take "the necessary action," it requested "all states to provide appropriate support for the actions undertaken." Thus all states were called on to assist in defending one state, Kuwait, from aggression. Actions to be taken for this purpose would seem clearly to constitute "effective collective measures for the prevention and removal of threats to the peace, and for the suppression of acts of aggression" as foreseen in Article 1 of the charter.

But the procedure adopted is not without its difficulties. The Security Council has no means of controlling when, how or in what degree the collective measures are applied. In the gulf case, the states concerned were only requested "to keep the council regularly informed"; some measures taken might not have had majority support in the Security Council or the General Assembly. The state that is in command may have from the outset an interpretation of U.N. goals different from that of other Security

Council members, or its aims may become more expansive in the course of the operation. The latter happened in Korea with the U.S. decision to cross the 38th parallel and try to reunify the country by force. It would have been the case in the gulf had the United States pursued military action beyond the Kuwaiti theater of operations.

If the measures taken cease to have the endorsement of the majority of the Security Council, can they still be considered collective measures taken in the council's behalf? This problem is inherent in a procedure in which action is taken on behalf of the council but without any council control over the nature, timing or extent of the action. The major danger is that the entire undertaking will be identified with the country or countries actually involved in military action rather than with the United Nations. In any case, many U.N. members will not view the military action as an appropriate application of collective security if the action appears to conflict with the Security Council's goals.

The gulf operation and the terms for ending military action against Iraq offer a case in point. None of the 12 Security Council resolutions called for eliminating Iraq's war-making capability or deposing Saddam Hussein. But the former clearly became a goal of some coalition members, and the latter was widely suspected. President Bush and the coalition partners felt free to give their own interpretation to the Security Council resolutions. Those members, including the Soviet Union, that interpreted the resolutions more narrowly may be reluctant next time to give such unconstrained authority to member states acting on the council's behalf. In any operation, if the Security Council has asserted no control over the military action authorized, will it be possible for it to assert control over the terms of peace?

Such questions indicate the problems that can arise when a procedure such as that developed for the Gulf War is followed. Moreover the approach adopted in the gulf case is not likely to be viable unless vital interests of one or more major military powers are at risk. For example, the United States might not be interested in deploying substantial forces, even if authorized to do so by the Security Council, to deter or repel an Egyptian attack on Libya.

V

There are alternative procedures that might in the future be followed by the Security Council, ones that would offer the prospect of effective enforcement action without the disadvantages and problems associated with according responsibility to individual member states.

One would be a variant of the procedure followed in Korea. National forces could be brought together in ad hoc fashion under a unified U.N. command, with the commander designated by whichever happened to be the major troop-contributing country. The problems that arose in the Korean case could conceivably be alleviated if the unified commander were required to consult with the Security Council, or with some form of military authority appointed by the council, on the mission of the military operation and the basic strategy to be followed in achieving it. The country supplying the major troop contingent can be expected to resist such a procedure as inhibiting unacceptably the freedom of action of the commander and subjecting its forces to perilous uncertainties. But if favorable relations among the permanent members of the Security Council persist, such a consultative, though not command, procedure might be feasible. It would have the distinct advantage of maintaining a close U.N. identification with all action taken and of giving the Security Council some influence, if not control, over any military action.

The other alternative is the procedure defined in Articles 42 and 43 of the U.N. Charter, according to which all members of the United Nations undertake "to make available to the Security Council on its call in accordance with a special agreement or agreements, armed forces, facilities and assistance." In the Korean War, the "uniting for peace" resolution of 1950 recommended that each member maintain within its armed forces earmarked units so trained that they could promptly be made available for service "as a United Nations unit or units."

The hostile relations between the United States and the Soviet Union were long perceived as the major obstacle to implementing such provisions. If after the Gulf War the two countries remain in accord on using the United Nations, that obstacle may be lifted. The willingness of member states to commit themselves in advance to provide troops and facilities at the request of the Security Council for enforcement purposes has never been tested. It can be argued that such commitment is inherent in U.N. membership, a condition for which is acceptance of the obligations contained in the charter and ability and willingness to carry out those obligations. For such a commitment to be reliable, however, it must be embodied in agreements between the Security Council and those member states prepared to assume the obligations. Such commitments will not be undertaken lightly.

The subject was discussed in detail in 1945 in the U.S. Senate when the U.N. Charter was under consideration. John Foster Dulles, a member of the U.S. delegation to the San Francisco conference at which the charter was signed, told the Senate Foreign Relations Committee that an agreement with the United Nations on the provision of troops should be regarded as a treaty requiring approval of a two-thirds majority of the Senate. The recorded comments of the senators indicate wide agreement with that interpretation. It was also discussed whether the president would need to obtain the consent of Congress to provide troops, when called upon by the United Nations after completion of an agreement. No consensus emerged on the question, but one senator suggested at the time that the size of the force requested could be decisive. Two or three thousand troops for "police action" would not need congressional approval, whereas a battle force would.

Soviet representatives have recently expressed a positive view of a U.N. agreement on the provision of troops for enforcement purposes, but they have emphasized that in no case could the troops be provided without the specific approval of the Soviet parliament.

Once agreements on the provision of troops were completed with a fair portion of member states, the Security Council would have the capacity to call into being a multilateral force (land, sea and air) under a U.N. commander "to maintain or restore international peace and security." In military operations the commander would presumably have full tactical authority but would operate under the guidance of the Security Council or a body established by the council to serve this purpose. Subsequent understandings would be required on command, intelligence, logistics and other more or less centralized functions. The Military Staff Committee could, as foreseen 46 years ago, "advise and assist the Security Council on all questions relating to military requirements." It could do this without acquiring any command authority, which would be inadvisable since it functions on the basis of consensus.

In some ways a U.N. force of this type would be quite similar to a peacekeeping force, since it would be made up of troops provided by member states and would have a U.N. commander. It would differ markedly, however, in mission, armament, composition and command.

A U.N. force of this nature would not entail the problems and disadvantages that the other identified approaches could present. Identification with the United Nations from initiation to end of any operation would be assured, and control could be clearly in the hands of the Security Council. The likelihood of sustained support among U.N. members for the action undertaken would be strong. Yet in this approach, too, likely problems can be identified.

First of all, it is not clear how many states will be willing to conclude the agreements foreseen in the U.N. Charter—or how long this will take. It can only be said that international circumstances, especially in the wake of the Gulf War, appear more favorable than at any time since 1945. It is also questionable whether a force as large and elaborately equipped as one needed to maintain peace in the gulf, for example, could have been organized quickly on this basis. Any very large operation is bound to depend heavily on a major contingent from one or more of the principal military powers; the larger and more sophisticated the contingent provided, the less likely the contributing country will be willing to place it under non-national command.

Organization and deployment of a multilateral force by the Security Council would likely require more time than if action were delegated to one or more member states, especially if a large-scale operation were foreseen. To shorten the lead time, the secretary general might be given authority, not subject to the veto, to send an unarmed observer corps to any international border at any time. According to Article 99 of the U.N. Charter, the secretary general "may bring to the attention of the Security Council any matter which in his opinion may threaten the maintenance of international peace and security." To do so he needs to be informed. An authorization to send observers without specific consent of the parties raises difficulties, but it would allow the Security Council to be forewarned and to make quick preparations if an enforcement action were required. The very presence of observers can have a deterrent effect, possibly avoiding the need for subsequent enforcement.

Then, too, there is a very basic question as to whether a military action can be successfully carried out under multilateral strategic command, or as successfully as under national command. Administrative aspects of managing the use of force by the Security Council have received little attention. Save for peacekeeping and the peculiar conditions permitting the Korean operation, the prospects of using U.N. forces were nil during the Cold War.

Nonetheless important multinational dimensions characterized U.S. military plans during the Korean War, in the U.S. commitment to NATO and notably in the Persian Gulf.

The force of the NATO and Korea precedents must not be exaggerated. In both instances there was virtual consensus on the nature of the military threat, decades-long experience of close cooperation and, in Europe, a high degree of cultural and political homogeneity—far more than likely in most future U.N.-sanctioned operations. If the United States should put its forces under another state's commander, one would have to expect a relatively much smaller contribution of U.S. troops and financing than in the gulf operations. By its treaty commitments and geographic deployment, however, the United States stood a great chance of being involved in any military operations in Europe and Korea. Any U.N. enforcement action would have to be authorized by the Security Council and would thus be subject to U.S. veto. This fact should reassure Congress.

One question inherent in any big multilateral action concerns the level at which integration of command of multinational forces would occur. The distinction in U.S. military terminology between command and operational control (OPCON) is useful in this respect. Command applies to such matters as discipline, pay, morale and logistics; most of these (perhaps not logistics) would be carried out at the level of the national military contingents. OPCON is likely to be different. If U.S. troops were involved there would probably have to be, under an overall U.N. commander from some country, a U.S. "component commander" operating with substantial independence. OPCON can be decentralized by confining each member's forces to a specific sector, physically dividing up the ground, as has been done in most U.N. peacekeeping operations.

Some other functions may be even harder to divide than OPCON. Intelligence gathering, for example, will be dominated by states with vast technological capacities for overhead and electronic surveillance. In the gulf operation other coalition members presumably accepted U.S. control of intelligence, but if there were substantial Soviet participation the Soviets would likely not accept it. Secure communications would be required among participating forces in the field, either through sharing encryption (politically very sensitive) or cumbersome procedures for transmission and delivery. It is likely that some states will be unable or unwilling to provide adequate logistical support for their troops, and that those with the motivation and ability to do so will have to provide for others. Some U.N. "headquarters" personnel and facilities will be required for these functions, probably drawing on the experience and capabilities of the secretary general's staff.

The problem of financing such military actions demands careful attention. The history of financing past peacekeeping efforts by voluntary contribution is, to say the least, not encouraging. The gulf operation was heavily dependent on the willingness and ability of the most deeply involved states—the United States, Saudi Arabia and Kuwait—to pay most of the immediate costs, and in turn their willingness depended upon their ability to control the means and ends of military operations. A future operation that less directly engaged the interests of such states would have to rely on broader support, probably through an assessment of all member governments. Reasonably complete and prompt payment of those assessments would have to be assured.

Such problems may be equally severe for the peacetime maintenance of standing earmarked forces. Unless any additional costs incurred can be covered by the United Nations, Third World states may be unable to participate. Certain central (non-state-specific) services, such as administration, intelligence, command and control, perhaps logistics and transport, must be prepared and institutionalized in advance. Provision in the regular budget of the United Nations might cover such ongoing costs of multilateral readiness, with special assessments made to cover the cost of any enforcement actions undertaken.

VI

The credibility of U.N. action to repel aggression and restore international peace and security, as foreseen in the U.N. Charter, has been profoundly affected by the response to the Iraqi invasion of Kuwait. The Security Council showed itself capable of taking decisive action. Its ability to impose comprehensive sanctions and see them enforced was clearly demonstrated, even though the ultimate effectiveness of the sanctions was not adequately tested. By authorizing the use of military force the council gained compliance with all of its relevant resolutions. The Security Council has shown that it has the capacity to initiate collective measures essential for the maintenance of peace in a new world order.

This development can enhance the United Nations' ability not just to restore the status quo as it existed prior to a breach of the peace, but also to change the parameters of the global order to something more favorable than existed under the prior status quo. In this it may even go beyond the vision of the U.N. founders. Furthermore knowledge that the United Nations has such a capability will also enhance its ability to deter breaches of the peace, and so make actual enforcement or later peacekeeping less necessary. Collective security may suppress incipient acts of aggression as well as defeat or punish those that do emerge.

Nevertheless it should not be assumed that any U.N. role in enforcement during the 1990s will be automatic. It will require a deliberate political judgment that can only be made by members of the Security Council acting collectively, and will depend on some continuing commonality of interests among the five permanent members of the council—the United States and the Soviet Union in particular. The effectiveness of the United Nations in dealing with international security problems, whether by enforcement measures, peacekeeping or mediation, will always be sensitive to the nature of relations between these two superpowers. A United Nations whose credibility in dealing with aggression and threats to peace has been restored, however, can serve to moderate any revival of tension between them by lessening the need for, or likelihood of, unilateral intervention in regional crises.

The manner in which the gulf military action was executed by the United States and its coalition partners will likely limit the willingness of council members to follow a similar procedure in the future—a procedure that leaves council members little control over the course of military operations and over the conclusion of hostilities. Neither the United States nor any other country will be ready to act under all circumstances to preserve or restore peace. Nor will other states always be ready to endorse unilateral actions. Some states may not wish to contribute to an operation, and the council may not always wish to depend disproportionately on a particular state's contribution.

Some U.N. capacity to carry out these functions on a permanent basis will therefore be desirable. For this reason, as well as others previously mentioned, the Security Council should be able to mobilize a force to serve under U.N. command for enforcement purposes. That capacity may be virtually indispensable in an emergent world order. The chance to achieve it should not be missed.

WHOSE COLLECTIVE SECURITY?[4]

The founders of the United Nations (UN) had it right, but it took 45 years and the end of the Cold War to prove it: given the proper international environment, the entire global community can mobilize a collective response to aggression through the UN. The international community was determined to oust Iraq from Kuwait by diplomatic, political, economic, and, finally, by military means, but it was, in the end, a Security Council authorization to use force—even if it was not a "UN force" itself—that provided the mandate to the 28 nations allied with the United States to undertake the Persian Gulf War. After the ceasefire agreement was signed, the UN returned to center stage to carry out that agreement's disarmament provisions, especially the dismantling of Iraq's nuclear, chemical, biological, and ballistic missile capabilities, its restrictions on the sale of Iraqi oil and the use of funds for humanitarian purposes, and its procedures for returning properties taken during the occupation of Kuwait.

The UN's founders had hardly intended, however, that one member state should play such a dominant role in marshaling the world's military might and that in doing so it should ignore the collective security mechanisms outlined under chapter VII of the UN Charter. Moreover, they would have been shocked to witness the collapse of the Soviet Union just when the possibility of U.S.–Soviet cooperation in defense of peace—for four decades the dream of every supporter of a more activist UN—seemed within reach.

If the original vision of the United Nations has new life, then, there are also many unanswered questions about the shape of future international security arrangements. Indeed, by turning to the United Nations as a critical component of its Gulf strategy, the United States brought to the surface both the hopes and the fears surrounding any discussion of collective security. If today's transformed international environment raises the hope that the collec-

[4]Article by Edward C. Luck and Toby Trister Gati, president and senior vice president for policy studies, respectively, of the United Nations Association of the USA. From *Washington Quarterly* 15/2:43–56 Spring '92. Copyright © 1992 by the Center for Strategic and International Studies & MIT. Reprinted with permission.

tive might of the international community can protect the weak against the strong, as originally intended in the UN Charter, it also raises concerns that the strong will seek to impose their vision of world order on the weak, without regard for the principles of national sovereignty and noninterference in domestic affairs also enshrined in the UN Charter. The ambivalence of many states toward a stronger UN is now coupled with apprehension about a pax Americana, even a UN-centered one, without a Soviet counterweight.

If collective security has a future, it is not yet clear what it will look like. Americans are far from eager to assume the role of global policeman, but neither are U.S. political leaders ready to suggest putting even part of U.S. military forces under an international or UN command. Other countries have similar concerns. During the Persian Gulf War, national leaders of the major contributing states hailed the new era in international relations, but none expressed a willingness to cede authority to the UN so that it might implement existing provisions of the charter regulating the use of force. The detailed structures for implementing collective security outlined in the UN Charter need to be reviewed in light of the changing international security environment of the world after the Cold and Persian Gulf wars. For if a "new world order" is to be created, a way must be found to strengthen the institutional capability for responding to global threats to the peace.

Here, the role of the United States is crucial. It is the only country with the combination of political, economic, and military strength necessary to defend the interests of smaller countries against powerful neighbors. At the same time, as seen in the Gulf, preponderant military power cannot always be brought to bear without the active support, both political and increasingly financial, of other states in the international community. Not every crisis will rivet U.S. attention as did the Iraqi invasion of Kuwait or call for a massive U.S.-led response. But if the United States does not take the lead, then who will? In a world characterized by repeated outbreaks of low-level fighting between neighboring states and disregard for the welfare of civilian populations caught in the cross fire, by mistreatment of ethnic or national minorities, and by large-scale human rights violations, the greatest threat to international stability may be a situation in which everyone knows something should be done but no one wants to take the lead.

It is at this point that "the system" should take over—a system of collective responsibility that would engage the international community in tasks ranging from preventive diplomacy, to economic sanctions, and to joint military action as needed to maintain international peace and stability. The UN Charter provides for such a system and it is the purpose of this paper to consider ways in which its collective security provisions can be strengthened and reinvigorated to take advantage of exciting new possibilities in the post–cold war world.

National decision makers in many parts of the world, not least in Washington, D.C., are rediscovering the potential utility of the range of coercive actions permitted the UN Security Council under the charter's chapter VII, with its 13 articles detailing the possibilities for a concerted multilateral response to threats to international peace and security. There is no lack of authority or tools, as amply demonstrated in the diplomatic, economic, and military efforts to expel the Iraqi invaders from Kuwait. But this was a highly unusual situation that provides no clear precedent for the future. If the UN's full potential as an instrument of collective security is to be realized, four clusters of questions need to be addressed with some urgency:

• Who should have the authority to decide when to invoke the charter's collective security provisions, or more precisely, which countries should be represented on the Security Council and how should it take its decisions?

• Who should be authorized to oversee the implementation of sanctions and the use of force once these steps have been mandated by the council?

• When should the UN decide to become involved in a local conflict and when should it leave this burden to regional organizations or to the parties themselves?

• Who pays the bill when the UN is asked to serve as world policeman and how are the funds to be raised?

The UN Charter speaks to all of these concerns to some extent, of course, but fuzzy answers that seemed acceptable in the days when the UN was usually left sitting on the sidelines are inadequate as the organization enters the center ring of international security politics for the first time. In the days ahead, these provisions are likely to be tested as never before.

Who Decides?

It is clearly the Security Council—the subject of all 13 articles of chapter VII—that has full and unrivaled responsibility for determining when and how collective security steps will be undertaken. Only the council has the authority under international law to make decisions that are binding on all member states. So with the new-found cooperative spirit among the five permanent members—none has cast a veto on a substantive issue in almost two years—has come increasing discussion among the whole UN membership about the composition of the council itself. The more active and assertive the council becomes, the more the 150-plus member states not on the council will mutter about decisions it makes in their name but without their input.

The Persian Gulf War was a striking case in point. Although initially there was widespread excitement in the UN about the close collaboration of the five permanent members of the Security Council, over time the disenfranchised expressed growing apprehensions. They included both developing countries, concerned about their exclusion from UN decision making, and leading developed countries like Germany and Japan, which were expected to shoulder much of the cost of the UN-authorized operations but were largely excluded from key decision-making sessions. Simply put, during the Gulf crisis most UN members were left out of the process of consultation and deliberation that led up to the resolution authorizing the use of force. Even the 10 elected, nonpermanent members of the Security Council professed frustration that the permanent five met alone under U.S. leadership to design security policy and then presented them with a fait accompli to be voted up or down. For the rest—more than nine-tenths of the UN's total membership—the system seemingly afforded no say at all. They were not involved in the consultations, and their assent was unnecessary according to the charter even on decisions that could bind their actions.

This is particularly galling to the larger states in the developing world that exert enormous influence over events in their regions and in the General Assembly yet have no comparable input into UN security policy. Because it is in the developing world, after all, that the UN again and again becomes involved, developing countries large and small are uneasy about the way future decisions on critical war and peace issues may be resolved at the UN. The fact that U.S. power is no longer counterbalanced by another superpower only heightens these concerns. Paradoxically, the renewed emphasis on consensus in UN decision making has resulted not only in a less acrimonious process but also in suspicions in some developing countries of a more subtle, behind-the-scenes dominance by the United States. Even the low-key, restrained U.S. stance in the selection of a new secretary general in the fall of 1991 was at first misinterpreted by some of the smaller countries as a U.S. device for getting its way without having to express its preferences publicly.

Even some American allies, who once complained that the United States failed to use the UN, now fret that it may use the world body too much, turning it into a mere instrument of U.S. foreign policy. On the other hand, if the middle and smaller powers seek to make the UN a mechanism for constraining U.S. power, then trouble could lie ahead. The UN cannot succeed without strong, constructive U.S. leadership, while the United States needs the UN to manage and promote a fair international division of labor and burden-sharing arrangements on security as well as development issues. The Security Council could not work under cold war conditions, but sustaining a balance of interests in a post–cold war world in which the United States is the only remaining superpower will also be a challenging proposition for all concerned.

The larger economic powers in the industrialized world do not fear UN encroachment on their domestic order, but, like many developing countries, they too resent their exclusion from decision-making circles. Because they are assessed substantial amounts for UN operations that the Security Council authorizes and they are obliged to suspend economic relations when the council imposes sanctions, UN enforcement actions have real consequences for them. Accustomed to being part of the inner circle that makes decisions in other areas of international policy-making, some of the Group of Seven (G-7) economic powers complain that this is tantamount to "taxation without representation." Japan has been especially vocal in recent years in insisting it should be part of the Security Council circle; Germany has also begun to voice similar concerns. Certainly if key economic powers like Japan and Germany showed a greater willingness to participate directly in peacekeeping and enforcement operations, as the British and French did in Desert Storm, it would enhance their claims for permanent Security Council seats.

The case of Japan demands special attention. The Persian Gulf War shook politics in Japan more than in any other country and raised questions among the Japanese about their country's status in the international community. The question of whether or not Japan should send support troops or even nonmilitary personnel to the region was especially divisive. The Japanese government did agree to send minesweepers to the Persian Gulf after hostilities ceased. The promised legislation to permit not only greater logistical, communications, and medical support of UN peacekeeping operations, but also participation of the Japanese Self Defense forces in peacekeeping has failed to pass in the Diet for the second time. For many, this is just one more sign of Japan's unwillingness to accept its global responsibilities. At the UN, whose charter still refers to the Axis "enemy states," the Japanese are particularly sensitive about being excluded from levels of decision making commensurate with their economic influence. A permanent voice in the Security Council might prod Japan to consider more seriously how and toward what ends its influence will be used in the world, although China is likely to resist a permanent seat for Japan, and France and the United Kingdom have opposed any changes that would bring their special status into question. All three, of course, can veto any amendments to the charter, including changes in the composition of the Security Council.

The issue of the council's composition is clearly coming to a head. The corridor talk on this question at the UN is far more serious than in the past and, with the organization's rapidly expanding security role, it is framed with a good deal more urgency. Amending the charter may be tantamount to opening a Pandora's box, but it was accomplished on several occasions in the 1960s and 1970s without significant harm. In each case, moreover, the primary purpose was to increase the size of UN bodies to more fully reflect the organization's growing membership. The Security Council, for example, was enlarged from 11 to 15 members in 1965.

A number of formulas are being floated that would keep the council to a manageable size, retain the same veto-carrying permanent members, and give both major donors and major developing countries a more permanent voice in the council's deliberations. We would recommend that, first, Japan and Germany be given permanent but not veto-bearing seats and the "enemies clause" (article 107) be deleted and, second, that Africa, Asia, and Latin America each be given an additional rotating seat, also without a veto, so that big countries like India, Nigeria, and Brazil can sit on the council with greater regularity. These steps would raise the total membership of the council from 15 to 20. The future of the Soviet seat, with its veto, depends on developments within the Commonwealth of Independent States, as well as on the ultimate legal and political judgment of the international community. It seems to us, however, clearly preferable on both international legal and political grounds to have Russia as the legal successor state to the Soviet Union and the other republics as independent, separate UN members. Giving the council seat to Russia would be the best way to ensure the continued excellent cooperation of Security Council members. In any case, the break-up of the Soviet Union has spurred a more urgent look at the makeup of the council and has whetted the appetite of other large countries for a permanent seat.

Over the longer term, a more radical restructuring of the Security Council might be contemplated. Although the whole structure of the UN is based on the member state system, the growth of regionalism is likely to persist in both the economic and security realms. With the end of the global competition between the United States and the USSR, international politics are increasingly defined in regional terms, especially on security issues, and here the biggest problems are local, not global. This suggests two steps, one simple and short term, the other complex, controversial, and long term. The easy part is for the five permanent members to expand consultations within their respective regions on the major issues that are before the council or likely to arise in the foreseeable future. To a certain extent this has already taken place within the European Community (EC) and among the G-7, but the process should be regularized. Over time, if the sense of regional identity grows and regional organizations begin to assume a larger security role, the UN Charter might be amended to give a voice and possibly a veto to each major region (North America, Latin America, Western Europe, East Central Europe, Africa, East Asia, and South Asia) on UN intervention in that area. The current permanent members would retain permanent seats, at least in the near term.

Who Enforces the Peace?

The war with Iraq displayed both the strengths and the weaknesses of the UN system of collective security for all the world to see. The UN itself proved to be a remarkably good forum for rallying an international political response to naked aggression, yet when it came to using force, the carefully laid out provisions in chapter VII of the UN Charter were never invoked. The UN's authority was proclaimed everywhere—including most vividly in the U.S. Senate—up to the point of authorizing the use of force, and again the UN came front and center in the effort to clean up the mess left by Desert Storm. But the world body seemed to fade once again into irrelevance when the fighting was in progress.

There were, of course, good reasons for this pattern: after all, the evolution of international relations has not yet reached the point at which most nations are ready to accept international command of their forces in combat. And there is reason to question whether a UN command could have prosecuted the war as efficiently as the coalition and with as little loss of life among allied troops. But there were political costs to excluding the world body completely, including a loss of credibility both for the United Nations and for the concept of a "new world order."

Clearly, the international community is still improvising rather than institutionalizing mechanisms for dealing with regional crises. The mobilization of a global consensus was possible in the Persian Gulf not only because the Iraqi actions were so egregious but also because the United States was willing to take the lead politically, diplomatically, and militarily (although not financially). Future crises may follow a similar pattern, but many states feel that eventually the role of world policeman should rightly belong to the world community as a whole rather than to any one country—no matter how strong—and that authority and responsibility should be shared more equitably among all nations. A number of recent opinion polls, moreover, have shown that the U.S. public is not eager to have the United States play the role of global policeman and would far prefer to send the UN's blue helmets to handle regional crises rather than the U.S. Marines. Whether this represents a growing confidence in the UN, a desire to have other countries carry more of the burden, or a new isolationist spirit remains to be seen.

For all its shortcomings, no one has been able to advance a more credible plan than the UN Charter for carrying out collective security. Moving beyond "pacific settlement of disputes" under chapter VI of the charter to enforcement actions under chapter VII, however, has put the UN into largely uncharted territory. The Kuwaiti crisis of 1990 led to a highly improvised application of the collective security *principles* in the UN Charter, while the charter's *provisions* for UN enforcement of security (Military Staff Committee, UN troops, UN command) were circumvented.

Whether the UN collective security structures envisioned almost half a century ago, with the various peacekeeping mechanisms that have evolved since, can be reshaped to make the UN a potent agent for international security—and whether the major powers have sufficient commitment to making them work—is an open question. The resistance of major military powers to consideration of a unified or UN command and the general reluctance of member states to negotiate "special agreements" for standby forces under article 43 of the charter bespeak the difficulties involved.

Article 43 goes to the heart of the matter because the UN at present has no forces automatically at its disposal and must appeal to the members to volunteer forces even for noncombatant peacekeeping missions. This sometimes results in significant delays in responding to urgent crises, reducing the world body's credibility as a potential deterrent to would-be aggressors. In a long-forgotten passage of the 1945 UN Participation Act, which defined U.S. relations with the new United Nations organization, Congress acknowledges that article 43 agreements, should they be concluded between the United States and the UN, could well turn the command of those U.S. forces over to the Security Council and thus possibly to non-American officers. This might be seen today by many Americans as ceding too much of the president's authority as commander-in-chief to a multilateral body. Certainly, in an operation as large and risky as Desert Storm, to do so would seem unrealistic, although it would be less so in more limited operations of less strategic importance to the United States.

It should not be forgotten, however, that the United States would retain a veto in the Security Council over the commitment of any UN forces. There are no precedents, moreover, so it would be quite possible to consider negotiating article 43 agreements with the UN that would stipulate that the standby forces would be put at the UN's disposal only under conditions and circumstances specifically agreed to by the president and/or Congress, and only with their consent. In other words, the United States could designate certain units, and perhaps give them special training for participation in prospective UN collective security operations, without committing them to the UN in advance.

This topic remains controversial, but we believe it is time for the United States to open quiet consultations with the other permanent members of the Security Council about the possibility of all five nations negotiating simultaneous article 43 agreements with the UN. As the countries protected by the veto, as well as by their nuclear deterrents, the five are best positioned to open this new chapter in collective security. The size of the designated forces need not be enormous, but they should fit the needs of rapid deployment and force projection missions. Logistical support, communications, and intelligence capabilities should be shared with the UN whenever possible. Although it might take some time to negotiate such agreements, as well as to get all five permanent members on board, the very suggestion that these major military powers were consulting on how to bring force to bear under the UN umbrella should in itself serve as a powerful deterrent to potential aggressors, especially after the experience of the Persian Gulf War.

Other UN member states should also be encouraged to negotiate standby agreements. Because these countries would not be able to veto the deployment of their article 43 forces by the UN, it was suggested at a UNA–USA [United Nations Association of the United States of America] meeting in Moscow in spring 1991 that these countries be given the right to determine whether or not their forces would take part in a particular enforcement operation. This would provide them with essentially the same assurances that possession of the veto gives the five permanent members, while making it possible for them to prepare for future enforcement operations.

A second key building block of the UN collective security system was meant to be the Military Staff Committee, consisting of the chiefs of staff of the five permanent members or their representatives. Again, the elaborate article 47 provisions regarding its operation were largely set aside during the cold war era. In the buildup to the Persian Gulf War, the committee met once at a relatively high level, chiefly to scare the Iraqis by showing the determination of the major powers, but no real efforts have ever been made to create a unified command structure under UN auspices. Should article 43 forces ever come into existence, command and control questions—and the role of the Military Staff Committee—would take on greater urgency.

In the meantime, the committee could undertake more modest, but important, roles to test the prospects for cooperation and to prove its utility. Its first task under the charter, "to advise and assist" the Security Council on military matters, makes considerable sense, especially if the UN's security role is to expand in the future. It has been said that war is too important to be left to the generals, but surely questions of how to maintain the peace should not solely be the preserve of diplomats unaided by the best professional military advice the military has to offer. Among the questions on which the Military Staff Committee is to proffer advice is "the regulation of armaments, and possible disarmament." In the case of Iraqi disarmament, the UN is taking unprecedented steps to disarm a major military machine. As the whole body more and more approaches arms control and disarmament as an integral component of peacemaking and peacekeeping efforts specific to regional conflicts, the technical expertise of military specialists will be increasingly important to its work, as has been the case in Iraq. Activating the Military Staff Committee to aid in these tasks, in other words, need not represent a commitment to, nor even a step toward, multilateral command and control of national forces—something the charter says would "be worked out subsequently" in any case. If the committee had been functioning fully prior to Iraq's invasion of Kuwait, it might have been helpful in several ways. First, its very activity might have been a useful deterrent, suggesting the possibility of a broad-based international response to Iraq's aggression. Second, the charter states that the committee shall be responsible under the Security Council for the "strategic direction of UN forces." This could have included, first, sorting out the general division of labor among the various national contingents deployed in the Gulf theater and, second, laying out overall military and strategic objectives in the Gulf operation, possibly including limits on the use of force against largely civilian targets. Even modest results from general consultations on these subjects could have proven beneficial politically, particularly in the uncertain months leading up to the commencement of hostilities. Third, a little-noticed clause in article 47 speaks of the establishment of "regional subcommittees," to which local UN member states would presumably send military representatives. This might have proven a politically acceptable way to expand the commitment of the moderate Arab states and others in the coalition with less political arm-twisting by the United States and less need for these Arab leaders to defend their cooperation with the United States to skeptical domestic advisers.

When Should the UN Intervene?

With increasing opportunities for UN intervention has come a growing need to choose when UN involvement is most appropriate and a renewed debate about where national sovereignty ends and international responsibilities begin. The UN Charter gives the Security Council considerable freedom to "determine the existence of any threat to the peace, breach of the peace, or act of aggression . . . and to decide what measures shall be taken" (chapter VII, article 39). And, under article 99, the secretary general is authorized to bring to the attention of the Security Council those items that "in his opinion" may threaten international peace and security.

Although the preamble lays out a series of principles and purposes that sound universal, the remainder of the charter describes a decision-making structure that is highly political and selective. In practical terms, then, most of the responsibility for deciding when, where, and how these sweeping principles will be applied rests with the members of the Security Council. Theirs necessarily must be a subjective rather than an objective judgment. Thus, council members chose to respond vigorously to the Iraqi invasion of Kuwait, but they showed no inclination to get involved in the strife in Liberia, Ethiopia, or the Sudan that raged at the same time. To some observers, this selectivity undermines the credibility and integrity of the institution as a global peacekeeper, but to others it is a sensible bow to reality in view of the UN's limited capabilities and capacity for influencing events. A keen sense of when to get involved and when to stay out, moreover, helped to sustain the organization through such politically difficult times as the Cold War.

In the past, Soviet–U.S. tensions—reflected in the penchant of the two states to use their vetoes—ensured that the UN would get involved in relatively few crises. Today, the unprecedented cooperation among the permanent members, as well as their more narrowly defined interests in the developing world, could provide—in fact already has provided—a much wider menu of problem areas calling for UN attention. With the UN's continuing physical and financial limitations, however, this growth of tempting opportunities calls for a corresponding sense of restraint and for selectivity.

Will it simply be, as many smaller nations complain, that the UN will get involved only when the interests of the five permanent members are demonstrably involved (Kuwait being a case in point) but when none of them can or wants to handle the situation unilaterally? In that case, how will the security interests of developing countries that are not deemed strategically important get addressed? There is a growing danger, for instance, that conflicts in Africa will be essentially excluded from the map of Security Council interests. Over time, it may be useful to try to develop generally applicable rules of intervention regarding when the collective security provisions of chapter VII should be invoked. For example, specific kinds of events, threats, or situations might automatically trigger Security Council action, such as the possibility that weapons of mass destruction might be used in a regional dispute, clear evidence of genocide, a huge flow of refugees that threatens to destabilize neighboring countries, massive human rights violations, the overthrow of democratically elected governments, or flagrant violation of earlier Security Council decisions. Not one of these questions has a simple answer, but each is worth grappling with if the concept of a new world order is to be based on sustainable and broadly credible political and legal norms.

The increasing demand for UN security services, especially in internal or transnational conflicts, has also raised pointed questions about the capacity of the organization to deal with so many security problems simultaneously. Some of these questions deal with the personal time, talents, and priorities of the secretary general, who cannot be everywhere at once, while others deal with the organization, staffing, and communications capabilities of the UN Secretariat for overseeing so many far-flung operations. These issues are especially timely at a point when restructuring the secretariat is being given serious attention by the member states, and a new secretary general, well-versed in international diplomacy, seeks to put his stamp on the organization. The old question of the relationship between the UN and regional organizations takes on a renewed urgency under these conditions.

The UN Charter does not assume that the Security Council will address all security problems or that it will necessarily be the first recourse in case of threats to international peace and security. Article 52, in fact, calls on member states to "make every effort to achieve pacific settlement of local disputes through . . . regional arrangements or by . . . regional agencies before referring them to the Security Council." Chapter VIII, probably the least explored territory in the charter, addresses the possibilities for coordinating the efforts of regional bodies and the Security Council aimed at both peaceful resolution and enforcement of council decisions.

Such coordination of global and regional action might have been a politically, and perhaps militarily, attractive option in the Gulf crisis, especially given the symbolic importance of bringing Arab states into the coalition. Unfortunately, in the Middle East as in other areas of strategic importance, adequate regional partners for the UN do not yet exist. In the past, when regional organizations were weak and divided or where a superpower had a clear interest, the venue for action more often than not was the Security Council. Where regional organizations exist, as in Africa, Latin America, or Europe, the track record of regional-global cooperation has been mixed at best. The recent crises in Haiti and Yugoslavia, on the other hand, engendered a greater degree of cooperation between the UN and regional organizations in dealing with stubborn local conflicts. Developing a fuller global-regional partnership would also help address the endemic problem of alienation among developing countries within the UN security structure.

One of the most fundamental questions facing the UN today is whether principles of collective security—and other global norms—apply to individuals and groups within states or only to relations between member states themselves. If the latter, then nations could be allowed to do to their own people what international norms do not permit them to do to other nations. On the other hand, if the international community can tell states how they should treat their own populations, how are these verdicts to be enforced? Many still feel reluctant to condemn the violation of human rights or disregard for basic human needs when these result from internal political breakdown or civil war. It is only in recent years that the international community has come to accept the idea that certain domestic policies (e.g., apartheid, genocide, and other massive human rights violations) should not be tolerated by the community of civilized nations. Yet the Security Council remains cautious about labeling even gross rights violations within established borders as "threats to international peace and security" requiring chapter VII action, at least beyond economic or arms transfer sanctions in especially egregious and persistent cases.

The aftermath of the Kuwait crisis dramatically raised these issues in a way that was distinctly unwelcome to many governments. The intervention by the Western powers to create "safe havens" to protect Iraq's Kurds and other minority groups from their government, for example, may have set a precedent with

far-reaching consequences for traditional notions of state sovereignty. Recent suggestions by the French that international law
recognize a "duty to intervene" in cases where a government's
actions are creating a humanitarian catastrophe has set off alarm
bells in a number of capitals, especially in the developing world.

With refugee crises around the globe and famine present or
looming in parts of Africa, this controversy will not go away. Many
governments assert that the "duty" concept is a dagger directed at
them, threatening to formally reduce their sovereignty and af-
fording the great powers, through the Security Council or worse
yet unilaterally, an excuse to intervene in domestic conflicts. The
dilemma posed by the conflict between government claims to sovereignty and human claims to survival will almost certainly become one of the major issues of international law and security in
the 1990s.

Who Will Pay the Bill?

There has clearly been no "peace dividend" for the UN peacekeeping, arms monitoring, and collective security budgets. The
more these services are demanded by the international community, the higher the costs to the world body. Once a small fraction
of UN spending, with the launching of the Cambodia operation
the costs of peacekeeping operations alone may soon exceed the
whole regular budget of the United Nations. Although puny
compared to the costs of national defense or of local conflicts
prevented or contained, these expenditures loom very large in
UN eyes. If the UN begins to undertake collective security operations directly, then its expenses will multiply many times. Operation Desert Storm, for example, cost 10 times as much as the
annual outlays of the entire UN system, including all of the specialized agencies. Even a more modest collective security operation would be very expensive by UN standards.

These new demands come at an awkward time for the UN,
which is still struggling to overcome the painful effects of massive
U.S. financial withholdings during the mid-1980s and of smaller
delinquencies by other member states. The United States has
begun to pay off its arrearages, but they still exceed $500 million
(or one-half of the UN's regular annual budget), of which more
than $100 million (as of October 1991) is owed to peacekeeping
alone. The United States is clearly a lot more ready to enunciate a
new world order than to help pay for it. And although the Rus-

sians are clearly supportive of the principles of the UN Charter and supportive of recognizing the right of the international community to intervene, they may not be able to contribute even their assessed dues on time, much less extra for new peacekeeping operations in the next few years.

Although separate assessments are made for most new peacekeeping operations, the prospects for successfully completing new assignments are inevitably affected by the overall financial health of the institution. The most obvious problem has been the virtual elimination of the UN's modest reserve funds, leaving no discretionary funds that could cover the start-up costs for a new operation until the hat can be passed around the member states for longer-term support. Subsequent delays in payments from major donors, like the United States, tend to compound the problem. There is a built-in nine-month mechanical delay in the payment of U.S. regular dues, which are due each January but paid at the earliest when the next U.S. fiscal year begins in October. And U.S. funding for peacekeeping operations is particularly problematic when new operations, unanticipated by the federal budget cycle or the agreement to reduce the budget deficit are begun. Although the United States cannot solve the UN's financial problems alone, it could at least set a good example for others.

When the United States and other major contributors are unable to come up with the funds in a timely fashion, the ability of the UN to maintain peacekeepers in operation is dependent largely on the willingness of countries contributing troops to wait for compensation or on emergency supplemental support by a few states. When it was time to dispatch UN observers to the Iraq–Iran front following the UN-brokered armistice, for example, there were no funds to get them there until a member state agreed to make an extraordinary payment. More recently, the efforts of the UN Special Commission to ferret out Iraqi weapons of mass destruction were hampered by the lack of adequate transportation and logistical support from member states, which otherwise professed keen interest in the operation. Many months after the operation had begun and had proved its extraordinary value, still no funds had been appropriated by the UN member states to fund it.

The issue of financing looms even larger when one moves from peacekeeping to enforcement actions. Although Operation Desert Storm demonstrated a clear U.S. willingness to provide military leadership and troops for collective action, a central aim of U.S. foreign policy was to share the financial burdens more broadly. The Bush administration appears to have persuaded its coalition partners to pay more than $48 billion in cash and other contributions toward an estimated $60 billion in war costs, with additional Saudi Arabian payments likely. In future crises, however, the countries that foot the bill may be unwilling to allow the United States the degree of military and political control it had in the Persian Gulf and may link issues of financing to greater participation in strategic decision making. The UN, of course, can offer a forum both for sorting out the division of labor in carrying out such operations and for developing a formula for sharing the financial burden.

Another endemic problem has been the separation of substantive and budgetary decision making within the UN. Under the charter, the Security Council has authority over the former and the General Assembly over the latter. This anomaly in the UN's structure—a bit reminiscent of Washington's system of checks and balances but more clumsy in practice—could cause serious difficulties down the road, especially if the resentment of the council's prerogatives grows among those countries excluded from its deliberations. Haggling between the council and assembly over the size and cost of the Namibian operation delayed the deployment of the peacekeeping forces and almost jeopardized the success of their mission. Japanese officials have complained that their minor role in the decision-making process for the UN-brokered peace agreement in Cambodia, which looms as the largest, riskiest, and most complex security mission ever undertaken by the UN, has not been commensurate with the financial burden Japan will be expected to carry in the implementation of the agreement.

There have been many creative suggestions for producing a larger and steadier flow of income for UN peace and security operations, which often cannot be anticipated in the regular budget cycle. These proposals have ranged from a tax or assessment on international commerce or on arms sales, to a renewal of the UN's reserve fund, to shifting U.S. contributions from the State Department to the Defense Department budget. Rebuilding the reserves should be the first priority, especially as the United States begins to pay its arrearages. Although it might be unwieldy in practice, the concept of an international levy on arms transfers is very appealing because the greater the volume of weapons proliferation, the greater the funds available to the UN to contain the consequences of their use. The possible establishment of a UN arms trade registry might provide a data base for such an undertaking. Developing countries, which depend on arms supplies from the major arms producing countries, are likely to have strong objections to such a system, however, because it would let countries with indigenous arms manufacturing capabilities off scot-free. Whether or not this is the best approach, clearly some kind of regular financing mechanism is needed, given the increasing number and importance of UN efforts at both enforcement and peacekeeping. Anything approaching a "new world order" cannot be obtained on a shoestring, especially an ad hoc one.

Conclusion

Global threats to the United States have receded, perhaps creating a false sense of security. Regional instabilities, many based on ethnic hatreds and thwarted national aspirations, are multiplying at an alarming rate. Certainly the United States cannot resolve all of them with the use of force, nor should it aspire to do so. Multilateral crisis management, peacekeeping, and collective security should be as fundamental to the defense of U.S. national security interests in the 1990s as participation in the North Atlantic Treaty Organization (NATO) has been during the past 45 years. The threats we face are different today and so should be the mix of responses.

If the White House and Congress are serious about a new world order, they should begin by putting their own house in order. A first step would be to put some real money and political capital behind their lofty rhetoric. Just as the U.S. government mobilized an international coalition against Iraq, so, too, it can energize international diplomacy to develop at least a rudimentary collective security system based on broader consultations, modest commitments of forces to the UN, and financial burden sharing.

Certainly there is the risk of failure. But the unprecedented opportunities to build new security structures that are present today will not last forever. Untapped potential is wasted potential. Without U.S. leadership in forging a new collective security system based on the UN Charter, the only alternatives when the next bully comes along will be another large-scale commitment of U.S. troops or letting an aggression go unpunished. Surely the political and security risks of either of these outcomes are greater than

those inherent in a determined effort to bring the UN Charter
back to life.

PEACEKEEPING IN THE NEW EUROPE[5]

Yugoslavia has imploded. Peace seems irretrievable as blood
feuds threaten to make that area—it can no longer be called a
nation—a semipermanent battleground. Military force has been
deployed and sometimes used in several cities of the former Soviet Union, including Moscow. Ethnic claims and quarrels have
erupted in the Czech and Slovak Federal Republic. Romania and
Bulgaria are wrestling with minorities problems that threaten a
breakdown in public order. The use of military force is obviously
no less unthinkable in the new Europe than during the depths of
the Cold War. Is the contradiction between order and justice
in Central and Eastern Europe so profound that violence will
become more commonplace and more intense than during the
Cold War?

In this essay, I will first point out some of the difficult issues
posed by intrastate conflict. To illustrate the problems in concrete
terms I will then describe the experiences of European and United Nations (UN) mediators in Yugoslavia during the latter half of
1991. These experiences add up to a valuable—and tragic—case
study in peacekeeping in the new Europe. Yugoslavia may be a
sad example of the kinds of security problems Europe will be
facing in the post–cold war era. If so, it will be of crucial importance to absorb and act on its lessons. I will discuss some of the
lessons that I think emerge from six months of trying to stop the
fighting between Serbia and Croatia. One of these lessons is that
Europe and the United States should be better prepared the next
time. That includes being better prepared to exercise diplomacy's
military instrument. In the last part of this essay I will outline
some steps that might be taken to begin contingency planning for
the use of peacekeeping forces in Europe.

[5]Article by James E. Goodby, Distinguished Service Professor at Carnegie Mel-
lon University. From *Washington Quarterly* 15/2:153–169, Spring '92. Copyright ©
1992 by the Center for Strategic and International Studies & MIT. Reprinted with
permission.

New Threats to Peace and Stability

The Cold War was peaceful in the important sense that war did not break out between the Soviet Union and the United States or between the nations of Eastern and Western Europe. It was not a peaceful time in other respects. Aside from repressions imposed by the former regimes in Central and Eastern Europe in which blood was shed—sometimes secretly, sometimes openly—military force was used by the USSR in East Germany in 1953, in Hungary in 1956, and in Czechoslovakia in 1968. Poland was threatened with military force in 1981, and the former regime itself imposed martial law. Shoot-to-kill orders were carried out by East European border guards against people trying to flee to the West. Obviously, Central and Eastern Europe were hardly models of tranquillity during the Cold War.

One difference stands out between conflict in the cold war era and in the present period. During the Cold War some sovereign states were invaded and, in effect, occupied by others. In the post–cold war period, that kind of conflict seems very unlikely. Violence on a large scale will certainly occur, however, because internal instabilities are likely to persist for at least the next generation in Central and Eastern Europe, and almost certainly for longer. The breakup of Yugoslavia has created conditions that the *Economist* very early on quite rightly labeled "war in Europe." The coup in Moscow came perilously close to precipitating a civil war; such conflict seems almost inevitable in parts of the former Soviet Union.

Internal struggles, it is important to note, may become threats to international peace and security. This was the principle adopted by the UN Security Council in deciding to authorize intervention in Iraq to aid the Kurds. The principle is equally valid in Europe, especially since the Helsinki Final Act and subsequent documents negotiated by all participants in the Conference on Security and Cooperation in Europe (CSCE) have made a government's treatment of its citizens a matter of proper international concern. But acting on the principle is extremely risky when it involves the use of armed force. During the period when the Bush administration was considering its options for dealing with the growing war in Yugoslavia, many advisers thought that civil war in that country would pose a threat to international security only if the major powers became involved. For them the right solution was simply to isolate or quarantine the war zone.

This is realpolitik logic. In the face of intractable differences between Serbs and Croats, this may have been prudent advice but it seems likely that dangerous precedents are being set in Yugoslavia that will endanger future peace and stability. At the end of 1991, after 10,000 people have been slaughtered, it is evident that it is a miscalculation to think that a war in the center of Europe can rage on indefinitely without harmful effects beyond the war zones. The poisons released by the Serbo–Croatian war have already seeped into the Western alliance.

It is prudent to recognize that intervention in an internal conflict could lead the nations of Europe to take sides against each other, with disastrous results. Although the major powers have shown little interest in having their own military forces become involved in any way in the ethnic or intrastate conflicts of Eastern Europe, statements by the pre-coup Soviet government came close to threatening war if other countries, for any reason, decided to intervene in Yugoslavia. A Soviet statement in early August 1991 referred to European considerations of peacekeeping forces in Croatia and warned that "to enter . . . on one side of the conflict would mean to come into conflict automatically with others inside and outside Yugoslavia. And the conflict would grow into an all-European one." That statement may have been the last gasp of military hard-liners, but it was intended to—and did—signal that intervention in internal quarrels carries the risk of a general European war. Even without any act of military intervention by the major powers, however, internal conflicts on the scale of the Yugoslav war may become threats to international peace and security. According to one report, the Hungarians have warned the Bush administration that they must consider intervening to help ethnic Hungarian communities in Yugoslavia if the lives of those people are endangered. Bulgaria and Greece have direct interests in the fate of Macedonia and so does Albania in Kosovo. As it became clearer toward the end of 1991 that Serbia intended to annex large pieces of Croatia, and the intensity of the fighting correspondingly escalated, the implications for other parts of Europe of a violent but successful Serbian seizure of territory began to come into focus. The KGB even described the scene in Yugoslavia as a harbinger of things to come in the former Soviet Union.

Neither the North Atlantic Treaty Organization (NATO) nor the European Community (EC) can be counted on to provide a stable haven for the Central and East European countries, not to mention the Soviet republics, for a long time to come. The region will continue to exist in a kind of security limbo while the construction of a post-Communist order in the former Soviet Union proceeds on its spectacularly disorderly way. This is the kind of environment that balance of power theorists and practical politicians alike would have no difficulty in identifying as a temptation to fate. So long as Central and Eastern Europe remain relatively unstable, incidents may occur there that will become threats to international peace and security. Quarantine, or nonintervention, might successfully isolate the fighting, but what kind of a new world order does this imply? Yugoslavia already has shown us the answer to this question.

European and UN Mediation in Yugoslavia

In the main, it was the European Community that bore the burden through most of 1991 of working for cease-fires, monitoring these cease-fires, and searching for formulas to get negotiations started between Croatia and Serbia. A review of the Community's efforts is instructive. It shows a Community divided over the fundamental question of whether it was worth saving a Yugoslav federation and at odds over whether armed force should be used under any conditions. The record reveals that the Community negotiated with few instruments of coercion, and chose to deny itself those it had throughout most of the period from July through October 1991. The voice of the United States, the world's only superpower and self-proclaimed advocate of a new world order, was muted, no doubt because of the realpolitik logic cited above. Even the task of orchestrating the sounds of public opprobrium was neglected. The picture that emerges is one of selfless, even heroic maneuvering by brilliant West European and UN diplomats harnessed to national commitments that can only be described as half-hearted.

The mission was truly heroic—it nearly led to fatalities among the mediators. It was certainly creatively and energetically carried out. From early July 1991 onward, it was one of the chief preoccupations of the Dutch foreign minister, Hans van den Broek, in his capacity as president of the EC Council of Ministers for the latter part of 1991. EC mediation was successful almost immediately in the case of Slovenia. The Community negotiated an agreement that called for the federal Yugoslav army to return to barracks in both Slovenia and Croatia and for the two republics to suspend for three months the declarations of independence they had made on June 25, 1991. The agreement was carried out in Slovenia, where EC observers were quickly introduced, but not in Croatia, where over 11 percent of the population is Serbian. Clearly a major reason for the success in Slovenia was the decision of the Serbian military leaders to concentrate their limited resources on Croatia.

The Community resorted to a whole arsenal of mediation techniques. As its efforts to resolve the Yugoslav dispute expanded, it organized a peace conference, invented an arbitration mechanism for the settlement of disputes, offered ideas for the reconstitution of Yugoslavia, and sent observer teams to monitor cease-fires that had been brokered by EC mediators between Serbia and Croatia. Repeatedly, Community spokesmen talked about economic sanctions, but over four critical months the EC failed to impose sanctions on Yugoslav republics that refused to end the fighting and seek a diplomatic solution to the war.

The peace conference was chaired by Lord Carrington, former British foreign minister, former NATO secretary general, and one of the most successful mediators of the past 40 years. The conference met for the first time on September 7, 1991, in The Hague and held several meetings over the next months. Its full complement of participants included the leaders of Yugoslavia's six republics, the eight-member collective Yugoslav presidency, and EC ministers. Those issues that could not be resolved by negotiation were to be handed to a five-member arbitration board whose decisions would be binding. The five members would be the heads of constitutional courts in France, Italy, and Germany, plus one judge each from Croatia and Serbia. The board would be required to reach a decision within two months after Carrington submitted a case to it.

The EC put forward formal proposals designed to nudge the Yugoslav republics not just toward a cease-fire but also toward a long-term settlement. The proposals would have replaced the Yugoslav federal structure with a "free association of republics with an international personality." Guarantees for the rights of minorities would be provided, ethnic enclaves would be disarmed, and a customs union and programs for economic cooperation would be established. There would be no unilateral changes in borders. Early in October 1991 an agreement along these lines had seemed possible, partly because it required Croatia to continue in some form of association with Serbia and required Serbia to renounce the use of force to change its borders. All the republics except for Serbia, Montenegro, and Slovenia (which considered itself fully independent) had accepted the EC plan for restructuring Yugoslavia. On October 7, however, the three-month delay in implementing their declarations of independence expired for both Slovenia and Croatia. They then proceeded to nullify their legal connections with the Yugoslav federal government. By the end of October, the president of Serbia, Slobodan Milosevic, was dismissing the EC plan as a violation of Yugoslavia's federal constitution.

President Mikhail Gorbachev's efforts at friendly persuasion were equally fruitless. On October 15, the presidents of Croatia and Serbia met with Gorbachev in Moscow and issued a communiqué calling for an immediate cease-fire and the beginning of negotiations within a month under the sponsorship of the United States, the Soviet Union, and the European Community. This promising opening failed to materialize.

At a meeting in Belgrade on October 23, the leaders of Serbia began to unveil their plans for a Greater Serbia as the successor state to Yugoslavia. On November 8, the European Community announced that it was imposing economic sanctions. These included suspension of a 1980 trade and cooperation agreement, limits on imports of Yugoslav textiles, elimination of benefits under the General System of Preferences, and exclusion of Yugoslavia from an EC-backed economic recovery program. A more direct blow to the federal army's war-making capability was the Community's intention to seek a UN-ordered oil embargo against Yugoslavia. Most of Yugoslavia's oil imports come from the Soviet Union and Libya. On November 9, President George Bush personally declared that the United States would support these sanctions.

Most of the Community's mediation effort had been directed toward the limited objective of a cease-fire. Getting agreement to cease-fires proved to be an easy thing to do, but none of the combatants took them seriously and none of them took hold. One problem was that irregular forces were not fully under the control of the Serbian or Croatian governments. Twelve cease-fires were brokered and broken before the EC decided to impose sanctions. A thirteenth was negotiated and ignored shortly afterwards. Observers were sent to Yugoslavia, however, and some precedents were set that may be relevant for future peacekeeping operations. For example, at a meeting in Prague on August 8 and

9, 1991, the CSCE's Committee of Senior Officials—Yugoslavia concurring—agreed "to include other CSCE participating states invited by Yugoslavia" in the observation teams. Yugoslavia agreed to accept observers from the Czech and Slovak Federal Republic, Poland, Sweden, and Canada. The observers are therefore CSCE sponsored, not just EC mandated. The costs are borne by the governments that furnish monitors. This is a model that is apt to be used again. It allows groups within the CSCE to engage in peacekeeping operations at their own expense while the full membership legitimizes the effort.

The EC did not want to send peacekeeping units to areas where a cease-fire had not yet taken hold. This has been one of the main obstacles to inserting peacekeeping forces into the war zone, and various ideas were floated to deal with it. For example, the EC mission to Yugoslavia in early August suggested that monitors of a cease-fire should consist of "units of the federal armed forces, representatives of the authorities in Croatia and representatives of the Serb population in Croatia in coordination and cooperation with European Community monitors." That EC suggestion failed when Serbia boycotted a scheduled meeting with the EC ministers and Yugoslavia's collective presidency.

Yugoslavia also had its own cease-fire monitors, charged by the federal government with enforcing an "absolute and unconditional cease-fire" approved by the six Yugoslav republics. The observers consisted in part of plainclothes federal police from Macedonia and Bosnia-Hercegovina. One of the members of the cease-fire commission reported on August 23 that the commission was unable to enforce a cease-fire because the federal army seemed unwilling to defend both Serbs and Croats. Instead, he said, he saw Serbian guerrillas wearing army uniforms and driving vehicles with army licence plates.

Recognizing that the Community was placing self-imposed limits on the effectiveness of its mediation efforts, some EC members understood almost at once that escalation of the EC commitment might be necessary. As early as August 1991, Hans van den Broek said that he had "no great objections in principle" to deployment of an armed European peacekeeping force in Croatia. The *New York Times* reported on August 1, 1991, that officials from France, Britain, and Luxembourg had privately acknowledged that military personnel might have to augment the EC observer teams. Croatia would probably appeal to the Helsinki Conference and the United Nations for peacekeeping forces to be sent to the country, said President Franjo Tudjman of Croatia in early August, also according to the *New York Times*. Nothing happened.

The president of the European Commission, Jacques Delors, remarked that "the Community is like an adolescent facing the crisis of an adult. It now only has the weapons of recognition and economic aid. If it were 10 years older, it might be able to impose a military peacekeeping force." France had suggested in July that EC observers should carry sidearms for their own protection. On September 11, 1991, French President François Mitterrand, referring to peacekeeping forces for Yugoslavia, stated that "if, for legal reasons, the United Nations excuses itself, France expects the European Community to take the initiative." On September 17, the *New York Times* reported that Dutch officials had proposed a "lightly armed" force for Yugoslavia, not to impose a cease-fire but rather to use a European show of arms to discourage a resumption of warfare after a new cease-fire had gone into effect.

John Tagliabue, the Balkans correspondent of the *New York Times*, perceptively summed up the situation as of September 15, 1991:

[E]fforts to establish a cease-fire, despite the presence of dozens of cease-fire monitors operating under the flag of the community, were failing miserably . . . the little war was increasingly becoming a test of the effectiveness of forging a common European foreign policy in a post–cold war world. With ethnic rivalries and nationalist conflicts like those in Yugoslavia abounding throughout newly democratic central Europe, the test was not going well at all.

As if to underscore this judgment, the European Community foreign ministers, meeting on September 19, failed to reach agreement on organizing an armed peacekeeping force. Germany, France, and Italy had backed the Dutch proposal but Britain had blocked agreement. The British foreign secretary, Douglas Hurd, drew on British experience in Northern Ireland to make two points that certainly need emphasis in considering peacekeeping operations: it is easier to put troops in than take them out; [and] the scale of effort at the start bears no resemblance to the scale of effort later on. It might be noted in passing that if the level of violence in Yugoslavia could be reduced to that prevalent in Northern Ireland the investment of peacekeeping forces for a few years would save thousands of lives.

The Western European Union (WEU), despite British hesitations, was asked by EC ministers to draw up contingency plans for the use of armed forces. Options developed by the military staffs of the WEU included a 30,000-man force, a lightly armed corps, and a force of 10,000 or fewer. None of these plans was ever activated. The possibility of intervening with naval forces was endorsed on November 18, when the WEU foreign and defense ministers offered warships to protect Red Cross ships evacuating the wounded from Yugoslavia. Britain, France, and Italy were prepared to make warships available. Foreign Secretary Hurd said, however, that the offer would have to be negotiated with Serbia and Croatia. The idea of small-scale intervention was discouraged by public statements by U.S. officials suggesting that the scale of any military effort to halt the fighting in Yugoslavia would be prohibitively large.

The Serbs and Croats have themselves at various times favored the interposition of external forces and have said so publicly. For example, in its response to the EC peace settlement proposals in early November, Serbia stated that the federal army would withdraw from Serbian-populated enclaves in Croatia following the deployment in those places of an international force adequate to protect the Serbs in Croatia. On November 6, President Tudjman reportedly said that "ideally some ships from the [U.S.] Sixth Fleet should be sent into the Adriatic and air traffic should be blockaded just as it was in the Persian Gulf war." The most serious proposal was a letter to the UN Security Council reported in the media on November 9, in which the remaining members of the Yugoslav federal presidency asked for UN peacekeeping forces to provide a buffer between Serbian and Croatian forces.

Chancellor Helmut Kohl of Germany and President Mitterrand, as early as September 19, had proposed that the Community seek a UN mandate for a peacekeeping force to establish a "buffer zone" between the warring forces in Yugoslavia. The federal army had flatly opposed the introduction of peacekeeping forces, but this position was overruled in the letter to the UN from Yugoslavia's federal presidency. The Croatian foreign minister immediately welcomed the idea of peacekeeping forces and on November 13, Lord Carrington pursued the idea in conversations with the Serbian and Croatian presidents. Not surprisingly, the Serbs wanted the peacekeeping forces to be inserted along the line established by the Serbian incursion into Croatia, while Croats wanted the forces to be placed along the republic's old borders. Nonetheless, when the three EC members of the UN

Security Council—Britain, France, and Belgium—drafted a resolution to implement the EC decision to seek an oil embargo, included in it was a request to the UN secretary general to seek a
cease-fire that would last long enough to permit the deployment
of UN peacekeeping forces between the Serbian and Croatian
forces. Included also was a proposal for a mechanism to tighten
compliance with a UN-imposed embargo on arms shipments to
Yugoslavia.

Activating the United Nations machinery created one immediate result. It shifted the burden of seeking a cease-fire from the
European Community mediators to a UN team headed by former
U.S. Secretary of State Cyrus Vance and Marrack Goulding, head
of the UN Secretariat's peacekeeping operations. Lord Carrington had stressed the requirements for a cease-fire before EC
peacekeeping forces could be introduced and Vance was just as
emphatic about this prerequisite. No UN peacekeeping forces
would be considered unless the warring factions had accepted a
lasting and effective cease-fire.

On November 17, the day that Vance arrived in Yugoslavia to
assess the prospects for introducing UN peacekeeping forces, the
defenses of Vukovar, a city of key importance to Croatia, were
overcome after three months of a siege conducted by the federal
army and Serbian irregulars. The federal army at once began to
move its tanks and artillery to the nearby Croatian cities of Osijek
and Vinkovci, inhabited largely by ethnic Croatians. This movement was accompanied by new cease-fire negotiations among the
Croats, Serbs, and the UN mission, which led to the signing of a
fourteenth cease-fire by Tudjman, Milosevic, and Yugoslav defense minister General Veljko Kadijevic in Geneva on November
23. The cease-fire conditions were similar to those of earlier
cease-fires. They included a requirement that Croatia should allow federal forces trapped at bases inside Croatia to go to Serbia.
Another condition was that all paramilitary or irregular forces on
either side would also observe the cease-fire, a very difficult objective to achieve.

Vance expressed the view that when they were deployed, UN
troops should be inserted in an "inkblot" fashion to deal with
"flashpoints," that is, areas where the situation was particularly
tense. This would sidestep the issue of whether UN forces would
form a buffer at the border between Serbia and Croatia, as
Croatia wanted, or between Serbian and Croatian forces where
they were as of the time of the cease-fire, as Serbia wanted.

The fourteenth cease-fire lasted long enough for Vance to report to the UN Security Council that it seemed to be working. Thus encouraged, the Security Council on November 27 unanimously adopted a resolution that enabled Vance to return to Yugoslavia to work out arrangements for the deployment of up to 10,000 UN peacekeeping troops. Two aspects of the Security Council's action require special note. The European Community decided not to press for an oil embargo, thus once again dropping any real element of coercion. Second, the support of the Yugoslav delegation to the United Nations was indispensable to win the votes of India and other like-minded countries. Significantly, the role of the UN in resolving internal—as opposed to external—disputes was seen by these countries as unwanted meddling in domestic matters.

Shortly after this hopeful action by the UN, Croatian President Tudjman announced that Croatia would accept UN troops in battle zones in the republic, not just on the border. Adding to the euphoria, federal army forces began a peaceful withdrawal from barracks near Zagreb. By December 1, however, coincident with Vance's return to Yugoslavia, the intensity of fighting had begun to increase. The UN mediator was obliged as soon as he arrived on the scene to express disappointment at the lack of progress.

Thoroughly frustrated by their experiences in Yugoslavia, the European Community's monitoring team in that country had drafted a highly critical report for the EC presidency. The report leaked as the fourteenth cease-fire began to collapse. The federal army's strategy, the report said, was to "pour heavy artillery fire onto a target . . . send in undisciplined irregulars, then move into the villages to reassume overall control." Military intervention by outside forces could deal with the situation, the report suggested: "There is good reason to believe that selective show and use of force—to intimidate and hit the J.N.A. [Yugoslav Peoples' Army] in places where it hurts can cow its bluster and bluff." The monitors accused the federal army of fighting only "for its own status and survival." At the same time, the German government renewed its threats to recognize Slovenia and Croatia by the end of the year, whether or not other members of the EC agreed to do so. Bonn also imposed a ban on air, sea, and land links with Serbia. Partly to encourage recognition, the Croatian parliament decided to grant ethnic Serbian enclaves in Croatia a degree of self-rule.

Meanwhile, as Vance worked to create conditions that would win the Security Council's agreement to deploy UN peacekeeping forces in Yugoslavia, the Serbs increased the pressure on Osijek. Touring the city on December 3, Vance was reportedly shocked by the damage and subsequently protested to the Yugoslav defense minister over the shelling of the city. Dubrovnik, too, came under renewed attack. In Bonn, Chancellor Kohl told the presidents of Croatia and Slovenia that Germany would grant them recognition before Christmas, a move opposed by the United States, Britain, and France. Some of Yugoslavia's neighbors, however, warned that they might follow Germany's lead. The concern of those opposing recognition was that this should await an overall peace settlement and that Serbia's response would be to escalate the conflict, rather than to negotiate. Stepping up its own pressure on all the republics, the United States announced on December 6 a series of economic sanctions, to take effect on December 21.

On December 12, UN Secretary General Pérez de Cuéllar announced plans for a UN peacekeeping force of more than 10,000 troops. The force would consist of 10 infantry battalions and police units. It would be deployed in regions where Serbs and Croats lived in proximity to one another and would assist in humanitarian work, including resettlement of displaced people. The federal army would be withdrawn from Croatia. But the secretary general stipulated that "an effective cease-fire" would have to be in place before the plan could be implemented. Clearly, from the secretary general's report, Serbian irregular forces continued to block an effective cease-fire.

Efforts in the Security Council to organize a peacekeeping force coincided with efforts by Washington to block German diplomatic recognition of Croatia and Slovenia. On December 12–13, Deputy Secretary of State Lawrence S. Eagleburger gave "stern warnings" to the 12 members of the European Community that premature and selective recognition of Yugoslav republics would damage prospects for peace and lead to greater bloodshed. These warnings followed letters to the EC from Lord Carrington and Pérez de Cuéllar also cautioning against early recognition. In the Security Council, the British and French sought to head off the German action by sponsoring a resolution calling for military observers to be sent to Yugoslavia to begin arrangements for deployment of the UN peacekeeping force once a cease-fire had taken hold. The two delegations also proposed a clause that would warn against "political actions," that is, recognition that would harm the reconciliation process. All this was to no avail. The German foreign minister, Hans-Dietrich Genscher, responded to the UN secretary general by asserting that denying recognition would only encourage the Yugoslav Peoples' Army in its "policy of conquest." The UN Security Council on December 15 adopted a resolution that watered down the nonrecognition appeal and authorized the dispatch of 18 to 20 military, police, and political observers to Yugoslavia. Reportedly, the United States had objected to a more ambitious French-British proposal to send as many as 100 military observers there.

President Bush added his voice to the debate on December 15 by saying "we want to see a peaceful evolution." Adding that the United States had been "strongly supportive" of the UN and of the EC, President Bush said "their advice has been to go slow on recognition, and I think they're right."

Germany's advice carried the day, however, in the EC foreign ministers' meeting in Brussels on December 16. The ministers agreed unanimously that they would extend recognition by January 15, 1992, to any Yugoslav republics that asked for it by December 23, provided certain criteria were met. These included protection of minority and human rights, adherence to democratic principles, and respect for existing borders. The decision, however, would permit EC members to extend recognition even if the standards had not been met. Thus, as the new year dawned, the conflict in Yugoslavia would cease being a civil war and become an international European war. The media speculated that fighting soon would spread to Bosnia-Hercegovina.

Lessons for the Future

Were there errors of commission or omission in the EC's mediation effort in Yugoslavia? The Serbs and Croats had irreconcilable agendas and seemed to prefer slaughtering each other to compromise. The general assessment of the leaders of the Yugoslav republics is that they are not men of great political stature and vision. The prospects for success—meaning a reasonably effective cease-fire accompanied by serious efforts to reconstitute the basis for relations among the Yugoslav republics—were never very bright.

Still, any critique of the EC effort must begin with an acknowledgment that the Community's hand was weakened by its apparent public repudiation of the use of armed force under almost any circumstances. In discussing the use of peacekeeping forces, it is essential to make a distinction between *peacekeeping* and *peace enforcing*. The former relates to a situation where a cease-fire has taken hold and where the principal parties to a conflict want help in preserving a shaky peace. Such forces are lightly armed and their mission may be compared to that of police forces. Peace-enforcing missions, in contrast, may operate in environments where a conflict is still raging. Their purpose is to impose a peace, rather than to preserve it. For such a purpose, well-equipped regular units are necessary and their mission is similar to that of a military campaign.

Some EC members, most notably France, seemed favorably disposed toward peace-enforcing operations but most of the EC debate was evidently focused on peacekeeping operations. It was the reluctance of some EC nations, particularly Britain, to authorize the use of peacekeeping forces under conditions of a shaky cease-fire that was most indicative of a lack of full commitment to the mediation effort in Yugoslavia. This meant, in practice, that the conduct of irregular forces, rather than republican governments, determined whether peacekeeping forces could be introduced. The tragedy of Yugoslavia was allowed to mount in intensity and to become a disastrous precedent for all the other disputes in Eastern Europe while the Community denied itself anything like the ultimate argument. The possibility that force would be used to deny military objectives to an attacker or to exact punishment for violations of a cease-fire by irregular forces was a consideration that neither Serbs nor Croats ever had to face. It was this void in the diplomatic process that obviously troubled the EC monitors and led to their cri de coeur to the EC presidency.

The risk of escalation to large-scale military involvement is always present once any military action is taken. Foreign Secretary Hurd was right to warn of that. The risks of not acting also may be serious, especially if Yugoslavia is a test case for how nations will behave in the post–cold war world. There were specific, quite limited tasks that could have been accomplished with the use of armed forces. These included protection of observers, reconnaissance overflights of disputed areas, constabulary duties, and protecting food and medical shipments to besieged towns. More open-ended and more hazardous tasks would have included overseeing the disarming of and providing protection for

Serbian enclaves in Croatia and relieving federal army troops blockaded in garrisons in Croatia. The Community also discussed the idea of inserting military units as a show of force to deter violations in areas where cease-fires had been negotiated. There were moments when that might have been feasible. Carrying out these tasks would not automatically have resulted in the need to deploy several divisions of West European combat forces. Yet an inordinate fear that this might happen seems to have prevented a rational exploration at the political level of limited military actions, whether peacekeeping or peace enforcing, even the threat of which might have made a difference.

A second and related factor that contributed to the EC's inability to halt the fighting was the very low profile assumed by the United States regarding Yugoslavia throughout the latter part of 1991. The Bush administration preferred to leave the running to the Community and was immensely pleased with the Community's agreement to this policy. Occasionally, the United States made clear its support for the EC's effort and occasionally it denounced the actions of Yugoslav republics, particularly Serbia. It *chose* this course; it was not obliged to. It is also true that the allies, through misjudging the situation, missed an opportunity to concert their policies when the idea was raised in the North Atlantic Council in the fall of 1990 by the United States.

The U.S. effort in Yugoslavia bore no resemblance, of course, to the successful diplomatic offensives by the president and Secretary of State James A. Baker III in the cases of the Persian Gulf War and the Arab–Israeli peace conference. It is hard to escape the conclusion that the absence of a high-profile U.S. involvement weakened the EC mediation attempts and discouraged some members of the Community from contemplating the use of limited force in Yugoslavia. The lesson could be pushed still further: it is probable that the West European nations, divided as they still are, will not engage in peacekeeping operations in Central and Eastern Europe that require the use of armed force unless the United States is at their side. "Where the United States does not tread, the alliance does not follow." The experience also showed once again that even the United States cannot set the rules of the game while sitting on the sidelines. Opposing recognition of Croatia and Slovenia was a policy that brought the United States into a head-on collision with its major European allies. The United States had little chance of winning that policy argument when it was contributing so little to the peace process.

There were two other factors that hampered the mediation effort, both questions of process, rather than principle. The first was the reluctance of the EC to escalate its pressure more rapidly than it did. It should not have taken 12 broken cease-fire agreements to persuade the Community that it had to raise the ante. By the time the Community decided to impose sanctions the war itself had caused at least as much damage to the country's economy as the sanctions were ever likely to cause. The time to impose sanctions probably would have been in July when the potential economic losses might have loomed larger in the minds of Yugoslav leaders. The indecision on this issue was another reflection of how difficult it is for 12 nations to conduct a common foreign policy.

Another process problem was the fact that other institutions that could have been actively and visibly engaged took a more passive stance than was necessary or desirable. The threat to international peace and security represented by the conflagration in Yugoslavia was not sufficiently dramatized or publicized during the latter half of 1991 in any of the forums that might have been utilized for this purpose.

The UN adopted an arms embargo, and the Security Council discussed Yugoslavia from time to time. "No one can tell us what the U.N. can do that would be useful," a U.S. official was reported to have said in September. Late in the year, however, as we have seen, the secretary general appointed a special representative, Cyrus Vance, who played a useful, even crucial role in developing the possibilities for application of peacekeeping forces in Yugoslavia. The UN was hampered, of course, by the worries of countries that wanted the UN to stay out of intrastate quarrels.

The CSCE's Committee of Senior Officials held several meetings in Prague without much notice by the media. The foreign ministers of the CSCE assembled only once, in June, for their inaugural meeting as the Council of Ministers in Berlin. The presidency of the CSCE Council of Ministers was held by German Foreign Minister Genscher, a strong supporter of the CSCE, but because of suspicions, especially in Yugoslavia, about German intentions in the Balkans Genscher was not able to be as effective in this role as his energy and skill would have indicated. The mandate that the nations fashioned for the CSCE Council of Ministers virtually precluded them from meeting for emergencies like Yugoslavia anyway. The result has been that the CSCE has been practically invisible throughout the Yugoslav conflict.

NATO, of course, issued communiqués but the Yugoslav issue was never portrayed as the main business of high-level meetings of the alliance. This was especially noticeable at the Rome NATO summit meeting of November 7–8, 1991. Assembling at a critical juncture in the Yugoslav agony and in a country adjoining Yugoslavia, the heads of state were preoccupied with whether U.S. forces should remain in Western Europe and with a new strategic concept for NATO. Of course they addressed the Yugoslav crisis by opposing the use of force to change existing borders. There was little recognition of the fact that Yugoslavia, not strategic concepts, was shaping the new world order.

The European Community had trouble making key decisions because of internal differences. Would things have gone better if one of the other institutions—NATO or the UN—had been handed the Yugoslav assignment at the outset? Considering the limits that the nations potentially involved imposed upon themselves respecting the use of military force, it does not seem likely that the Community's performance could have been much improved. It is, after all, national governments and not international institutions that determine what is possible. What Britain, France, or the United States were not prepared to do in one institution they were not likely to do in another.

Yugoslavia may be unique. But it also may be a paradigm for the kind of security threat that Europe and North America will face in the decades ahead. A central lesson of Yugoslavia is this: borders can be changed by force so long as the struggle is between successor states to a former union, and in such circumstances the international community will not react with force of any kind. This could be as deadly a lesson as Munich was in its time.

Steps Toward Contingency Planning

When anything like Yugoslavia happens again the international community should be better prepared for it. Among other things, a Europe-based peacekeeping force should have been trained and ready for use. The functions of such a force and the conditions under which it might be used should have been thoroughly studied. Realistic means should have been devised to help governments assess the risk of limited use of force as against the risk of major escalation of force on the one hand or the risk of no use of force at all, on the other. Facing unfamiliar problems in 1991, the governments that might have been effective in moderating the fighting in Yugoslavia shrank from taking resolute action. Next time, the kinds of problems that Yugoslavia presented should be seen in a broader perspective. If the pattern of Yugoslavia is repeated even once more, the road to war in Europe will be so well marked and the road away so obscure that war must become the norm. A commentary of Winston Churchill's comes to mind:

We shall see how the counsels of prudence and restraint may become the prime agents of mortal danger; how the middle course adopted from desires for safety and a quiet life may be found to lead direct to the bull's-eye of disaster. We shall see how absolute is the need of a broad path of international action pursued by many states in common across the years, irrespective of the ebb and flow of national politics.

And yet, a beginning toward international peacekeeping may have been made in the case of Yugoslavia. What positive lessons there are need to be taken to heart. The experience suggests that at least two levels of involvement by international institutions will come into play in this kind of situation. The first is the legitimizing action provided by the international community through a broadly based institution like the United Nations or the Conference on Security and Cooperation in Europe. The second is the operational responsibility assumed by some subset of those institutions. This has been the pattern tentatively established with regard to Yugoslavia and it seems likely to be repeated.

Thus, the UN or the CSCE in this model would give its approval to the principle that some action is necessary. Ideally, the state or states most directly concerned should join in this consensus. At this point, a smaller, action-taking institution or group of states would take over. This could be NATO, or the WEU, or a group of states that band together on an ad hoc basis, perhaps within the CSCE framework, for the purpose of mounting a peacekeeping operation.

This model could be important for the East Central European states and the Soviet republics, which need reassurance that collective security will work for them too. The former Warsaw Pact nations have not exhibited much interest in the CSCE as a security mechanism. They know that it is structurally impaired by its decision-making procedures. The requirement for unanimity almost guarantees that it will not be an action-taking operational organization. They also know that the United States almost never exhibits leadership in the CSCE in security matters and this, to them, is proof enough that there is no security to be found in this organization.

NATO could help correct this situation as an operating arm of the CSCE. But peacekeeping operations, as pioneered by the United Nations in many parts of the world, require skills that are different from those for which armies are normally trained. Because this is the type of operation that is likely to be most needed in East Central Europe, NATO should give priority to training some units in these skills. Indeed, if NATO is to be relevant to the real security problems of Europe, it is essential that the alliance accelerate such preparations.

The WEU also could prepare itself to take on such assignments. So could the CSCE, through its Conflict Prevention Center, if the nations authorized the center to undertake contingency planning and gave it a proper military staff.

There are five types of peacekeeping operations that might be needed in the future. The reality of these examples has been demonstrated in Yugoslavia. These are:

- to carry out humanitarian functions, such as organizing shipments of food and medicine under hazardous conditions;
- to observe a situation that contains some risk of conflict;
- to patrol borders or other sensitive areas;
- to establish a buffer zone between adversarial military forces; and
- to protect enclaves of ethnic minorities.

Such situations would probably subsume all of the possible crises that can be envisaged in Eastern Europe: ethnic disputes within one state, political subunits of one state on the verge of conflict with one another, and two states that are on a collision course over some unresolved issue.

The Yugoslav situation has highlighted the need to think through some of the practical organizational problems of peacekeeping that may arise in Europe. Contingency planning in NATO, the WEU, or the CSCE Conflict Prevention Center should be authorized so that governments will understand the issues that will have to be decided if they are ever to authorize military force in crisis situations. These include the authority to send and receive forces, national origins of forces, command arrangements, and readiness status. Three possible models for peacekeeping forces are illustrated in figure 1.

Model I is a system like the CSCE–EC relationship today. It is the most likely kind of peacekeeping because it assumes a UN or CSCE sanction for actions carried out by a smaller organization. A NATO peacekeeping operation sanctioned by the CSCE would be one example of how this model might work. Model II is a system based on the assumption that the CSCE itself could be-

Figure 1
Three Models of Peacekeeping Forces

Decisions Required	Model I	Model II	Model III
Authority to send forces	UN or CSCE	UN or CSCE	UN or CSCE
Authority to receive forces	Host central government approval or all factions involved	Host central government approval or all factions involved	Host central government or government of local jurisdiction
National origins of forces	NATO, WEU, and/or some CSCE members on ad hoc basis	Any CSCE member	Great powers only
Command arrangements	Commander appointed by NATO/WEU/subset of CSCE	Commander selected by director of Conflict Prevention Center with approval of states contributing	Commander selected for one-year term by contributing states. Each state serves in turn.
Readiness status	Responsibility of operational organization	Standards set by Conflict Prevention Center to permit deployment within 48 hours	Deployment possible within 24 hours. Joint exercises
Funding	Funding by nations contributing forces	Special assessment for all members	Great power funding

come operational through its Conflict Prevention Center. Model II envisages the possibility that the CSCE would develop its own peacekeeping capabilities relying, of course, on forces provided by member states but with a permanent and sturdy CSCE infrastructure that would provide some institutional glue. Model III assumes a case where the major military powers of Europe and North America jointly form peacekeeping units, under the aegis of the UN or the CSCE. Neither Model II nor Model III seems very realistic at present.

Each of these models assumes that the CSCE could supplement or substitute for the United Nations in future peacekeeping decisions, especially with regard to the very important legitimizing function. These expectations may not be realistic. The CSCE's role in the current Yugoslav crisis has been much more limited than might have been expected when the CSCE heads of government issued their "Charter of Paris for a New Europe" in November 1990. There are many reasons for this. Initial Soviet opposition to a peacekeeping role for the CSCE in Yugoslavia has been cited above. The aspirations of France and some other European nations for a common defense and foreign policy within the European Community tilted them toward the WEU. The unanimity rule in the CSCE gives Yugoslavia a veto over any decision in that body, thus suggesting that other institutions might better handle the operational aspects of peacekeeping in Europe. As for the United States, a press report claims that "European officials said the Bush administration has made clear that it wants no part of cease-fire monitoring efforts and only a passive role in mediation." This, of course, made the EC an ideal choice for the United States.

There are sound reasons for developing regional peacekeeping machinery in Europe. The UN debate on the Yugoslav question in November 1991 showed clearly that non-European UN members are prepared to block peacekeeping operations for reasons having nothing to do with Europe. Ideally, the UN should encourage issues to be handled in a regional context so that the UN itself will not become overloaded. Conversely, as Henry Kissinger argued recently, "if global collective security is pursued too literally, regional institutions like NATO will gradually wither, and a threshold will be created below which local pressures and even aggressions may flourish." If the UN were the only legitimate body for peacekeeping operations in Europe, the CSCE would gradually cease to have even a pretense to responsibility for security in Europe.

However it evolves, one of the main questions for countries participating in the CSCE is whether its requirement for consensus should be further modified in order to make this institution more effective in fast-moving crisis situations. If this cannot be done, the CSCE will probably be doomed to being a talk shop. Its crisis management potential, even in passing the operational baton to NATO or the WEU, will not be fully realized.

It does not have to be this way. It is not too late for the members to turn their attention to strengthening the CSCE as a peacekeeping instrument, even while giving operational responsibility for peacekeeping to other mechanisms. Changes in methods of reaching decisions are needed, probably to include a qualified majority vote under clearly defined conditions. Investing in the contingency planning and operational capabilities of the CSCE's Conflict Prevention Center in Vienna is essential. NATO can help enormously in this respect. There should be an infusion of NATO talent and experience in Vienna. If amour propre is a problem, let it be a joint NATO–WEU contribution. Links to the United Nations should be forged so that the CSCE can develop into a regional peacekeeping organization in the meaning of the United Nations Charter. All of this demands U.S. leadership. Providing this will also provide at least some of the reassurance needed by the nations of East Central Europe and by the republics of the former Soviet Union.

Conclusion

Experience in Yugoslavia points out the need to think about the unthinkable—international intervention in internal struggles. It bears repeating that intervention in civil wars carries great risks and usually should be avoided. International peacekeeping forces may be necessary, however, to help contain the conflict within the borders of the affected state and to avoid dangerous precedents concerning frontiers. Mediation efforts must be accompanied by some element of military coercion if they are to be successful. And if one accepts the dictum that "all wars must end," some wars might end with all the parties asking for peacekeeping forces. In such cases, third-party intervention with military force could be indispensable. Europe is very poorly prepared to deal with such problems. Furthermore, the involvement of the United States in maintaining peace not only in Western but also in Central and Eastern Europe is essential to long-term stability there. The evidence of traditional divergences of view between Germany, France, and Britain on East European issues has been quite clear in the case of Yugoslavia. It is equally clear that the voice of the United States cannot be heard very well if Washington is only offering advice from the sidelines. Most important, the unwillingness of the majority of the states directly concerned with the issue of peaceful change in the Balkans to consider the use of armed peacekeeping forces except under the most ideal conditions, and perhaps not even then, is a major setback to hopes for a new peace order in Europe. The stakes are too high to let this happen again.

II. REFORM AND FINANCE

EDITOR'S INTRODUCTION

Veteran critics of the U.S. government bureaucracy may take solace in at least one matter: the bureaucracy of the United Nations may be worse. The first article in this section, "Reforming the United Nations", by Professor Gene Lyons of Dartmouth College, analyzes recent efforts to streamline the United Nations organization. Ideally, the large U.N. bureaucracy should be composed of politically neutral, highly qualified civil servants, but Professor Robert S. Jordan, writing in *Public Administration Review*, finds instead a highly politicized staff, reflecting the biases of individual member states.

The third article, "Can the U.N. Stretch to Fit Its Future?", by Tad Daley, a Fellow of the RAND/UCLA Center for Soviet Studies, speculates on whether the U.N. will need to expand the provisions of its original charter to accomplish new goals, such as peacekeeping during an internal civil war.

In the concluding piece, "U.N. Dues: The Price of Peace", Enid C.B. Schoettle, a senior fellow at the Council of Foreign Relations, discusses the growing costs of the U.N.'s expanding range of activities.

REFORMING THE UNITED NATIONS[1]

Introduction

The 41st General Assembly of the United Nations met in September 1986 with the usual long agenda. The issues ranged

[1]Excerpts of an article by Gene M. Lyons, Professor of Public Affairs at Dartmouth College, from *International Social Science Journal* 120:249–266 My '89. Copyright © 1989 by the *International Social Science Journal*. Reprinted with permission.

from conflict in the Middle East and apartheid in South Africa to strategies for economic development and legal principles to regulate remote sensing from outer space. But major attention focused on a more mundane issue entitled: 'Review of the efficiency of the administrative and financial functioning of the United Nations', which had long been hovering over the organization. It was now forced on the agenda by the threat by the United States to reduce its contribution to the UN unless it could meet a congressional mandate that the one state—one vote formula be changed to give greater weight in voting to major contributors. Over the years, other members had been delinquent in paying their assessed contributions and some had held back payments from specific programmes they did not support. But the US action was particularly significant both because the United States, assessed at 25 per cent of the regular budget, is the largest contributor to the UN and because any change in the method of voting attacked the principle of the sovereign equality of all member-states.

Throughout the autumn months, debate concentrated on the report of a group of eighteen experts set up a year earlier to present recommendations for 'improving the . . . functioning of the Organization'. The Assembly had no difficulty in unanimously supporting a series of recommendations by the Group of Eighteen for severely cutting back UN staffing at the top levels and simplifying what had become very cumbersome procedures for dealing with the organization's business. There was less success in finding a formula to satisfy the American demand for weighted voting in the UN budgetary process. The expert group itself had been split on the issue, finally presenting three formulae that had been discussed, none gaining full support. The ball was thrown back onto the main playing field.

The compromise worked out was to provide for consensus voting early in the budgetary process when the projected programme for the next financial period is reviewed by the Committee for Programme and Coordination (CPC). Proposed programmes move from the CPC, where content is examined, to the Advisory Committee on Administrative and Budgetary Questions (ACABQ) for financial and administrative review. During the Assembly itself, the programme and budget are then reviewed by the Fifth Committee on their way to the General Assembly for approval. Consensus voting at the CPC stage gave the United States (which, as a major power, always has a seat on the 21 member CPC) a virtual veto on projected programmes without forcing a revision of the principle of one state—one vote in the Charter. The problem was that it also gave a veto to every other member of the CPC. The Iraqi Ambassador emphasized the risks of consensus if applied too broadly:

If every Member of the Assembly or of any group has to vote positively for everything, consensus means something worse than weighted voting; it means transferring the veto of the five permanent members of the Security Council to others—going back to the League of Nations where every member of the Council . . . had a veto.

In the end, the formula stood. Whatever may have been the views of the members of even the American delegation about the potential dangers of consensus, they were faced with a mandate to which they had to find an answer if the assessed contribution of the United States was to be appropriated by the Congress. At the same time, the practice of consensus voting had become widely prevalent in the UN as a practical way of avoiding North–South divisions on many issues. Indeed, the chief American representative reminded the Assembly that both the CPC and the ACABQ 'have traditionally taken their decisions by consensus'. The difference was that the requirement for consensus was now made explicit under what some members considered to be conditions of duress.

The budgetary questions were only the tip of the iceberg, however. 'The United Nations is at a critical juncture', the American delegate said, 'it is facing a crisis of reform, the root causes of which are political and bureaucratic.' His diagnosis was shared by others, however much they might have disagreed about the sources of the crisis, let alone the ways of reforming the organization. In his report to the General Assembly, the Secretary-General also sounded the alarm. 'Regrettably', he wrote, '1986 has witnessed the United Nations subjected to a severe crisis challenging its solvency and viability'. The immediate problem was the failure of member-states (and especially the United States in this instance) to pay their obligated contributions. But, more deeply, he recognized the need for 'the strengthening and revitalization of the present structure of multilateral institutions . . .' and went on to explain:

Various factors have contributed to the present difficulties of many multilateral organizations. We are still adjusting to the new and uneasy distribution of forces in the world resulting from the Second World War, from the revolution of decolonization, from demographic and technological changes, from the mixed patterns of development and, of course, from the advent of nuclear weapons.

The Secretary-General is correct: the international system has not yet fully adjusted to the dramatic forces for change that have been generated since 1945. He may also be correct when he argues that 'the United Nations should be, and is, a central element in bringing . . . the necessary adjustments' to these changes. Nevertheless, the role of the UN today is considerably different from what it was intended to be in 1945, when the United Nations system was the only framework within which states could become engaged in multilateral diplomacy in pursuit of their interests. This is no longer the case. The UN system itself is highly decentralized and the United Nations is now only part of a larger framework of international organizations within which the goals of peace and security and economic and social stability are being pursued.

The movement for reform in the UN, beyond 'improving administrative and financial functioning' will thus also have to address the question: What is the role of the United Nations in today's world? This was already evident in the report of the Group of Eighteen experts when it called for 'a careful and in-depth study of the intergovernmental structure in the economic and social fields'. Quite significantly, the words 'intergovernmental structure' extends the study not only beyond the central UN organs to the specialized agencies in the UN system, but also through the entire system of international economic relations. The issue is not simply to find ways of increasing the efficiency of the UN, however important. The issue is to find an effective role for the UN in an international system in which governments now organize their political and economic relations through a highly decentralized complex of multilateral arrangements.

The problem, moreover, is two-fold and that makes it that much more difficult. It is, on the one hand, to identify the essential role for the United Nations in a world that is greatly changed from the time when the Charter was written. At the same time, it has to be a role that the majority of member states can support. Over the years, the Charter has proved to be a flexible document, permitting the UN to respond to new problems. When the original provisions for collective security were weakened by superpower rivalry, the UN assumed an important peacekeeping role that was widely supported. When the colonial systems began to fall apart, the UN provided considerable stability to the process of decolonization by the political support the vast majority of its members gave to independence and by the platform that the organization itself offered to new states on which to pursue their interests in international relations.

The weakness of the UN in recent years has been largely rooted in the deep divisions between the North and the South, the developed and the developing countries. The earlier split between East and West had prevented the full implementation of the Charter's security system. But the United States and its allies not only retained a majority in the principal organs, but also had the means for and interest in supporting peacekeeping operations and the transition of the UN toward policies of preventive diplomacy. Until very recently, the interests of the Soviet Union have always been defensive in the UN and particularly marginal in economic and social affairs. Once the developing countries attained a majority in the UN, the organization could continue to function effectively so long as there was a common interest on the part of the countries of the North to continue to carry the major financial costs whatever their disagreements with the countries of the South. Since the mid-1970s there has been a deterioration in North–South relations that has now put the United Nations at risk. The US Ambassador to the UN was quite blunt, yet quite accurate when he said: 'In plain terms, there is a lack of understanding and a lack of confidence among different groups of Member States concerning the motives of other groups. It is my view that the United Nations cannot continue to function in this fashion. . . .'

The observation is accurate whether one attributes the lack of understanding and confidence to the demands of the South, the recalcitrance of the North, or trends towards unilateralism in American foreign policy. In his report, the Secretary-General suggested that the divisiveness may be abating with the 'emergence of a widening constituency of basically pragmatic Governments with a firm grasp of the economic, social and technological characteristics of our time. . .'. He too may be right. If he is, then a new political consensus might emerge for reforms that could result in an effective United Nations. But what should those reforms be? The purpose of this article is to attempt to set out guidelines for the reform of the UN system. But, first, it will review what is being suggested by those who are studying the present crisis and recommending remedies.

Efforts to Begin the Reform Process

The mandate of the Group of Eighteen was deliberately limited. It was called upon to recommend immediate measures to meet the financial crisis accelerated by the American threat to withhold a substantial part of its contribution. The Group was created at the end of the 40th General Assembly and worked during the early part of 1986 to try to work out a series of recommendations. The Secretary-General already had to begin to cut back expenditure by freezing appointments and taking emergency measures to curtail administrative activities. A major purpose of the Group's report was thus to support the actions the Secretary-General had already taken. But it also specified further cuts at the higher levels of the Secretariat which had become 'too top-heavy', 'too complex' and 'too fragmented' and recommended a sharp reduction in meetings and conferences and in service costs and new facilities.

Beyond its mandate, the Group of Eighteen was limited by other factors. Its time was short and it was caught up in the controversial issue of voting procedures on which there were deep differences. The group was chosen to represent broad constituencies among UN members and many of the eighteen were members of national delegations. They could not therefore completely play the part of disinterested 'experts'. Their major contribution was, in effect, political: to demonstrate a willingness to undertake drastic cuts in the short term and a genuine determination to begin a process of reform. Thus, their report left major issues largely unresolved. They could only recommend that a longer range study of 'the inter-governmental structure in the economic and social fields' be carried out and urge that the Secretary-General assume 'greater leadership in personnel matters', especially to ensure that 'the selection of staff is done strictly in accordance with principles of the Charter'.

Besides the Group of Eighteen, the UN financial crisis led to two other efforts to begin a process of reform. The first was a private initiative by Sadruddin Aga Khan and Maurice Strong, both of whom had served in high-ranking UN positions: Prince Sadruddin as UN High Commissioner for Refugees and Strong as Director-General of the UN Environmental Programme and, more recently, as UN Co-ordinator for relief operations in Africa. They commissioned a separate study of UN financial problems by George Davidson, a former Under Secretary-General for Administration, and convened a consultative meeting to review his findings. Not only did several members of the Group of Eighteen participate in the review, but the Davidson study was made available to them before they completed their final report. It thus served as additional material in the deliberations of the Group of Eighteen, as well as a set of separate proposals that were subsequently more broadly circulated in order to contribute to the longer process of reform.

In dealing with the immediate need to find cuts in the budget, Davidson, like the Group of Eighteen, emphasized over-staffing at the top echelons, excessive and repetitive meetings and the need to combine functions and staff services. But, more broadly, he suggested that the regular budget, to which UN members contribute in accordance with their obligations under the Charter, could not be examined without also looking at the budgets of closely related operational programmes to which governments contribute on a voluntary basis. These include the UN Development Programme (UNDP), the UN Fund for Population Activities (UNFPA), and the UN Environmental Programme (UNEP). For the year 1986, these so-called extra-budgetary programmes amounted to $1.25 billion, as compared to the regular assessed budget of some $700 million.

Davidson argued that the UN secretariat continued to carry a number of functions under the regular budget that could reasonably be charged to extra-budgetary programmes or, in some instances, to specialized agencies that have budgets of their own. There was, in effect, a broader base within which to absorb current costs and where functions could not be cut, their costs might be transferred to operating programmes to which they are related. Taking this wider perspective means more than shifting charges for convenient budgetary purposes, however. It reflects the changes in the UN over the years, the increase in programme activities, the decentralization of operations, and the general unwillingness of governments to apply fixed assessments to funding operational programmes. What Davidson recognized was that 'governments prefer to direct their contributions to . . . programmes which they themselves select as deserving of their support'.

The principle of voluntary contributions could, of course, be carried too far and deprive the UN of an assured base of financial support as an obligation of membership. But taking a broader view of the organization and its budget provides a more compre-

hensive basis for coping with the immediate shortfall and project-
ing more long-range changes in how the UN functions. The
scope of UN activities has expanded dramatically since 1945 and
certainly justifies an increase in the UN programme and budget.
There are more ways in which states interact and more problems
that they can only deal with through co-operation. But the expansion has often led to tasks that Davidson calls 'marginal activities'
and 'incremental tasks [added] . . . without full consideration of
whether they are susceptible to meaningful international action'.
While there may be some truth in Davidson's characterization, it
should be recognized that the purpose of new tasks has usually
been highly political so that efficiency is not necessarily a measure
of their utility. They have frequently been pushed by the Third
World majority to amend the international agenda or to satisfy the political needs of certain governments and thus strengthen
the fragile unity of such a large and diverse group of states.

The Davidson study also took a bolder approach to the question of contributions. Davidson pointed out that the choice was
not only between the principle of one state—one vote and
weighted voting. There were other alternatives. The most significant was to reduce the maximum percentage that any member
can pay from 25 per cent to 15 per cent or 10 per cent of the
budget. A reduction to 15 per cent would only affect the US
contribution. A reduction to 10 per cent would also affect the
contributions of the USSR and Japan, both of which are slightly
above that figure. Making up the difference, moreover, would not
require heavy increases if it were distributed over a number of
middle-sized states and if the present momentum for reform suc-
ceeds in keeping limitations on the growth of the UN budget.

The proposal to limit any single contribution to 10 per cent
had actually been advocated by Sadruddin Aga Khan and
Maurice Strong almost a year earlier. The immediate effect
would be to free the UN from very substantial reliance on the
contribution of a single member. But Prince Sadruddin and
Strong also argued that, by assuming more of the financial responsibility, middle-sized states might also be encouraged to play
a bigger role in the UN. 'The United Nations', they explained, 'is
often their principal diplomatic outlet'. They therefore have an
incentive, that would now be backed by their more important
financial role, in rationalizing the structure of the organization
and actively supporting long-term changes to make it more effective.

The initiative to commission the Davidson study was intended to supplement the Group of Eighteen with a privately-sponsored effort that would be able to open up options upon which an essentially political body might not be able to agree. Another review of the UN under private auspices, this one more long-term and comprehensive, was undertaken by the United Nations Association [UNA] of the USA, a two year study to examine 'United Nations management and decision-making'. It was intended not only to provide guidelines for action at the UN, but also to serve as a process through which to renew the American commitment to the organization. It was under the direction of a 23-member panel of eminent persons, nine of whom are from the United States, five from other industrialized countries and nine from the Third World. The final recommendations reflected the experience of the panel members, all of whom had had long periods in political office and international assignments, as well as the views of two principal staff assistants, Peter Fromuth, the study director, and Maurice Bertrand who served as a consultant.

Longer-Range Studies: The Fromuth and Bertrand Reports

As study director, Peter Fromuth produced an early report under the title, *The UN at 40: The Problems and the Opportunities* to lay out the scope of the problem for the panel. Fromuth did not deal with specific and immediate remedies, as did both the Group of Eighteen and the Davidson study. But his prognosis was quite the same. The present situation, he said, is 'marked by disarray, lack of direction, and near paralysis'. There is a kind of 'identity crisis'. His main intent, moreover, was to establish criteria for more specific recommendations the study panel might subsequently adopt:

What the UN needs is a sense of purpose that (1) is inclusive and collaborationist, (2) exists at a level of specificity that is meaningful, and (3) can be translated into programs that undertake important yet achievable tasks . . . [there needs to be] a simpler role for the United Nations: (1) to identify areas of consensus among its members; (2) to convert that consensus into practical, desirable specific results; and (3) to seek to expand the margins of consensus by providing places for the exchange of views and vehicles for the incremental narrowing of differences.

In his analysis, Fromuth emphasized the need for political agreement among member states if the UN is to be effective. Certainly the problem rests primarily with member states and how they perceive their interests in co-operating with others. But Fromuth also points to a number of institutional inhibitions to consensus-building: the over-lapping mandates of various UN agencies and committees, especially in the field of economic and social affairs; the repetition of issues in different committees; and the frequent failure of the secretariat to help find a basis for consensus. As a result, issues get debated over and over, the positions of delegates become rigid, and staff papers do little more than repeatedly summarize the views of member states. Reform, Fromuth argued, can contribute to consensus building by reducing and sharpening the role of principal committees and providing more active leadership by the Secretary-General and senior staff.

The role of the Secretary-General was also emphasized by the Group of Eighteen and in the Davidson study and is critical to any proposals for reform. The Group of Eighteen, for example, urged the Secretary-General to provide 'greater leadership', especially in staffing the organization in accordance with the high standards of competence set down in the Charter. The recommendations of the Davidson report rely heavily on decisive action by senior staff under the leadership of the Secretary-General. Fromuth agreed but also recalled that 'traditionally, the permanent members of the Security Council have had reservations about an activist U.N. leader. . . .' Not only must the Secretary-General be nominated with the concurrence of all permanent members of the Security Council, but the nomination must also satisfy the Third World majority if the incumbent is to be fully accepted.

As a result, any Secretary-General is severely limited by the political burdens he inherits from the selection process. From the beginning, moreover, the great powers have insisted on being represented at the Under or Assistant Secretary-General level and, more recently, other groups of states have pushed for high-ranking posts for their nationals. There is thus a heavy layer of essentially political appointments at the highest levels of the organization.

Very much like Davidson, Fromuth showed that there are several ways to deal with the disparities that have developed between financial contributions and voting majorities. One option, he suggests, is to amend the Charter to provide for weighted voting or otherwise to adjust the process of budget review to insure principal contributors substantial formal control. But he also offered two other options which parallel Davidson's approach. One is to narrow disparities by reducing the maximum assessed contribution to, say, 10 per cent; and another is 'by contracting the regular budget category and enlarging the number of activities funded by extra-budgetary . . . voluntary . . . means'. But by approaching the issue as Davidson did, the two latter options are not mutually exclusive. There may be considerable merit in both reducing the maximum assessed contribution and shifting many UN activities to programmes, like the UNDP, to which governments make voluntary contributions.

One of the major consultants in the UNA project was Maurice Bertrand who was also a member of the Group of Eighteen and, prior to retirement, had served for many years with the UN Joint Inspection Unit. The Unit had been set up in 1968 to provide the UN with an independent audit staff through which to evaluate the effectiveness of operating programmes. Bertrand had been involved in assessing the effectiveness of any number of individual programmes and took the occasion of his retirement to prepare a broad evaluation of the UN system as a whole. His report, published late in 1985 and available to the Group of Eighteen, also served as a basis for his contribution to the UNA project.

In the beginning of his report, Bertrand put his 'reflections' in the broadest perspective. Reform of the UN is not simply a question of devising administrative changes to cope with problems of structural complexity and fragmentation of effort. It is rather a problem of creating what he calls a 'third generation world organization' after the experiments, first, with the League of Nations and, then with the UN during its first forty years. Like Fromuth, Bertrand suggested that we have come to an important point of transition. The UN now has to be seen in a world in which many other organizations have been created and are now performing functions originally anticipated for the UN. He also agreed that it is only possible to think in terms of effective management in cases where there is substantial consensus on what the role of the UN should be. The aim of reform, therefore, should be as much on facilitating political consensus as on improving administrative capacity.

Like the other reports, Bertrand concentrated on economic and social affairs which has been the area of greatest expansion in UN activity and consumes the highest portion of the budget. He recalled that there have been a series of efforts to reform the system over the years with mixed results. The so-called Jackson report in 1969, for example, gave the UNDP a more central role in development activities by giving it leverage at the level of field operations. Governments had to project development programmes over a period of five to ten years to qualify for UNDP grants and UNDP representatives had authority to co-ordinate the activities of the specialized agencies in the field. The position of Director-General for Development and International Economic Cooperation was established directly under the Secretary-General in order to provide greater central control and integration throughout the UN system. Here less was accomplished; new central offices were created but the Director-General has few resources through which to assert his authority. The UNDP, on the other hand, has an annual budget, financed through voluntary contributions, with which to fund technical assistance and pre-investment projects. It thus has the means to gain the attention of governments in need of assistance and to co-ordinate the activities of specialized agencies that propose to expand their development role by serving as executive agents for UNDP-financed projects.

At one level, Bertrand's recommendations emphasized 'regional development agencies or enterprises', concentrating the resources of the UN system in the field in the countries and regions where development assistance is being carried out. Here, his position was consistent with the intent of the Jackson report and, indeed, with the recommendation of the Group of Eighteen that 'the central co-ordinating role of the . . . UNDP . . . should be reaffirmed'. But Bertrand stressed that reform and effectiveness at the level of the central organs ultimately depend on a stronger consensus, particularly between developed and developing countries, on exactly what role the UN should play in economic and social matters. And, like Fromuth, he suggested that, while consensus can only emerge from a sense of shared interests among major states, structural reform can enhance the quest for political agreement. His most central recommendations, therefore, involved a fundamental restructuring of the Economic and Social Council into what he calls a new 'Economic Security Council'.

The creation of the Economic and Social Council (ECOSOC) was one of the innovations of the UN Charter. It signalled a priority for economic and social affairs that had not been emphasized in the League Covenant. But it was, in part, based on the experience of the League (as analysed in the 1939 report of the

Bruce Committee) in providing for a negotiating forum that was separate from the more political organs of the UN. From the very beginning, however, the ECOSOC has proved to be an empty vessel. Major economic and social programmes were developed through the specialized agencies which operated autonomously even though they were obliged to submit annual reports to the ECOSOC. The IMF and the World Bank especially operated independently and, by the 1960s, became central agencies in international economic relations. At the same time, the ECOSOC, first set up as an eighteen-member group to facilitate negotiation, was twice expanded in order to represent the expanding UN membership. Even when the ECOSOC grew to fifty-four members, the developing countries still opted to bring economic questions to the General Assembly and its committees where they had an overwhelming majority.

Thus, from the beginning, the ECOSOC was never able to perform that co-ordinating role, the 'central brain', that was constantly called for. The specialized agencies went their separate ways except where their activities could be harnessed through the UNDP and the World Bank, on which they largely depended for funding their participation in development projects. Issues that were discussed at annual ECOSOC meetings, moreover, came up again in the committees of the Assembly and in the plenary sessions. They also emerged in the tri-annual United Nations Conference on Trade and Development, established in 1964 by the Third World majority as an alternative forum to the ECOSOC and as an alternative source of economic information and analysis to the IMF and the World Bank. As a result, Bertrand concluded: 'The present forum, exaggeratedly ideological, seldom makes it possible to organize genuine negotiations. . . .'

Bertrand's remedy was what he called a 'Council-Commission', borrowing from the experience of the European Economic Community. A Council of limited size, representing those members with the largest economies and populations, would be paralleled by a Commission of highly qualified experts. These experts would be selected for fixed terms by the Council and serve as heads of the principal services, as well as working as a collegial body to present issues for Council discussion. Such a scheme, Bertrand argued, would bring the Council down to manageable size and minimize political pressures in staff appointments by raising the expectation of competence and professionalism. It would focus the UN, not on issues that are being dealt with elsewhere in the system of international organizations, but on identifying new problems that require co-operation and new areas where the interests of member-states are converging.

Bertrand's suggestion for a new council was the most fully elaborated recommendation for structural change in the several reports. In many respects, he anticipated the request for a broad study of 'the intergovernmental structure in the economic and social fields' that emerged from the General Assembly discussion of the report of the Group of Eighteen. At the same time, many of the functions that he stipulated for an Economic Security Council correspond to the broad areas for UN activity that Fromuth outlined, but did not yet fully develop, in his report: 'the UN as humanitarian agent', as 'global watch organization', 'development catalyst', and 'global economic forum'. There is, indeed, a convergence in all the reports on the pressing need to find an alternative to the ECOSOC structure. The Bertrand concept of a Council–Commission is one alternative. . . .

The Basis for Reform

All the reports reflect four fundamental changes that need to be taken into account in thinking about reform in the UN: first, the evolution of a complex and highly decentralized system of international organizations in which the UN is essential, but not always central; second, the changing character of international conflict and the emphasis on UN mediation and good offices rather than enforcement; third, the growth in UN activities over a broad range of economic and social issues; and, fourth, a major change in UN membership which is now universal, made up of states with great differences in cultural background, historical experience and economic and technological development. The reports also insist that the organization must concentrate on activities on which there is greater agreement among member states than there has been in recent years. All well and good. But none of the reports indicates what those areas of agreement are or how to go about finding what they might be. This, in many respects, remains the largest lacuna.

One way to try to approach the question about what governments want the UN to do, or to be, is to understand something about the evolution, not only of the UN, but of international organizations as a whole since the Second World War. Almost from the beginning, for example, the UN was not able to play a significant role in questions of peace and security, the field in which, ironically, it was originally intended to be dominant and for which it was primarily established. Instead of being centred in the UN, matters of peace and security have become diffused through three sets of complex networks of which the UN is only one. The first and most important network is based on bilateral relations between the super-powers from which they both then reach out to other governments through multilateral alliances. This network is governed by what might be called a 'nuclear regime'. Within the framework of their otherwise antagonistic relations, the behaviour of the superpowers is guided by rules and procedures to further their common interest in preventing the outbreak of a nuclear conflict. The rules are broadly two: to maintain a balance of power between the NATO and Warsaw Pact alliances; and to prevent the spread of nuclear weapons not only among their allies, but also outside the European theatre in which they confront one another. These rules largely shape the policies of deterrence followed by the United States and the Soviet Union, the conduct of arms control talks between them, and their political relations with their allies.

A second and more diverse set of networks is to be found in the regional defence arrangements provided for under Article 52 of the Charter. NATO is, by far, the most advanced of regional defence organizations, but is essentially integrated into the nuclear regime dominated by the super-powers, as is the Warsaw Pact. The Organization of American States (OAS) and the Organization of African Unity (OAU) are both relatively ineffective, the first because the overwhelming presence of the United States makes it less of an alliance and more an instrument of American policy and the second because the African members lack the unity to take action against even the most flagrant act of aggression. The League of Arab States has also lacked the unity to play an effective role in regional collective security and no regional defence organization has been established in Asia, vast and expansive as it is, where agreements would have to overcome the rivalry between India and Pakistan, the long fighting between Vietnam and its neighbours, and the imposing presence of China. In some regions, more *ad hoc* sub-regional arrangements have emerged to try to mediate conflicts. Such efforts, like the Contadora group in Central America and the so-called 'front line states' in southern Africa, may prove to be more efficient, involving as they do fewer governments that, by their self-selection, have a common interest in resolving the conflict and a readiness to contribute to the solution, if necessary.

The third network in the area of peace and security is the UN itself. The collective security provisions of the Charter were stillborn and peacekeeping operations were successful when they served the purpose of hastening the process of decolonization for which there was broad support. Such peacekeeping forces as remain, in Cyprus and Lebanon, are involved with persistent and bitter political conflicts and continue to exist only because they were established earlier and their removal could unleash even greater acts of violence than already occurs. Future peacekeeping, during the transition to independence in a liberated Namibia, for example, can only be initiated if there is broad agreement among governments. As the UNA panel emphasized, the most promising role for the UN is to provide avenues for the peaceful settlement of disputes where contending parties are looking for a way out. The major UN organ that can command the level of perceived objectivity and respect that peacemaking requires, however, is the Office of the Secretary-General. The Security Council can only be effective if the super-powers have a meeting of minds and the General Assembly is too large and unwieldy and too often divided. This is but another reason why, as the reports of the Group of Eighteen and the UNA panel recommend, an essential element of UN reform is an active Secretary-General.

A kind of division of labour among these three networks has evolved over the years and needs more to be confirmed than worked out. But it would be a mistake to minimize the role of the UN in matters of peace and security and put it essentially in a narrow residual category. Not only are regional instruments for the peaceful settlement of disputes generally weak, but there is considerable merit in the attention given in the UNA panel report to the role for the UN in the field of arms control and disarmament. The objective of the super-powers to stop the spread of nuclear weapons, for example, requires the negotiating forum of the UN and the monitoring services of the International Atomic Energy Agency (IAEA). Devising rules and inspection systems for demilitarizing outer space also requires a universal organization, as do efforts started as far back as The Hague Conventions and the League of Nations to prohibit the production and use of chemical and biological weapons. The UN Charter gives little attention to arms control and disarmament, entrusting the maintenance of peace to the collective security responsibilities of the great powers. But these provisions of the Charter have long since become obsolete under the impact of both super-power rivalry and military weapons developments. There is a new urgency for arms control and disarmament not only to rid the world of weapons of mass destruction, but also to control the wide-spread trade in conventional arms.

A second area of UN reform, in addition to peace and security, is usefully illuminated by Oran Young's notion of 'free standing' organizations. Young's formulation is an important step in clarifying the links between organizations and regimes, with regimes defined as 'principles, norms, rules and decision-making procedures around which actor expectations converge in a given issue area'. The concept of regimes has provided a way of examining international organizations without getting trapped between 'realism' and 'idealism', as was the case for many years. 'Particular international organizations may come and go', Inis Claude said in an early text, but 'international organization' as a characteristic of international relations, 'is here to stay'. In this sense, international organizations are seen not as idealistic responses to international anarchy, but as part of the 'real world' of international politics. By the same token, there is increasing evidence (especially in international economic relations and environmental issues) that states may learn that co-operation under a regime can satisfy their interests as much, if not more than competition and conflict. The task now is to relate organizations to regimes.

The clearest connection is the role of organization as a forum for the negotiation of rules and, subsequently, for the implementation and monitoring of regimes. But Young point out that regimes may also operate without organizations when states actually follow rules that have been agreed upon and are, in one way or another, self-regulating. An example is the regime for Antarctica where activities are carried on under an international treaty without any large administrative apparatus. By the same token, there are organizations that function independently of regimes, that is, international organizations may be set up not to contribute to the functioning of a specified series of rules and procedures, but rather to provide services that facilitate the practice of diplomacy and help governments solve problems that they cannot otherwise contend with on their own. 'Free-standing' organizations may also provide the arena within which governments negotiate regimes that may then 'spin off' and become quite separable in how they are administered.

The idea of 'free-standing' organizations is extremely useful in capturing an essential role for the UN in an increasingly inter-dependent world. On the one hand, the UN provides a forum for the growth and adaptation of traditional diplomacy to a world of more numerous and more divergent states. Not only do governments confront those issues that are on the formal agenda, but they have facilities to deal with others in multilateral sessions rather than through numerous and time-consuming bilateral communications. The UN also provides facilities for the creation of political coalitions and for integrating new members into the business of international affairs. Coalitions may, on the one hand, lead to greater confrontation, but they also contribute to the organization of international politics in much the same way that political parties contribute to stabilization in national politics. It is difficult, moreover, to think how states that became independent after the Second World War could have become effectively engaged in international relations as broadly and widely as they have without the facilities of the UN system, which also provides an infrastructure for developing a world-wide system of information and communication and for codifying international law, equally essential to bringing the minimum of order to a decentralized system of politics in which there is no government.

In the broadest sense, the UN system is also a principal channel for opening up the international agenda so that governments can be confronted with problems whose transnational implications might not emerge from their own more narrowly oriented policy processes, something of the 'global watch' function developed in the UNA report. The whole issue of the global environment is a prime example of how a 'free-standing' organization operates to serve just such a purpose. Environmental concerns were growing in almost all industrialized countries in the 1960s. The huge increase in industrialization after the post-war recovery and the application of new scientific and technological advances to industrial production were beginning to threaten the quality of air and water and disturb the rhythm of many natural processes. The transnational effects of environmental change also began to show up in international programmes like those of Unesco and on the initiative of the Swedish government, the General Assembly voted to convene a global conference on the human environment in Stockholm in 1972. The Stockholm Conference spawned not only a new UN Environment Programme, but also a series of regional projects and the development of environmental standards to serve as a guide and target for national environmental programmes.

The Stockholm Conference was the first in a sequence of global conferences and special sessions of the General Assembly that expanded the international agenda, some bringing significant issues visibly to the surface, others more narrowly serving the political purposes of particular countries that could carry the majority along with them. There is, unfortunately, a down-side to the UN functioning as a free standing organization with an open agenda. Many of the overlapping and often competing activities that both Davidson and Bertrand document in their reports originate in these large conferences, each of which usually closes with the approval of a statement of principles and an action programme to implement its goals.

Proponents of conferences like those on population growth and the application of science and technology to development, understandably want to create political pressures for increased activity. They are, in one sense, an indication of the flexibility and vitality of the UN system. But the conferences are also a sign of the failure of the existing structure, especially in the workings of the ECOSOC and the General Assembly, to serve as an effective vehicle for systematically adding new problems to the international agenda or dealing with changes to old problems. They thus contribute to the growth of meetings, administrative units and committees that not only weigh down the UN itself, but often exceed the capacity of all but the very largest governments to follow their progress and participate in their deliberations.

The loss of control over the international agenda is related to a third area of UN activity, economic and social affairs, in which there has been the greatest expansion and which was the principal focus of the recommendations of the Group of Eighteen and the reports by Davidson, Bertrand and the UNA panel. The loss of control over the international agenda, however, is often not so much a loss as it is a conflict for control. This has particularly been true with regard to economic matters since the 1960s as the North and the South have increasingly clashed over what issues should be on the agenda, what the priorities should be, and even where, within the system of international organizations they should be taken up. The countries of the North have given priority to the requirements for economic growth and liberal economic policies, maintained the centrality of the Bretton Woods agencies which they can control through weighted voting, and urged the countries of the South to base development programmes on their effective integration into the dominant world trading system. The South, beginning with the establishment of UNCTAD

[United Nations Conference on Trade and Development] in 1964 and working through its overwhelming majority in the UN, drew up an alternative strategy for economic co-operation and development. Under the rubric of a New International Economic Order (NIEO), it called for substantial increases in development assistance through multilateral agencies, a system of trade preferences to give Southern manufactured goods a boost in Northern markets, and international price supports for commodities which are the major exports of many developing countries.

What, in essence, happened is that the countries of the South tried to use the organs of the UN to influence the international monetary and trade regimes which the highly industrialized countries control through the IMF, the World Bank and GATT [General Agreement on Tariffs and Trade]. They pushed the NIEO proposals through UNCTAD and the General Assembly by completely outvoting the United States and its allies. At the same time, the developing countries have been continually frustrated since votes in the UN only constitute recommendations and have no binding force. They have also been dissatisfied with the extent of response to the NIEO proposals outside the UN. Multilateral lending to developing countries more than doubled between 1975 and 1985 and trading preferences, extended by schemes like those of the European Community under the Lome Accords and agreements between producers and consumers to stabilize prices, have been drawn up to cover a number of commodities. But development assistance from the OECD [Organisation for Economic Co-operation and Development] countries has still failed to reach the 0.7 per cent of GNP voted in the International Development Strategy and the economies of developing countries were hard hit by the recession in the North in the early 1980s. They have found it impossible, despite their voting strength, to get the industrialized states engaged in UN-sponsored 'global negotiations' to revise the regimes that govern economic relations. The standoff was summarized in a preview of the 40th session of the General Assembly in 1985:

Smarting from dependence in a system where external markets, terms of trade and interest rates greatly influence their economic fate and yet remain outside their control, Southern governments . . . will renew their efforts to improve their individual and collective bargaining power. Northern governments will resist.

The North–South stalemate in economic issues has been further aggravated over the years by what has come to be called 'politicization'. Politicization is, essentially, the process of attaching a statement on a controversial issue to a resolution to which it does not necessarily have direct relevance. Most such statements have to do with contentious problems like the cause of Palestinian nationalism, apartheid in South Africa and the urgency of nuclear disarmament. These are issues that have their own place on the UN agenda and are subjected to fierce controversy when they are debated on their own terms. By and large, there is a general Third World position on most of these issues which is in opposition to what might be called a 'Western' position, and especially the position taken by the United States in recent years. But they have also often deliberately been pushed onto the economic agenda by the need of the Third World majority to maintain unity among a very large number of countries with increasingly divergent interests of their own. The price of unity on broad issues like the NIEO frequently involved an agreement to include reference to the special interests of various constituencies, like Palestinian nationalism in the case of the Arab states and apartheid in the case of the African states south of the Sahara. But politicization has particularly alienated the United States which has felt itself the target of most politicized resolutions. It is this alienation which spilled over into American public opinion and the Congress and contributed to the decision to withhold a large part of the US contribution and seek a change in UN procedures for voting on budgetary questions.

Controversy over economic regimes and politicization occur at the level of what Fromuth calls 'the UN as global economic forum'. In practice, however, the 'action', so to speak, has become more centred in the financial agencies as development issues are increasingly related to the problems of economic growth and stability in world markets. Developing countries have, in fact, been drawn into the dominant world economy as they increasingly pursue export-oriented economic policies and as the largest and most important rely on private sources of capital investment. What has become concentrated in the UN have been those problems that cannot be left to market forces but require concerted community effort. Thus at the operational level, a cluster of economic and social programmes has grown up in the UN that have a distinct identity and enjoy wide support. These include the UNDP, the UN Children's Fund (UNICEF), technical assistance activities, emergency relief operations and the UN High Commissioner for Refugees. Broadly viewed, they all focus on the least developed countries and on humanitarian activities to respond to the basic needs of the poorest and homeless in the world.

There is, in effect, a division of responsibility in economic and social affairs which has been obscured by the controversy over the NIEO and the practice of politicization. But, deliberately or not, it is recognized in two of the recommendations of the Group of Eighteen. The first is the recommendation to reaffirm the central co-ordinating role of the UNDP for field operations. The second emerges from the recommendations to consolidate and rationalize the large number of departments and programmes that have been established pragmatically over the years and have come to form a kind of social 'safety net'. The search for 'identity' that Fromuth rightly insists is essential to give new purpose to the UN may lie in accepting primary responsibility for those peoples most in need of international assistance.

The broad directions for UN reform, in economic and social affairs as in other areas, emerge from the special characteristics of the organization and its place in the very extensive universe of international organizations that has evolved since 1945. It is universal, but being so has both advantages and disadvantages. The UN is the only universal forum that is not limited by function, subject or participation. It can provide the most comprehensive view of what is happening in the world and how the different parts are inter-related. In political terms, it is like a satellite in orbit in outer space, focused down on the earth and photographing its essential unity. The UN is therefore the central arena for establishing the international agenda and this is its advantage. The disadvantage stems from the lack of a central 'vision' of what the world should be like. 'There are', to repeat Robert Cox's warning, 'rival visions of a future world order. . . .'

The international agenda, like the UN itself, is thus fragmented and overloaded. What is needed is rationalization, a set of orderly procedures and strong management from an active and broadly supported Secretary-General, as the recommendations of the Group of Eighteen and the reports of Davidson, Fromuth, Bertrand and the UNA panel all encourage. But the UN as a world forum will continue to be wide ranging, free flowing and expansive as it must if it continues to be open to all and if there continue to be 'rival visions'. The place for serious realignment is in operational activities where the role of the UN can be assessed more clearly now that we have a better understanding of the scope and variety of organizations that exist. In the issues of peace and security, the realignment has, in fact, taken place. The real problem here is that the role of the UN may be reduced too far as a practical response to reality. The role of the Secretary-General, especially, needs strong support in facilitating the peaceful settlement of disputes as regional arrangements are weakened by local animosities. At the same time, a broader role for the UN in matters of arms control and disarmament has to develop as the super-powers themselves increasingly incorporate arms control into their strategies for security. Finally, in economic and social affairs, realignment is beginning to emerge as UN programmes increasingly focus on the least developed countries and on building a 'safety net' to enable the international community to respond to human needs in times of disaster and catastrophe.

Finding a Consensus on Reform

The UNA panel, like Fromuth and Bertrand, emphasizes that UN reform will require a new consensus if it is to stick and be in any way meaningful. They all also argue that, in Fromuth's terms, 'structural reforms may be necessary' to improve the way 'the UN conducts the search for consensus and converts consensus into useful outcomes'. There is great common sense in what they say, but they nonetheless pose a dilemma. There are certainly structural changes that would enhance consensus-building. But where is the consensus to decide which structural changes to make in the first place? UN reform, as Bertrand rightly emphasizes throughout his report, is neither technical nor managerial; it is essentially political. Structure and substance are integrally connected. Controversies over international economic regimes and the primacy of one set of international organizations over another, for example, involve more than economic policies and organizational adjustment. They are also disputes about political power.

Building consensus to support the initial proposals for UN reform is thus no easy task. The early response to the recommendations of the Group of Eighteen is certainly hopeful and the Secretary-General's observation about a growing attitude of pragmatism in member-states may identify a potentially new basis for political agreement in the future. The Soviet Union has also paid up its past debts to the UN and seems to be seeking a more positive role, especially in the resolution of regional conflicts. But there are also danger signs. The debate on voting procedures uncovered considerable resentment at the pressures being exerted by the United States. At the same time, the Group of Eighteen left the most substantive areas of reform unresolved when they only recommended 'further study' on economic and social programmes and called for a stronger role for the Secretary-General without suggesting any change to the process of his election. The UNA panel proposal to limit the Secretary-General to a single term of seven years is constructive, but still leaves broad agreement on what kind of chief executive is needed and wanted, first, to the permanent members of the Security Council who nominate the candidate and, then, to the majority of members who must confirm their nomination.

Nevertheless, even those who follow a generally realistic position acknowledge that international politics is not entirely a zero-sum game and that states co-operate as well as compete in pursuit of their interests. There is no reason for assuming that finding a consensus to support UN reform will be impossible—though it is certain to be extremely difficult. The concept of international regimes is based on the proposition that states may take on the habit of co-operating, of following rules and procedure over time, and therefore do not always need to be prodded by a hegemonic power to follow an agreed pattern of behaviour. The UN, however, is a 'free-standing' organization, not closely related to a specific regime. But member-states have now been engaged in the UN for a number of years, some over four decades, and most, for admittedly different reasons, have a stake in its continuing to operate.

Is a stake in the UN a sufficient basis for building a consensus for its reform? Robert Axelrod finds that co-operation can evolve through repeated interaction during which a learning process goes on. Most important is what he calls 'enlarging the shadow of the future', making participants more aware of the future, longer range consequences of their acts. 'There are two basic ways of doing this', he says, 'by making the interactions more durable and by making them more frequent'. Beyond 'enlarging the shadow of the future', co-operation is also promoted by 'changing the payoffs, teaching people to care about the welfare of others, and teaching the value of reciprocity'. Whether or not Axelrod's findings are applicable to UN reform is not altogether clear. They are, however, suggestive. So is Robert Keohane's elaboration of reciprocity as an 'effective strategy for maintaining co-operation'. Building on Axelrod's work, Keohane differentiates between 'specific reciprocity' and 'diffuse reciprocity', the latter involving not a specific exchange of benefits, but a general balancing of reciprocal obligations over time. Specific reciprocity, he cautions, is more relevant to international politics since the norms of obligation are weak. Reciprocity is also more difficult in multilateral than in bilateral relations because of the temptation of those not centrally involved to 'free ride' on the agreement of others.

If it is to succeed, a consensus for UN reform will have to unite both developed and developing countries, at least key countries in the North and the South that can provide leadership. The USSR has expressed a new interest in the UN, but it still has to prove its credibility and, in any case, its resources are limited and its interests and capacity largely in the area of international security. It is the North that has the financial resources that the UN system needs, while the South has the votes, and both are necessary to make the system work in all of its many faceted parts. Both North and South also have a stake in what the UN has to contribute to the world of the future. The North needs a rule-bound world of greater certainty and stability to protect its wealth and power. The South needs an open world in which it can more effectively participate in world politics. But the stakes are different and can only serve to create a new consensus if the two sides have something to offer each other on the issues that have divided them so sharply. They will have to find some way to reciprocate.

The United States is in a particularly critical position in this whole process. It was able to bring the UN crisis to a head because of the organization's financial dependence on its contribution. But the United States cannot bring about UN reform completely on its own. It will nevertheless have to be part of the agreement to support reform, even a leader in building the consensus. But in so doing, it would be well to heed Charles Kindleberger's contrast between a 'hegemon' and a 'leader'. 'The differences between hegemony and leadership', he has written '. . . go considerably deeper than semantics . . . [A leader is] one who is responsible, or responds to need, who is answerable or answers the demands of others, is forced to "do it" by ethical training and by the circumstance of position . . . ' Whether American hegemony is over is a matter of considerable debate. What is certainly less debatable is the need for the United States to participate effectively in the political coalition for UN reform.

THE FLUCTUATING FORTUNES OF THE
U.N. INTERNATIONAL
CIVIL SERVICE[2]

The Problem

The debate over the nature and functions of the international civil service has gone on at least since the founding of the League of Nations in 1920, when Sir Maurice Hankey and Sir Eric Drummond disagreed as to how best to organize the League Secretariat. Drummond's announced conception of a politically neutral secretariat recruited internationally and loyal only to the organization appeared to prevail over Hankey's conception that the secretariat should be drawn from national delegations. But Drummond's successor as Secretary General, Joseph Avenol, apparently felt more comfortable with Hankey's view. Upon leaving office in 1939, as the organization was buffeted by the ideological and power clashes in Europe, Avenol commented: "In this heartbreaking hour, I found ease in the simplest duty: being faithful to my country."

Being loyal to one's country is still the primary ingredient of nationalism and is a value to which the member states of the United Nations have steadfastly held. Thus it is not surprising that even the United States has challenged the Drummond conception that an international secretariat should be composed of nationals of the member states who were loyal only to the organization in which they served. For the United Nations, the relevant provision is Article 100 of the Charter:

1. In the performance of their duties the Secretary General and the staff shall not seek or receive instructions from any government or from any other authority external to the Organization. They shall refrain from any action which might reflect on their position as international officials responsible only to the Organization.

2. Each member of the United Nations undertakes to respect the exclusively international character of the responsibilities of the Secretary Gen-

[2]Article by Robert S. Jordan, Research Professor of International Institutions, University of New Orleans, from *Public Administration Review* 51:353–357 Jl/Ag '91. Copyright © 1991 by the American Society for Public Administration (ASPA). Reprinted with permission.

eral and the staff and not to seek to influence them in the discharge of their responsibilities.

In Article 101, the pursuit of the "highest standards" in recruitment was intended to be paramount over due regard for "geographical distribution." As shown later in this article, this provision has been honored more in the breach than in practice; certainly this was true before but it was especially true after decolonization, when the Secretary General and the executive heads of the various United Nations agencies were under intense political pressure to make room in their secretariats for nationals of the new member states.

As to the fate of Article 100, the United States raised the issue of the "national loyalty" of its citizens employed as international civil servants when President Truman issued Executive Order 10,422 in 1952. This order, which appeared to violate paragraph 2 of Article 100 (quoted above), required a full field security investigation not only of all United States nationals to be recruited by the United Nations, but of all United States nationals already working for the organization. Not unexpectedly, this political "means test" aroused strong opposition, which came to a head when an American who was under investigation decided to invoke the Fifth Amendment and was subsequently dismissed from his position in the secretariat.

The reason this matter is cited here is that it demonstrates that virtually from the early days of the United Nations, ideological predispositions aside, the member states have resisted openly the provisions either of Article 100 or of 101. To put it bluntly, along with the earlier U.S. position and, until recently, the consistent Soviet Union rejection of Article 100 (China still objects), the progressive de-Westernization of the United Nations—a process that has gone on for at least the last twenty-five years—also brought a widespread challenge to Article 101. Obviously, for Western and non-Western member states alike, differing national conceptions of bureaucratic responsiveness to political authority are reflected. But also reflected is the fundamental fact that the U.N. international civil service can indeed be a hostage to politics, whatever the domestic political cultures may be.

Nonetheless, even in the breach of the principles, the notion persists that there is an international administrative norm as expressed in Articles 100 and 101 that sets the limits of acceptable bureaucratic behavior for international civil servants. This norm, even though often compromised and openly flouted, stands as an

alternative to the primacy of national loyalty as the ultimate measure of staff recruitment and of the conduct of their duties by
United Nations employees. Somehow, even when member governments of whatever political persuasion have insisted on political orthodoxy from their nationals serving in or nominated to
serve in the United Nations, a persistent, almost nagging impulse
on the part of the international bureaucracy can be perceived in
favor of at least nonnationalism, if not devoted political loyalty to
the organization.

A noteworthy example is the recent change in attitude by the
Soviet Union toward governmental control of its nationals serving
the secretariat and its apparent willingness to loosen its insistence
on vetting the appointment and tenure of all its serving nationals
and to relax its previous opposition to career appointments. The
Soviet Union has even come out as not opposed to direct recruitment, but still retains the right to review and to comment on such
applications from its nationals.

Career Conceptions and Values

Perhaps the most obvious relevant consideration in regard to
recruitment has to do with the dramatic change in the nature of
the membership of the United Nations since its founding. Of
particular importance, of course, has been the growth in membership derived from decolonization. This change has had an
immediate and direct impact on personnel questions through the
emergence of a strong interest in ensuring an adequate and equitable Third World geographical representation in the staff of the
organization. Thus, during the 1960s and 1970s there was sharp
disagreement as to whether the principle of geographical representation (sometimes called "distribution") should, at times, dom-
inate over the principle of merit in recruitment. It is constantly
asserted, of course, that the one need not be at the expense of the
other, but it has been generally recognized that trying to arrive at
a measurable concept of efficiency and productivity in order to
establish a uniform standard of merit has been made much more
difficult since the international civil service has become truly mul-
ticultural.

Alternative conceptions of what the international civil service
should be have been widely discussed as the political/cultural basis of the United Nations has expanded. More recently, this discussion has centered around the advantages and the disadvan-

tages of the practice of *seconding*—persons are loaned from their own government to work for the United Nations with the understanding that they can return to their previous position with promotion and retirement rights intact. This is one form of fixed-term contract; the other is through direct recruitment of persons not connected with their governments. The alternative recruitment policy is to make larger numbers of career appointments after an initial probationary period. The initial problem for the new Third World member states was to keep open positions until their nationals could qualify for career appointments.

However, when secondment is linked to fixed-term contracts, then the chance for nationals from member states who openly favor these types of appointments to escape from political influence in the conduct of their official duties is virtually nil. For example, three Soviet staff members recently appealed directly to the Secretary General to have their fixed-term contracts renewed, bypassing for the first time the Soviet mission. They objected to being "rotated" according to the wishes of their government, claiming that they were not given equal consideration for contract renewal with other, non-Soviet, staff members. As it was put by the representative of the Federation of Civil Service Associations (FICSA) to the Fifth Committee of the General Assembly in its fall 1990 session:

The issue is not secondment *per se,* which is simply a loan mechanism, but rather misuse of this practice. Secondment, coupled with rotation and fixed-term appointments has in effect put the appointment and extension of certain nationals in the hands of their governments.

On a broader plane, a serious attempt has been made to upgrade the "internal justice system." Responsibility for the justice system rests with the Office of the Under-Secretary General, Department of Administration and Management (working with the Office of Human Resources Management; the Office of Program Planning, Budget, and Finance; and the Office of Legal Affairs). Many of the personnel cases come before the Joint Appeals Board (JAB) or, in cases of misconduct, before Joint Disciplinary Committees (JDC). The general consideration of reform of the administration of justice takes place in the Staff Management Coordination Committee (SMCC).

One successful innovation has been the increasing use of Panel of Counsel to assist staff members in preparing their statements of appeal and in providing appropriate counselling. This informal procedure is designed to supplement rather than to replace the formal use of the JAB, the Administrative Tribunal, or specialized appeal bodies. Another innovation has been the invention of grievance panels. Both of these informal devices have speeded up the disposition of cases, partly because many Third World nationals have not had in their pre-United Nations careers the same access to or knowledge of legal formalities and due process procedures and partly because of differing cultural values. They may not share the same conception of professional responsibility in the conduct of their duties as presumably do nationals from member states who are heirs to the vision of Sir Eric Drummond.

Budgetary and Financial Considerations
of the International Civil Service

The global economic situation in recent years, as world inflation followed by recession and sharp currency fluctuations have taken their toll on the United Nations' ability to finance its activities, has reinforced negative feelings in some member states toward the United Nations, even as the organization has been called upon to assume more responsibilities. These financial pressures have been felt in a number of ways. Staff reductions or freezes in recruitment are becoming more common, and when recruitment does continue, often only fixed-term contracts are given. Also, programs of career development, whatever the good intentions are unlikely to have much credibility in periods of continuing financial uncertainty and the consequent retrenchment efforts and salary freezes.

Persistent efforts to "bend" the system have surfaced. An increasing number of member states are violating the charter (and the principle of equity) by paying additional allowances and compensation to their nationals on the U.N. staff, although, according to FICSA, most of these same countries are strongly opposing any improvement in the conditions of the staff (United Nations General Assembly, Doc A/C.5/45/23, 5 November 1990, p. 2). Another example concerns the granting of privileges and immunities to the staff: the freedom from arrest, detention, and abduction. The Secretary General, who is assisted by the United Nations Security Coordinator in dealing with these problems, can only be successful in his efforts on behalf of the staff if member governments will cooperate. Such privileges obviously affect the secretariats' sense of being "international" in a nonpolitical sense.

Furthermore, the stability of the United Nations' pension system has been a very real concern. Even though the system is by its nature worldwide in scope (prospective pensioners come to their jobs from everywhere), pension stipends are expressed in the local currency of the retiree. It is, for example, not assured that a guaranteed replacement income can be maintained for retirees from strong currency member states, because this guarantee may not have been reflected in preretirement contributions. The specific cause of this concern is the rapid decline of the dollar, in which the United Nations budget is denominated, in relation to other major currencies.

This, of course, contributes to a lowering of staff morale and a rising of staff discontent. Personnel administrators, and especially the Assistant Secretary General, Office of Human Resources Management, have had to cope with this discontent even as their colleagues have had to seek to accomplish rapidly changing organizational tasks with resources increasingly difficult to obtain. In this respect, perhaps the international civil service has been undeservedly criticized.

The Role of the International Civil Service Commission (ICSC)

The International Civil Service Commission (ICSC) at its creation was thought to have the potential for ameliorating, if not reversing, some of the negative trends discussed. First, the commission set for itself the task of making a serious effort to deal with questions of recruitment and career development. Indeed, both subjects have been continuously active parts of the commission's agenda. This being said, however, it is also true that the commission has been overburdened by other personnel policy and administrative questions, which have detracted from its ability to give adequate attention and time to recruitment and career development.

The membership of the commission is a balance of national positions and political interests, which differ widely at times, even though, as Article 3 of the statute provides:

1. The members of the Commission shall be appointed in their personal capacities as individuals of recognized competence who have had substantial experience of executive responsibility in public administration or related fields, particularly in personnel management. 2. The members of the Commission, no two of whom shall be nationals from the same State, shall be selected with due regard for equitable geographic distribution.

In addition, the commission is constrained by the apparent reluctance of the specialized agencies to pursue questions relating to the "career concept" within the framework of the United Nations common system.

One of the recurring debates in the commission, as in the General Assembly's Fifth Committee, has been as to what exactly is a "career concept." Some governments, as mentioned, favor fixed-term appointments over permanent contracts; other governments have favored the opposite, citing the "traditional" concept of an international civil service as justification. Whether a high turnover of staff meets the long-term interests of the organization or not, the pressure to continue to make opportunities for categories of persons (whether women, underrepresented countries, underrepresented regions, overrepresented countries, or underrepresented developing countries) appears to some persons to weaken the sense of self-identity that must underlie a career system. To other persons it appears to strengthen the diversity of a career service that draws on the human resources of virtually the entire world.

The commission has been concerned more recently with the impact of the United States Federal Employees Pay Comparability Act of 1990. This act provides local flexibility in setting salaries and annual raises. Specifically, a portion of a federal employee's annual raise is linked to the wage or salary scales of his/her local labor market, and the economy of New York City (and state) is in decline at the moment. Because United Nations salaries are set on a basis of comparability with the United States federal civil service wage structure, this could have an adverse effect on United Nations salary scales. Added to the uncertainty is the fact that the president of the United States is authorized to reduce the amount of the annual adjustments of federal employees in very serious national circumstances, such as a war or a negative gross national product growth for two consecutive quarters.

The Coordinating Committee for Independent Staff Unions and Associations of the United Nations System (CCISUA) has suggested that salary comparisons be carried out periodically with other employers of international staff, such as the European Community (EC), the Organization for Economic Cooperation and Development (OECD), or the World Bank, that compete with the United Nations system for staff as well as with expatriate nondiplomatic staff and the expatriate diplomatic staff of the United States federal civil service. Such periodic comparisons could be used as a barometer or indicator of trends. This might be one way out of the dilemma of linking United Nations salary scales with the United States federal civil service scales which has resulted in United Nations employee pay freezes. In fact, the General Assembly has asked the commission to undertake a study to determine which, in effect, is the "best paid national civil service," which could be another way out of this dilemma (United Nations General Assembly, Doc A/C.5/45/24, 9 November 1990). Disaffection has been expressed over the commission's practice of making decisions in executive session. Tensions eased between the commission and the CCISUA, when the commission decided that "as a general rule, on all issues affecting the conditions of service of UN common system staff, representatives designated under rule 37, subparagraph (a) of the ICSC rules of procedure might attend all the Commission's meetings, including those at which decisions were taken." Another positive move toward restoring trust in the commission was its decision to establish tripartite working groups on major issues, as determined on its own initiative or on the proposal of the representatives of the organizations or of staff. These working groups would ensure that representatives of management and staff would participate in the work of the commission.

Conclusions

It should be clear from the foregoing that an international U.N. bureaucracy, composed of politically neutral international civil servants, recruited on the basis of merit, and subject to uniform standards of appointment, promotion, compensation, and retention must be viewed as being more of an ideal than a reflection of reality. The reality more closely approximates the highly politicized civil services of most member states. If viewed in this way, then the attempts at interference in the administration of the U.N. international civil service by the member governments is not as noteworthy as the slow but persistent efforts to provide uniform standards of personnel management and flexible methods of adjudication, when grievances or alleged cases of improper conduct are at issue.

In summary, as former Soviet Under-Secretary General for Political Affairs Arkady Shevchenko put it: "The Secretariat not only has problems common to any large bureaucracy but suffers from some special headaches all its own. The big ones are conflicting loyalties, different administrative traditions, and lack of a cohesive executive comparable to that of national governmental institutions." A pluralistic political world is bound to create pluralism in the composition of an international secretariat and efforts to create uniformity in standards of personnel management and in various forms of equitable treatment must confront this fact of international life.

CAN THE U.N. STRETCH TO FIT ITS FUTURE?[3]

Shortly before the first-ever United Nations Security Council summit convened in New York on January 31, [1992,] a reporter asked British Prime Minister John Major whether he would recommend changing the composition of the council. The best response Major could muster was: "Why break up a winning team?" Following the summit, a reporter asked Russian President Boris Yeltsin whether he would propose permanent Security Council membership for Germany and Japan. "I think you're confusing me with someone else," he said.

Questions about the composition of the Security Council are often side-stepped these days. There is no good answer to them. The idea that the five great powers of the world of 1945 should forever retain the leading role in the maintenance of international peace and security simply doesn't play well anymore with the rest of the planet.

In a declaration issued at the summit, the Security Council invited Boutros Ghali, the new secretary-general, to recommend by July 1 steps the United Nations might take to strengthen its capacity for "preventive diplomacy, peacemaking, and peacekeeping."

Ghali may well produce some bold initiatives—all of which, as the declaration stipulated, will fall "within the framework and provisions of the Charter." But pressures to open the U.N. Charter have been building for many years, and they are likely to increase. The weakness of the arguments for indefinitely retaining the San Francisco Charter will likely soon produce other ini-

[3]Article by Tad Daley, fellow of the RAND/UCLA Center for Soviet Studies, from *Bulletin of the Atomic Scientists* 48:38–42 Ap '92. Copyright © 1992 by the Educational Foundation for Nuclear Science. Reprinted with permission.

tiatives that go far beyond those that Ghali is likely to suggest in July.

A Peace Army

Because the U.N. Secretariat must now improvise each new operation from scratch, support is growing for ideas such as a standing system of logistical and financial support for peacekeeping efforts, a military staff college for training peacekeeping officers, and even a standing rapid deployment force for peacekeeping actions. French President François Mitterrand proposed such a force in his summit speech, pledging French willingness to commit 1,000 troops within 48 hours in a crisis.

Mitterrand did not specify whether the troops for this U.N. force would remain with their respective national military establishments until mobilized by the United Nations, or instead form a standing U.N. army. He was also unclear whether the authority to dispatch such a force would lay with the Security Council or the secretary-general. Mitterrand did suggest, however, that the rapid deployment force could operate under the command of the U.N. Military Staff Committee, which consists of the chiefs of staff of the "Perm Five" states. The Military Staff Committee has never commanded a force in the U.N.'s 47-year history, and the Charter provides no guidelines for how the Perm Five might reach consensus decisions. Boris Yeltsin of Russia generally endorsed Mitterrand's proposal in his own summit speech, although he added that the "expeditious activation" of such a force should occur "upon the decision of the Security Council."

An effective U.N. rapid deployment force would possess several key elements: The United Nations must be able to discern that an outbreak of violence is imminent, either through its own intelligence sources or "borrowed" intelligence information from member nations. There must be authority to dispatch such a force, as Austrian Chancellor Franz Vranitzky's summit statement suggested, *before* a conflict ignites, and without necessarily obtaining the consent of all the parties to the potential conflict. Most important, the secretary-general must have the blanket authority to dispatch the force on his own initiative, without Security Council authorization. Such authority is essential to avoid "telegraphing the punch," even if that might sometimes act as a deterrent. Other mechanisms exist for such public deterrent efforts. While a July 1990 Security Council debate might have deterred Saddam

Hussein's invasion of Kuwait, it might also have moved him to invade earlier.

Deployment of a U.N. force could be followed by compulsory U.N. mediation or by a hearing before the World Court. If a U.N. rapid deployment force had existed in the summer of 1990, and if the World Court had been prepared to hear the kinds of disputes (slant drilling, maritime access, and the like) that Iraq had with Kuwait, and if the world community had previously displayed a consistent commitment to the enforcement of international law, Iraq might never have invaded at all.

The summit declaration also noted with approval that the General Assembly had recently created a global arms registry for tracking transfers of conventional weapons (see March 1992 *Bulletin*). The British and the Japanese have gone further by pushing for a registry that would track both transactions and national inventories in conventional, nuclear, biological, and chemical weapons. Such an all-embracing register could deter both recipient and supplier, as in the famous phrase underlying American securities-disclosure laws: "Sunlight is the best of disinfectants." With the Perm Five countries accounting for nearly 90 percent of arms sales around the world, exposing the full range of arms trafficking ought to be a natural role for tomorrow's United Nations.

Beyond Peacekeeping

The U.N. role is likely to continue to expand beyond international security concerns into areas such as temporary governmental administration (now under way in Cambodia), election monitoring, humanitarian assistance, and disaster relief. The British have been pressing for the establishment of a new high-level U.N. position—a permanent undersecretary-general for disaster relief. The aid provided to victims of the May 1991 Bangladesh cyclone by American marines, who happened to be on their way home from the Persian Gulf, only underscored the inadequacy of the present system.

The maintenance of a healthy and sustainable biosphere may be the most important policy imperative facing the human community. Global environmental changes have made absolute national sovereignty over territories of importance to all of humankind—such as the Amazon rainforests—increasingly anachronistic. The U.N. Conference on Environment and Development, which convenes in June in Brazil, may go a long way toward creating an unprecedented body of global environmental law, as well as the enforcement mechanisms that global environmental protection will probably require.

Other problems, including drug trafficking, terrorism, AIDS, and sundry financial flim-flams—such as those perpetrated by the Bank of Credit and Commerce International—increasingly transcend national boundaries, and demand U.N. attention. But some attention must also be focused on the nearly universal Third World fears that the U.N.'s renaissance will be dominated by a First World perspective. The concerns of developing countries—such as debt, low prices for raw materials, and economic development—cannot be brushed aside. At the summit, several leaders of developing nations spoke passionately of the vast waste of human capital engendered by perpetual poverty.

In the broadest sense, the coming decades will demand larger roles for international institutions in the *management* of environmental degradation, population growth, energy exhaustion, and the global movements of capital, goods, services, information, and people. Will the scale of management of human affairs keep up with the continuously increasing degree of global interdependence? The international community must address that question today, not tomorrow.

Fading Sovereignty

Article 2, Paragraph 7 of the U.N. Charter prohibits U.N. intervention "in matters essentially within the domestic jurisdiction of any state." Nevertheless, we may be seeing the creeping emergence of a doctrine of humanitarian intervention in the internal affairs of sovereign states. An important theme in the speeches of the fifteen leaders gathered for the summit was the need to protect human rights everywhere. While most of the leaders spoke favorably of human rights as a common global value, some suggested even more directly that this value could be superior to national sovereignty.

Russia's Yeltsin, for instance, said that human rights "are not an internal matter of states, but rather obligations under the U.N. Charter," and maintained that the Security Council had a "collective responsibility for the protection of human rights and freedoms." And Secretary-General Ghali, echoing his predecessor, Javier Perez de Cuellar, said that "the misuse of state sovereignty

may jeopardize a peaceful global life. Civil wars are no longer
civil, and the carnage they inflict will not let the world remain
indifferent."

Although Germany was not represented at the summit, Foreign Minister Hans-Dietrich Genscher had gone even further last
fall in a speech to the General Assembly: "Today sovereignty must
meet its limits in the responsibility of states for mankind as a
whole. . . . When human rights are trampled underfoot, the family of nations is not confined to the role of spectator. . . . It must
intervene."

The most notable event to date on the sovereignty front has
been the haven for Kurds carved out of northern Iraq. Although
the sponsors of U.N. Resolution 688 in April 1991 argued that
the situation with Kurdish refugees threatened international stability, in reality external military intervention was used inside Iraq
to prevent the Iraqi government from committing acts of aggression against its own people on its own territory.

Saddam Hussein's behavior also revived the idea of establishing an international criminal court that could not only try violators of international conventions regarding such matters as terrorism and drug trafficking, but also heads of state who violate
international law through acts of international or internal aggression. Security Council Resolution 731, issued in January, also
stepped into this territory. The resolution demands that Libya
surrender the two intelligence agents accused of the bombing of
Pan Am Flight 103. Not only does the resolution call upon Libya
to subordinate its own procedures regarding extradition, but it
implies, perhaps for the first time, that the writ of the Security
Council extends not just to states, but to individuals anywhere in
the world.

But the use of economic sanctions as a mechanism to pressure
states to mend their ways may soon come up for reexamination.
Economic sanctions are generally thought to be a lesser form of
coercion than direct military action. Yet, as British journalist Edward Pearce has pointed out, although the international community condemns biological warfare, the economic sanctions preventing the repair of damaged Iraqi power plants and sewage
treatment facilities have resulted in epidemic levels of cholera in
Iraq. "That is different from deliberately seeding and spreading
the cholera virus," says Pearce, "in the same way that manslaugh-
ter is different from murder."

The economic embargoes against Iraq—and now Haiti—are

aimed directly at the removal of their governing regimes. But it is unclear how these sanctions can accomplish their desired ends. If Iraqi opposition forces could not overthrow Saddam Hussein at his weakest moment in the spring of 1991, sanctions that harm rulers less than the ruled seem hardly likely to increase the opposition's prospects.

In Haiti, where the economic embargo is hitting the general population far harder than the rich and well connected, the policy, rather than giving Haitians the incentive and the wherewithal to overthrow the military regime, has instead resulted in a massive refugee crisis off the coast of the United States. Something has gone awry in the international system when we impose harsh and effective economic sanctions on a country, and then repatriate the consequent refugees because their motives are economic rather than political.

If it has become legitimate for the international community to endeavor to remove a governing regime, direct international removal efforts may be undertaken in the not-too-distant future. It may soon become widely accepted that world standards and laws apply to every individual on the planet, and that the international community will intervene to enforce those standards and laws. Whether this process continues in an evolutionary or revolutionary fashion, we may be witnessing the beginnings of a sea change in human history.

Taxation Without Representation

As the U.N.'s role in world affairs continues to expand, so too will pressure increase to bring the composition of the Security Council in line with the contemporary realities of international power. The framers of the Charter envisioned a dynamic institution that would evolve over time. Article 109 provides for the convening of a "General Charter Review Conference" upon the approval of the two-thirds of the member states, including any nine members of the Security Council. And Article 108 allows Charter amendment upon the approval of two-thirds of the member states, including all five permanent members of the Security Council.

Japan and Germany, the second and third largest financial contributors to U.N. activities, are the two states most commonly cited as deserving permanent membership on the Security Council. Indeed, Japan contributes more to the United Nations than

Britain and France combined, and thus already has considerable clout. The new secretary-general's first high-level appointment was Japan's Yasushi Akashi, who was named special representative to oversee the multibillion dollar U.N. peacekeeping operation in Cambodia. Tokyo's U.N. ambassador, Yoshio Hatano, reportedly reminded Ghali beforehand that Japan had pledged to pick up fully half the tab for the massive operation.

But Japan is not satisfied with only this intangible influence in U.N. decision making. Although the possibility of a Security Council membership for Japan has been long discussed, Japanese Prime Minister Kiichi Miyazawa was particularly direct at the summit, saying that membership on the council must be "more reflective of the realities of the new era." In case anyone failed to get the message, his press secretary, Masamichi Hanabusa, later said Tokyo expected a Security Council seat by 1995, the U.N.'s fiftieth anniversary. Otherwise, he added, Japan would increasingly resent "taxation without representation."

Germany's approach is more low-key. In the short term, Germany seems to hope that Britain and France will informally "Europeanize" their seats as the European Community draws closer together. (Bonn, however, was reportedly miffed that it had not been consulted by London or Paris in preparation for the summit.) In the long term, German Chancellor Helmut Kohl said shortly before the summit that he was "strictly opposed" to Germany itself putting the Security Council issue on the table, but that he could imagine the European Community acquiring a permanent seat at some point.

Merging British, French, and German interests into a single European Community seat would require amending both Article 23 (which names the permanent members of the Security Council) and Article 4 (which limits U.N. membership to "states"). Once that Pandora's box is opened, all sorts of issues emerge. What about developing nations of increasing weight—such as India, Brazil, Nigeria, Egypt, and Indonesia? Indian Prime Minister P. V. Narasimha Rao made a strong case at the summit for expanding the Security Council's representation if it hopes to maintain political and moral effectiveness. And shortly after the summit, Nigerian President Ibrahim Babangida said that "to retain the structure of the Security Council in its present form is to run the risk of perpetuating what is at best a feudal anachronism."

What exactly are the criteria for selection as permanent members of the Security Council? Political power? Economic power? Military power? (The Perm Five happen to be the five major nuclear-weapon states.) Regional representation? Perhaps most important, if the Security Council expands its permanent membership, how can it retain the ability to act decisively?

Decisiveness or Democracy?

Italian Foreign Minister Gianni de Michelis called for major Charter revisions in a speech to the General Assembly in September 1991. He proposed expanding the number of both permanent and rotating members of the Security Council, but not necessarily extending the right of veto to the new permanent members. He also suggested "a system of weighted voting in both the General Assembly and the Security Council."

Over the years, many weighted voting schemes have been discussed. Some would give added weight to the population of a member state, or to its financial contribution. Some would award a degree of representation to stateless ethnic groups—Kurds and Sikhs, for example. Others envision a bicameral system much like the U.S. Congress, with citizens all over the world electing local representatives to a "U.N. House" and national representatives to a "U.N. Senate."

Many U.N. watchers argue that any conceivable recomposition of the Security Council would tremendously complicate the process of reaching consensus, and might paralyze the United Nations again, just when it is beginning to fulfill its post–Cold War potential. Although the veto has become a rarity in recent years, it is not difficult to imagine circumstances in which it could again be regularly employed. In November 1990, the "Soyuz" group of deputies in the Supreme Soviet stated plainly that they would have vetoed Resolution 678 on the use of force against Iraq. Conservative Soviet commentator B. Zanegin said after the war that "the U.N. Security Council can serve as an instrument for legalizing unilateral decisions by the U.S. and imposing them on the world community." The new world order, he added, basically amounts to a "U.S. dictatorship or hegemony" that is exercised through the Security Council.

But if a more conservative leadership should again come to power in Moscow, it is not clear that they would fail to cooperate in the Security Council. A conservative Russia would still be a nation in decline. Even a single Security Council veto might lead

Western states to reconsider the large-scale aid programs now under way. And a return to a "Mr. Nyet" approach could simply cause the United States and the West to again pursue their interests outside the U.N. framework, leaving Russia with virtually no voice in global political affairs.

Nevertheless, objective perceptions of national interest are seldom the sole determinants of a state's foreign policies. A central objective of a right-wing Russian leadership, however harmful to Russian interests, might be simply to reverse the national humiliation stemming from the recent Russian subservience to the United States in the international arena. Future Russian Security Council vetoes, exercised as a means of demonstrating national pride and independence, are far from inconceivable.

In addition, Chinese Prime Minister Li Peng struck a discordant note at the summit when he insisted that China would consistently oppose all external interventions in the internal affairs of sovereign states "using human rights as an excuse." The stridency of Li's speech suggests that we could see the emergence of the Chinese veto as well. Many Third World nations are deeply disturbed by the sovereignty issue. China may see an opportunity to stand at the head of the developing world as the great defender of sovereignty, opposing and vetoing all proposed U.N. interventions in "domestic affairs."

The various democratic decision-making structures around the world today are rarely paralyzed into complete inaction. Though often contentious in their procedures, they usually manage to produce some kind of public policy, however imperfect. Is there something fundamentally different about a global decision-making structure? If "decisive action" were the sole U.S. value, the president would be allowed to act, in all cases, without congressional authorization. "Democratization, at the national level," said Ghali in his summit statement, "dictates a corresponding process at the global level."

If Not Now, When?

The post–Cold War world will require global institutions with the power and authority to address the increasingly global issues of the new millennium. That is why, shortly after the Gulf War ended, the Stockholm Initiative on Global Security and Governance received the endorsement of international luminaries including Benazir Bhutto, Willy Brandt, Jimmy Carter, Vaclev

Havel, Robert McNamara, Julius Nyerere, and Eduard Shevardnadze. The initiative proposes measures such as "the elaboration of a global law enforcement mechanism," "the levying of fees on the emission of pollutants affecting the global environment," "a review of both the composition of the Security Council and the use of the veto," and the convening of "a World Summit on Global Governance, similar to the meetings in San Francisco and Bretton Woods in the 1940s."

Any new world order centered around the San Francisco Charter stands hostage to the prevailing political winds in Moscow and Beijing. Any opening of the Charter must endeavor to at least limit the Security Council veto so that some types of collective U.N. action can be undertaken even in the face of disagreement among the great powers. The protracted conflict between the United States and the Soviet Union was, after all, why the United Nations was essentially irrelevant for its first four decades.

The international community can pretend that the potential for paralysis-by-veto no longer exists, and it can keep bringing more and more issues to the Security Council in the hope that all will go well. Or it can begin seriously laying the groundwork, perhaps to coincide with the U.N.'s fiftieth anniversary in 1995, for an Article 109 Charter Review Conference.

"I am not an advocate for frequent changes in laws and constitutions," said Thomas Jefferson, in words inscribed on the Jefferson Memorial. "[But] as circumstances change, institutions must also advance to keep pace with the times. We might as well require a man still to wear the coat which fitted him when a boy, as require civilized society to remain ever under the regimen of their barbarous ancestors."

The San Francisco coat of the 1940s no longer fits the world of the 1990s. There are few worse things we could do to the legacy of Roosevelt, Churchill, and the U.N.'s other founders than to cast in stone the global structures they created for the world of their day. Politics, as every undergraduate knows, is the art of the possible. A great deal more is possible today, as we emerge from the Cold War era, than was possible when we entered it a half century ago.

U.N. DUES: THE PRICE OF PEACE[4]

In the new post–Cold War world, the United Nations has moved to center stage. Conflicts fueled by superpower rivalries are ending, often with U.N. help. Meanwhile, internal conflicts long suppressed by rigid Cold War alignments are erupting. As these conflicts widen and spill over to neighbors, warring parties are increasingly turning to the United Nations. The Security Council has authorized an unprecedented number of complex peacekeeping and military observation operations since 1988: in Afghanistan, Iran-Iraq, Namibia, Angola, Central America, Iraq-Kuwait, the Western Sahara, El Salvador, Cambodia, and—for the first time in Europe—Yugoslavia.

Indeed, the U.N. Security Council held a summit meeting of heads of state in January 1992—its first since 1945. In their final statement, these leaders stressed the importance of strengthening the United Nations, and they pledged their determination "to assume fully their responsibilities within the United Nations Organization in the framework of the Charter."

Unfortunately, the reality is different. Their ringing endorsement masks a growing financial crisis that is paralyzing the U.N.'s ability to act in ways the world's leaders say they want. And their increasing reliance on the United Nations is straining its already meager resources and seriously jeopardizing its ability to resolve conflicts.

For example, in 1988 the military observer force on the Iran-Iraq border was held up for three weeks for lack of $150,000 to charter a plane to transport signal units needed to link observation posts. In 1989, a three-month debate over lowering the budget for the peacekeeping force to oversee Namibia's transition to independence delayed deployment of the force. As a result, the United Nations had virtually no forces on the ground when a clash between returning SWAPO guerrillas and South African forces almost derailed the operation. Today, the U.N.'s early warning unit has so few fax machines that detailed information about developing crises cannot get through, and the secretary-

[4]Article by Enid C. B. Schoettle, Senior Fellow at the Council of Foreign Relations, from *Bulletin of the Atomic Scientists* 48:14–16 Je '92. Copyright © 1992 by the Educational Foundation for Nuclear Science. Reprinted with permission.

general, lacking a plane of his own, must often resort to borrowing from generous governments to visit crisis areas.

This spring, debates at the United Nations and in the U.S. Congress about cutting the projected budgets for new peacekeeping operations in Cambodia ($1.9 billion over 15 months) and Yugoslavia ($616 million over 15 months) delayed full deployment of peacekeeping forces, despite urgent requests from both countries to get peacekeepers in place quickly. Meanwhile, fragile cease-fire agreements hung in the balance.

Since Iraq continues to refuse to sell oil under strict U.N. supervision, which was supposed to finance the dismantling of Iraq's weapons complex, there is no regular funding for the U.N. Special Commission. To meet the roughly $3 million monthly cost of this unprecedented effort, the Special Commission must solicit emergency funds from interested governments, often at the last minute. And as of yet there are no funds for special and expensive tasks facing the commission: notably, the destruction of Iraq's chemical weapons and the removal of irradiated nuclear fuels from Iraq.

If world leaders—and especially the United States—want to strengthen U.N. peacekeeping and peacemaking, serious and systematic financial arrangements are needed. At the very least, member governments should meet their existing obligations by paying their annual assessments for the regular budget and for peacekeeping operations. At the end of March [1992], only 35 countries were paid up. The remaining 140 U.N. members owed $2 billion in unpaid assessments: $1.14 billion for the regular budget and $859 million for the U.N.'s eleven current peacekeeping operations.

In the mid-1980s, as a result of a general disillusionment with the United Nations, the Reagan administration and Congress began to withhold substantial fractions of the U.S. assessments owed the United Nations in order to wrench reforms from the organization. In principle, the Bush administration has now committed the United States to full payment of U.S. assessments, but it has undertaken to pay over a five year period, and there have been delays in even this elongated payment plan. As Secretary of State James Baker has been saying since September 1990, the United States remains the "world's biggest deadbeat."

At the end of March 1992, the United States was responsible for $863 million or 43 percent of the U.N.'s outstanding assessments. The other four permanent members of the Security

Council—China, France, Russia, and Britain—owed a total of $444 million, or 22 percent. Germany and Japan—the other two largest U.N. contributors—owed $267 million, or 13 percent. Given its acute economic crisis, it is unlikely that Russia will soon pay up. But the other major contributors should put their money where their mouth is—they should pay their arrears, and stay current. The United States should pay its entire overdue account now, rather than stretching repayment over the next three years. And it should begin to pay its yearly assessments at the beginning of the U.N.'s fiscal year rather than at the end, as has been U.S. practice since 1982.

Former Secretary-General Javier Perez de Cuellar, in one of his last reports in November 1991, suggested five sensible, business-like ways to reform the U.N.'s present hand-to-mouth financing:

• **Increase the U.N. working capital fund** to provide sufficient liquidity to temporarily finance ordinary operations and unforeseen expenses. Established in 1946, this fund has been eroding steadily since the early 1970s. In 1991 the fund averaged about a three-week reserve, but it was sometimes completely depleted. From August to October 1991, the secretary-general was forced to borrow from the few peacekeeping accounts with excess cash to meet regular budget obligations. No business could operate on such a narrow-to-vanishing margin.

• **Charge interest at commercial rates on all assessments in arrears** for 60 days or more. Governments collect interest from delinquent taxpayers and businesses collect interest on customers' debts; the United Nations ought to have the same right to collect interest when governments don't pay bills.

• **Grant the authority to borrow commercially** to cover cash-flow problems when the working capital fund is depleted. In the past, this request has been denied, although several specialized U.N. agencies have such authority. The secretary-general, who manages a complex organization, should have the same freedom that any small businessman has.

• **Establish a peacekeeping reserve fund**. By their very nature, peacekeeping operations are hard to predict and budget for in advance. But when the need arises, peacekeeping forces must be deployed quickly. Standby financing could meet start-up costs in the crucial first weeks of operations, and wrangling over final budgets would be less likely to derail fragile cease-fires.

• **Establish a U.N. peace endowment fund**, with an initial target of $1 billion. The fund's income could be used to cover the costs of small peacekeeping operations and the initial costs of larger ones, or of unanticipated peacemaking activities that might go beyond regular budget projections. When fully established, it could absorb the peacekeeping reserve fund.

Raising a billion dollars, as Perez de Cuellar suggested, may seem like a major undertaking. But it may not seem so great when compared with current endowment drives at major U.S. universities. Stanford has just completed a $1.2 billion drive, and several Ivy League universities will soon be conducting capital drives at or above the Stanford level. At this unique moment in history, the United Nations might well be able to attract comparable amounts.

Individual and foundation gifts to international efforts for world peace are not without precedent. Before World War I, Andrew Carnegie donated the Peace Palace in the Hague, and the Rockefeller family and its related philanthropies contributed heavily to the construction of both the Palais des Nations in Geneva in the 1920s and the United Nations in New York in the late 1940s.

Funds for the peace endowment should be solicited from both foundations and individuals. For instance, if the 40 largest U.S. philanthropic foundations made a one-time contribution of 1 percent of their assets, their combined contributions would equal 50 percent of the goal. Additional contributions might come from transnational corporations.

In addition to de Cuellar's recommendations, the United Nations should introduce less traditional methods of financing to give it a reliable stream of resources for the longer run. The authority to issue bonds is one possibility. Another might be user fees on industries that rely on peace to remain profitable—perhaps a one or two percent surcharge on international airline tickets and maritime insurance premiums. (Losses incurred by the airline industry during the 1990–1991 Gulf War and the astronomical insurance rates charged oil tankers operating in the Gulf during the Iran-Iraq War make it clear that some industries pay dearly when peace breaks down.) Other means of bringing in cash might include some kind of international lottery or a voluntary check-off on tax returns.

U.N. members might also consider putting a cap on the scale of assessments so that no country would pay more than, for example, 15 percent of the U.N.'s regular and peacekeeping budgets. (A percentage cap was proposed by the late prime minister of

Sweden, Olaf Palme, and by former Secretary-General Perez de Cuellar in the mid-1980s, but was rejected by the U.S. government.) Such a cap would lower the U.S. rates, which now stand at 25 and 30 percent respectively, and reduce the organization's heavy reliance on its largest but lately unreliable contributor. Other wealthy countries could easily increase their assessed contributions.

The General Assembly might also consider whether peace-keeping operations have now become such a normal part of U.N. activity that they should be incorporated into the regular budget and paid for as part of a single annual assessment. This would streamline the financing of operations and reduce the heavy rate of assessment now levied on a few states.

Major reforms along at least some of these lines are needed now. They would go a long way toward relieving the organization of its crippling financial constraints and enable it to do the jobs it has been assigned. No reorganization or reform of the United Nations will work unless its financing is rationalized. Perhaps the time has come to appoint an international commission of financial leaders to propose specific financial reforms to Secretary-General Boutros Boutros-Ghali, his new undersecretary for administration and management, Richard Thornburgh, and member governments.

In the end, the most important factor in resolving the U.N.'s financial problem is gaining a realistic perspective. Critics of the United Nations have long called it a "bloated bureaucracy," claiming it was full of inefficient underachievers drawing exorbitant salaries. Certainly, cases of waste, inefficiency, and duplication should be reformed or eliminated. But the overriding fact is that U.N. costs, including those for peacekeeping operations, are puny. The U.N.'s regular 1992 budget is $1.04 billion—less than the 1992 budget of the New York City Fire Department. The projected 1992 costs for the 11 military observation and peace-keeping missions now under way are approximately $2.5 billion, or about that of the New York City Police Department's 1992 budget. Surely the U.N.'s peace and security missions are worth this scale of investment.

III. VIEWS FROM THE UNITED STATES AND ABROAD

EDITOR'S INTRODUCTION

The articles in this section bring together different perspectives of the U.N. from around the world. In the first piece, "The Limits to Sovereignty", former Under Secretary General of the U.N. Brian Urquhart discusses how the U.N. will cope with the growing conflict between national sovereignty and interdependence. In the next two essays, U.S. Assistant Secretary of State John R. Bolton stresses the need for the U.S. and other nations to support U.N. peacekeeping efforts, and former Secretary of State Lawrence Eagleburger hails the repeal of the Zionism-is-racism resolution.

In "U.N. Role in Establishing a New World Order," Li Luye, the former Chinese Ambassador to the U.N., discusses his country's attitude to the world body. Japanese views of the United Nations and its human rights declarations is a generally under-reported topic, which is discussed in an article from *Asian Survey*. The next article, a translation of a piece that originally appeared in *Izvestia*, discusses Russian representation in the U.N. in the wake of the breakup of the Soviet Union.

Michael J. Berlin, a former U.N. correspondent for the *Washington Post* and *New York Post*, reviews press coverage of the United Nations. Finally, the *U.N. Chronicle* reports on the results of opinion polls conducted in more than a dozen countries to measure public attitudes toward the U.N.

THE LIMITS TO SOVEREIGNTY[1]

Under Secretary General of the United Nations from 1974 to 1986, Brian Urquhart is presently scholar-in-residence at the Ford Foundation.

[1]Interview with Brian Urquhart, Under Secretary General of the United Nations, from *New Perspectives Quarterly* 8:24–27 Fall '91. Copyright © 1991 by *New Perspectives Quarterly*. Reprinted with permission.

NPQ spoke with him about how the chief global organization, the United Nations, will face the growing conflict between national sovereignty and interdependence that has emerged with a vengeance in the post-cold-war era.

NPQ: The Gulf war began after it was sanctioned by the UN in the name of defending the national sovereignty of Kuwait. Yet the whole episode ended by contravening the same principle through the sanction of intervention in Iraqi internal affairs to rescue the Kurds.

Justification of these two actions, based on contradictory principles, reveals the conflict between the concept of national sovereignty and the universality of human rights. Along with the realities of economic and ecological interdependence, which also come into conflict with national sovereignty, this will be a central issue of the post-cold-war era.

You've said that it is time for the UN itself to ask the basic question about national sovereignty.

What is the basic question?

Brian Urquhart: How the contemporary world community is going to reach a working agreement that balances national sovereignty, the foundation upon which the United Nations is built, and international responsibility, the mission with which the UN is charged.

But if we are going to start changing the ground rules, which is necessary for both humanitarian and environmental reasons, the only way is through the promulgation of universally applied, and enforceable, international law. If intervention on behalf of human rights and environmental principles are to be sanctioned, it must be done without anyone—for example the G–7 powers—having the deck stacked in their favor.

That is why I take the much publicized initiatives for Kurdish rescue, led by British prime minister John Major, with a grain of salt. A lot of the enthusiasm for this rescue mission was tied to domestic politics.

How would Britain respond if the majority of the world community decided to call for international intervention in Northern Ireland?

You will recall that the Chinese and the Soviets, fearing world intervention concerning Tibet and the Baltics, respectively, balked at violating Iraqi sovereignty in order to save the Kurds.

One must also understand that in the developing world there

is much suspicion of this newfound interventionist enthusiasm on the part of the more advanced industrial nations. It is seen as a cloak for the perpetuation of great power meddling, which they have engaged in all too much over the past two centuries.

So, while I believe it is time to start developing legal norms for overriding national sovereignty in humanitarian cases, it is going to be a slow business.

NPQ: How in your own mind do you see the balance between sovereignty and responsibility?

The nation-state is not yet obsolete, but is surely *becoming* obsolete. Ethnic rebellion is eroding the nation-state from below; interdependence and new norms of responsibility from above.

Urquhart: Obviously, the nation-state remains the building block of the international system. It can't just be abolished. But it is being increasingly eroded by the general advance of technology and its functional imperatives.

The classic example of this is telecommunications. The International Telecommunications Union approves radio frequencies worldwide. Everyone accedes to this functional authority, since there could be no clear radio communication at all if everyone took whatever frequency they pleased.

Increasing numbers of common areas—global commons if you will—will emerge that must function according to international, not national, arrangements.

Natural resources, like the air waves, are another area of the global commons. The Treaty of the Law of the Sea embodies this principle of international responsibility over the fate of a common sea bed. It seeks, in the name of all humanity, to protect it from being irreparably plundered.

NPQ: In your view, then, would it be appropriate for the UN-sponsored Earth Summit in Brazil next summer to declare the Brazilian rain forest—in effect the planet's lungs—a resource of the human race that ought to be protected from development by Brazil or anyone else?

Urquhart: Above all, this question points up precisely why we need legal norms that apply to all equally. Otherwise we will get nowhere at all on global issues.

After all, we in the industrialized North have made the maximum contribution to environmental degradation, and we continue to do so. Not only have we already destroyed all our rain forests long before the Brazilians even started to degrade theirs, we also spew more pollutants into the air and are primarily responsible, through chlorofluorocarbon emissions, for the break-up of the ozone layer.

Given that reality, the Brazilians are going to resist any political machinations to finger them as the villains of ecocide, which is understandable.

Having said this, I applaud the effort of the Brazil conference to produce generally agreed-upon norms under which environmental behavior will be regulated. It will be a first step in the long trek toward the kind of global environmental regime that will be necessary for survival.

NPQ: A regime with jails and police powers to enforce the law?

Urquhart: Environmental risks are already so great that urgent action is of the utmost importance. I wish we were at the point where the law could be enforced. But I'm afraid we're not anywhere near that point now.

There is already a large body of unenforceable international law and conventions. For example, the convention against cleaning tankers at sea, a process that pollutes the ocean with oil sludge, is an especially serious problem in enclosed seas like the Mediterranean. But shipping crews continually flaunt the law because it is much cheaper to clean them at sea than in port.

At what point will an authority emerge—the UN or some other institution—that, first of all, has the surveillance capacity to detect this illegal activity, has the power to issue warnings, and, if the tanker ignores the first warning, has the authority to go out and sink that ship?

There is little question that sinking one tanker would discourage all other tankers from cleaning their hulls at sea.

If the new world order were built around that kind of international authority instead of some kind of self-appointed posse of great powers that goes around telling the bad boys to be good, then we would be getting close to a world order that works equitably for everyone. What we need is a new world order based on legal norms for the defense of the global commons, backed up by the force to ensure compliance.

Establishing some kind of hegemony of the seven industrial powers, which dictates to others, is not the right way to proceed.

Much of the world—the G–70 or whatever—is already resentful of the permanent members of the UN Security Council who they see as having manipulated the Security Council in the course of the Gulf war.

NPQ: When you say the UN or "some other institution" must emerge, do you envision that a new global organization could be more effective?

Urquhart: We are not living in the world of 1945, when the UN was conceived and founded. The challenges are entirely different. The world is now facing slow strangulation through population growth—world population has doubled since 1945—and the consequences of uncontrolled technology. We are threatened not only by nuclear and biochemical warfare but by pollution from mundane sources such as the automobile. The microchip and the telecommunications satellite were inconceivable at the time the UN was founded.

If someone could think of a better arrangement than the UN it would be wonderful. But whatever international machinery is set up, it will have to face the same problems vis-á-vis sovereignty and North-South inequality as has the UN.

In my view it would be better to build on an organization that has in some ways a considerable track record than to start an alternative one from scratch.

But the UN must be radically reorganized; it has to become less a global political forum and more a global management organization with strong executive leadership. It has to extensively expand its monitoring capacities and to prevent conflicts and disasters, not simply react to them after the fact.

The UN must stop being a kind of Sunday morning exercise where one goes only when already in real trouble. It has to work consistently 365 days a year.

NPQ: Would you specifically seek the repeal of Article II.7 of the UN charter, which states that the ability of the UN to act is based upon the sacrosanct nature of national sovereignty?

Urquhart: UN activity should not so much be constrained by the terms of its original charter as it should be an organically evolving organization shaped by the demands of the actual situation.

Rather than take on the political hornet's nest of revoking that section of the charter, it would be more fruitful to pursue the promulgation of conventions that embody the new principles and, as such, supplant rather than uproot claims of national sovereignty.

Again, the difficulties are immense. Think only of the Law of the Sea treaty, which the Reagan administration refused to ratify because it regarded a deep sea authority as a form of international socialism.

The question really comes down to whether governments can get enough support from their own people to lift their sights from short-term concerns to the long-term project of safeguarding the future.

NPQ: And there seems little evidence that states, or their subjects, are willing to abandon sovereignty. Indeed, the trend is in the other direction. Once they've gained their democratic rights in the former Soviet bloc or elsewhere, people are claiming ethnic and national sovereignty, not abandoning it. That's true from Eritrea to Croatia to Russia.

Urquhart: Well, I'm not sure the world is moving back toward nationalism, although there has obviously been an explosion of ethnic sentiments in the aftermath of the cold war.

The real challenge seems to be persuading a public to think in terms of future generations in the face of two particular obstacles: the selfishness of the haves and the extreme deprivation of the have nots.

And can you imagine running for Congress in the United States on the program of eliminating the single greatest polluting agent in the world: the automobile?

NPQ: How then can the interests of future generations effectively challenge the present interest of national sovereignty?

Urquhart: A battle over the domestic jurisdiction clause of the UN Charter can only be avoided by developing a basis for the future interest in international law.

It wasn't so very long ago that, even in states like the U.S. or Great Britain, we didn't have a system of democracy, equitable justice, and even the police, which appeared in England only in the 1830s. Now the U.S. and Great Britain have an executive, the legislature, and the courts. The courts are the arbiters of the law and the law is enforced as necessary.

Two hundred years ago what we have today was not even considered a remote possibility.

Now we have arrived at the point where the organized human community is larger than the nation-state. The very first institutions admitting this emergent reality—the United Nations and the World Court—are still very young. Conventions are promulgated, rulings are made, but, like the early days of the rule of law in England, the law is honored more in the breach than in its observance. But the time is coming, inevitably and inexorably, when a global legal regime will have to be enforced. . . .

U.N. PEACEKEEPING EFFORTS TO
PROMOTE SECURITY AND STABILITY[2]

I look forward to discussing with you a topic which I consider of great importance to the United States' national security, namely UN peace-keeping. To start, however, I would like to make a few brief remarks on three topics: the rapid expansion of UN peace-keeping, our attempts to control the costs of UN peace-keeping, and the outlook for the future.

Expansion of UN Peace-keeping

The last 2 years have seen an explosion in UN peace-keeping and peace-making activities. Since last April alone, the Security Council has created new peace-keeping missions in the Persian Gulf, the Western Sahara, El Salvador, Cambodia, and Yugoslavia. Indeed, the last 4 years have seen the creation of more new UN peace-keeping operations than had been undertaken in the previous 43 years of the organization's history.

Why has UN involvement in peace-keeping expanded so rapidly? The simplest answer is because the world has changed so much. The collapse of communism in Eastern Europe and in the former Soviet Union has led to breathtaking changes in the relations among countries and among peoples, most of which have been for the good. They have not only brought freedom to millions of individuals who lived under the yoke of tyranny but will also lead to greater global prosperity and stability. Some changes have, however, been pernicious and have led to the open expression of long pent-up hatreds. In varying degrees, these regional conflicts damage US interests and impact on our national security.

Overall, these changes in the world order have tremendously increased the importance of the UN's peace-keeping role. With the end of the Cold War, the Security Council is finally able to carry out the chief duty entrusted to it by the founders of the United Nations—the preservation of international peace and se-

[2]Excerpts of a statement by John R. Bolton, Assistant Secretary for International Organization Affairs, from *U.S. Department of State Dispatch* 3:244–246 Mr 30 '92.

curity. No longer do animosities between the Soviet Union and the Western members prevent the council from taking action to resolve threats to the global peace.

Now, the members of the council work together effectively to address international problems which would have been allowed to fester a few short years ago. In case after case, the Security Council finds solutions to problems which once seemed intractable. Those solutions are frequently imperfect, and they always cost money. They do, however, usually prevent the expansion of conflict, have saved countless thousands of lives, and cost much less than direct US involvement.

The end of the Cold War has not only made the Security Council a more effective institution for addressing threats to international peace, it has also meant that regional conflicts which were fueled by superpower rivalry are now ripe for resolution. In countries as diverse as Angola, El Salvador, and Cambodia, communist governments and guerrilla movements have realized that they can no longer count on outside support and must make peace. Given the long history of animosity, people in such countries naturally look for an impartial arbiter as they try to make the transition to a system incorporating all sectors of society. In many cases, the United Nations becomes that arbiter.

As I have mentioned above, the collapse of communism in Eastern Europe and in the Soviet Union, coupled with rapid democratization throughout the Third World, has had some undesirable side effects. Religious and ethnic animosities long crushed under the dictator's boot heel are now coming to the fore. Yugoslavia has already fallen apart because of such tensions; unrest is also palpable in various portions of the former Soviet Union. In some cases, the world community will be forced to turn to the United Nations to try to help cool things down.

New UN peace-keeping activities confront daunting obstacles to fulfilling their mandates. Each individual case presents unique logistical, financial, and underlying political problems. For example:

Cambodia. In Cambodia, the United Nations is beginning to implement its most ambitious peace-keeping effort to date— UNTAC [UN Transitional Authority in Cambodia]. Issues of immediate importance include establishing as soon as possible a viable, nationwide UN presence; initiating priority de-mining and infrastructural improvements essential for timely repatriation; preparing to demobilize as many of the factional forces [as] possible (at least 70%); and, finally, creating the conditions for free and fair elections. No less important is identifying sources to fund UN activities, especially an urgent need for accommodation, transportation, communication, and other support equipment and services.

Yugoslavia. On February 21, 1992, the Security Council established a UN Protection Force for Yugoslavia (UNPROFOR). UN estimates project a force of around 14,000 at a cost of close to $640 million [for] the first year. Security Council members have expressed concern over the high costs of UNPROFOR and authorized the dispatch to Yugoslavia of an advance mission to, inter alia, look at ways of reducing costs and creating the conditions necessary for UNPROFOR's full deployment. UNPROFOR will be charged with demilitarizing the three UN-protected areas within Croatia and overseeing the civil and police administration of those areas.

El Salvador. The UN Observer Mission in El Salvador (ONUSAL) was created May 20, 1991. ONUSAL's original mandate was to verify compliance with the San Jose agreement on human rights. The Security Council expanded ONUSAL January 14, 1992, to include separate peace-keeping (military) and police contingents. There have been accusations on the part of the Government of El Salvador that the FMLN [Farabundo Marti National Liberation Front] has violated provisions of the peace agreement on declaring its arms inventories, land seizures, and prompt entry into the zones of concentration. On the other hand, FMLN charges the government with trying to retain former paramilitary police units that it had promised to disband. We are looking into allegations by both parties and are working closely with ONUSAL to ensure that the process not lose momentum.

ONUSAL was able to deploy rapidly because its human rights unit had been in El Salvador since mid-1991 and because it inherited all resources, including military officers and equipment, belonging to the UN Observer Mission in Central America (ONUCA), which was dissolved shortly after ONUSAL/PK's [Peace-keeping] creation. ONUSAL has had problems, however, in recruiting sufficient numbers of qualified police officers.

Western Sahara. Although 185 UN cease-fire monitors deployed in the Western Sahara September 6, 1991, to observe the cease-fire between Morocco and the POLISARIO [Popular Liberation Front for Rio de Oro and Saguia El Hamra], the formal deployment of the full MINURSO [UN Mission in Western Sahara] peace-keeping contingent to conduct a referendum has been delayed because of the inability of the two parties to agree on the criteria to be used in selecting voters. The Secretary General has asked that the Security Council grant him until the end of May to resolve all outstanding impediments to the deployment of MINURSO.

Somalia. The Security Council approved last week the dispatch of a technical team to Somalia to discuss with all the warring factions the modalities of providing UN cease-fire observers and the effective distribution of humanitarian relief. The technical team must deal with the fact that there are many more opposing factions in Somalia than the two Mogadishu-based ones with which the United Nations has heretofore dealt. The team must also confront the fact that there has not yet been a respected cease-fire despite numerous agreements brokered either through regional or UN efforts. To be effective, UN peace-keepers in Somalia will have to oversee a continuing political process whose goal will be not only a cease-fire but a resolution of the fundamental political differences among the warring factions that will allow, in the first instance, the successful distribution of badly needed relief assistance.

Peace-keeping Costs

Strong support of UN peace-keeping activities has long been a basic tenet of US foreign policy. We must ensure the United Nations has the wherewithal to accomplish its very important mandate. The lack of adequate and timely financing for new and existing peace-keeping operations will pose serious problems for the United Nations and for the US leadership and influence in the United Nations.

We have requested an FY [fiscal year] 1992 budget amendment totalling $350 million in the foreign assistance bill to meet FY 1991 and 1992 unfunded requirements for the UN Iraq/Kuwait Observer Mission (UNIKOM), the UN Angola Verification Mission (UNAVEM II), the UN Mission in Western Sahara, and the UN Advance Mission in Cambodia (UNAMIC). Also included in this request is the initial funding for the UN Observer Mission in El Salvador, the UN Transitional Authority in Cambodia, and the UN Protection Force in Yugoslavia.

For FY 1993, the Administration has asked for $350 million

to meet new and anticipated peace-keeping requirements. This money will be used to fund UN peace-keeping missions in Cambodia and Yugoslavia, as well as continue the UN Observer Mission in El Salvador.

Benefits to the United States

We are keenly aware that our current appropriations request for US contributions for international peace-keeping activities represents a very large increase over our previous years' requests. However, while the costs are expanding rapidly, UN peace-keeping remains one of the best bargains there is with respect to the maintenance of world peace. Obviously, the amounts which the world spends on UN peace-keeping are only the minutest fraction of what the world spends on armaments.

UN peace-keeping serves US national security interests. Peace-keeping helps prevent regional conflicts from expanding and directly threatening US interests.

Admittedly, not all of those trouble spots would appear to be of direct interest to the United States. Many, however, are areas where US lives, money, and prestige have been on the line for years. In those instances, we appear to be making the last payment on investments which have succeeded brilliantly; failure to pay that last installment could, however, jeopardize the entire investment.

For example, our $20-million bill for UN peace-keeping in El Salvador looks high at first—until one compares it with the billions of dollars we have spent ensuring that that nation got to the point where UN peace-keeping could succeed. Similarly, the scores of millions of dollars we spent to ensure that a Marxist government did not stifle the will of the people of Angola more than offset the money we are asked to spend to ensure that the United Nations can help demobilize the rival armies and hold fair elections. Finally, who in good conscience could walk away from the last, best chance to resolve the tragedy of Cambodia, a tragedy with which the American people have been linked for years. The United Nations is the best insurance against a return to power by the Khmer Rouge.

Even those UN peace-keeping missions with which our ties are less obvious usually directly benefit US interests. For example, in many fields—investment, trade, strategic interests—our links to Yugoslavia are tenuous. Continuation of the war there, however, would have had a direct, negative effect on many important US interests in the area. To take one obvious example, the flow of large numbers of refugees could well have undermined the new, fragile democracies on Yugoslavia's northern and eastern borders.

Keeping Costs Down

While I continue to believe UN peace-keeping is a tremendous bargain, I am also painfully aware of the need to keep costs down. Our own domestic concerns demand it; so does the credibility of the United Nations.

How can we keep the cost of UN peace-keeping down? One way is to create as few new missions as absolutely necessary. The UN Charter makes it clear that regional organizations should take the lead in trying to resolve regional problems; we fully support this approach.

Let me assure you that we do not view UN peace-keeping as the savior of lost causes, to be thrown into a crisis willy-nilly when all else fails. If new peace-keeping missions must be created, they must have as clearly defined a mandate as possible. Preferably, the duration of a new mission should be set in concrete and tied to a process which will clearly lead to a resolution of the underlying problem. The current UN peace-keeping missions in Angola, El Salvador, and Cambodia and the one successfully concluded in Namibia all share these characteristics.

Even if the duration of a peace-keeping mission cannot be so sharply defined, we must make it clear to all parties that UN peace-keeping is not an end in itself; UN peace-keepers will not serve as the perpetual guarantors of an armed truce. For example, the Security Council resolution authorizing peace-keeping in Yugoslavia specifically tied the deployment of UN peace-keepers to the attempts to negotiate a resolution to the crisis at the EC [European Community]-sponsored conference on Yugoslavia. We expect those talks to succeed; if they do not, however, and if the parties abandon good faith efforts to resolve their differences, the Security Council will have to re-examine the mandate of that mission.

Another way to keep costs down is to ensure that each individual mission is as lean and efficient as possible. We are in constant communication with the UN Secretariat to make certain that the number of peace-keepers deployed in each mission is the absolute minimum needed to implement that mission's mandate. We also press the Secretariat to maximize voluntary contributions from the countries hosting peace-keeping missions and from countries with particular interests in the success of a given mission. These approaches have resulted in the savings of hundreds of millions of dollars from the estimates initially advanced by the United Nations for peace-keeping missions in Namibia and Angola. We expect that they will lead to even greater savings with respect to the upcoming missions in Cambodia and Yugoslavia.

Finally, let me assure you that we are examining the question of whether there is any honorable and equitable way to adjust the percentage that we pay of UN peace-keeping costs. We cannot escape the fact that our economy is more than twice as large as that of any other nation. We cannot deny that we are the world's only remaining superpower. We cannot escape the reality that our over-seas interests are broader and more compelling than those of any other country. Still, within those parameters, we will fight to ensure that the US share of UN peace-keeping is kept to an absolute minimum. To me, for the United States to continue to pay 30.4% of the total cost of UN peace-keeping does seem excessive.

The Future

We have reached one of the three great junctions of 20th century history. We have won the Cold War, just as we won the First and Second World Wars. Our prestige and influence in the world are at an apogee, but, in some ways, we are tired from the struggle and want to turn inward. Our domestic problems are myriad and cry out for attention. We want somebody—anybody—to take over the load overseas.

Over the long term, however, to turn our backs on the world we must live in would be disastrous. We all remember the isola-tionism of the 1920s and its evil twin, economic protectionism, just as we remember the chaos they helped create on the world stage. We must never let that happen again.

We have an opportunity to do great things:

• Help stabilize fledgling democracies in countries that have known only tyranny for decades;

• Promote human rights on a global scale; [and]

• Use the United Nations and the relevant regional organiza-tions to help create greater international peace and stability than the world has ever known.

The "good guys" are clearly winning right now; if we, the United States, abandon the fight, however, the outcome will become much murkier.

UN REPEALS ZIONISM-IS-RACISM RESOLUTION[3]

Mr. President, the United Nations was founded in 1945 at the close of one of the darkest chapters in recorded history. Two world wars, the massacre of untold millions, and a hideous attempt to exterminate an entire people formed the backdrop to the San Francisco conference. Mankind's hopes for a different fate in a better future rested almost entirely on the shoulders of the new international body—on its potential as a peacemaker and peacekeeper and on its moral authority as a voice for universal human values. One of the early acts of the United Nations was to assist in the realization of the national aspirations of that people—the Jewish people—who had so recently been the victims of one of the most barbarous acts known to man.

Those hopes for a better future were dashed with the onset of the Cold War. The international landscape was divided right down the middle between East and West. The two blocs stood poised on the brink of thermonuclear war. Totalitarian ideologies spread hatred and turned reality on its head by enslaving men and women in the name of liberating them.

And in the United Nations, confrontation replaced cooperation; paralysis prevailed over action. Ideological conflict eroded the UN's most precious asset—its claim to impartiality and moral honesty. The great parliament of mankind had become a forum for sterile rhetoric, feckless name-calling, and the willful distortion of reality.

At no time was this more evident than in 1975 when the General Assembly adopted Resolution 3379, which included a determination that Zionism was a form of racism. This determination demonstrated, like nothing else before or since, to what

[3]A statement by Lawrence Eagleburger, then Deputy Secretary of State at the U.N. General Assembly, December 16, 1991. From *U.S. Department of State Dispatch* 2:908–909 D 23 '91.

extent the Cold War had distorted the United Nation's vision of reality, marginalized its political utility, and separated it from its original moral purpose.

Resolution 3379 was one of this body's most ungenerous acts. It branded the national aspirations of one people, and one people only, as illegitimate—a people which had been homeless, dispersed, and exiled for the better part of 2 millennia. It labeled as racist the national aspirations of the one people more victimized by racism than any other.

My government rejected this characterization of Zionism in 1975, and it has hoped for and worked for its revocation ever since. Successive US Administrations—of Presidents Ford, Carter, Reagan, and now Bush—have been supported in this endeavor by our Congress and by our major political parties. And they have been supported overwhelmingly by the American people, who have never understood how the UN could let stand such a blatant repudiation of the charter's call for member states to practice tolerance and live together as good neighbors. In President Bush's call for repeal before this assembly last September, he recognized that the United Nations was at a historic watershed. "By repealing this resolution unconditionally," he noted, "the United Nations will enhance its credibility and serve the cause of peace."

Now the endeavors of 16 long years are about to come to fruition—not because of the United States, although we have never wavered in our determination, but because the era which produced Resolution 3379 has passed into history. With that era have gone many of the dictatorships whose repression was based on systematic lying and the distortion of reality. With that era have gone the confrontational ideologies which held much of the world in their thrall. They have been displaced by a revolution in truth-telling and openness which is truly universal in scope. They have been displaced, increasingly, by democratic governments committed to the universal human values for which this body, in principle, stands. Indeed, nothing more eloquently demonstrates the passing of the Cold War era than the fact that many governments whose undemocratic predecessors had supported or voted for the original resolution in 1975 have joined now in cosponsoring its revocation.

One of the signal features of the new era we have entered is that the UN is ever more frequently being asked to play a central role in making peace between nations and regions in conflict; in consolidating that peace through the deployment of military observers and peacekeeping forces; and, when it is necessary—as was so recently the case in the Persian Gulf—in leading the world in response to aggression.

We believe that with the world's and this body's passage into a new era, it is more than time to consign one of the last relics of the Cold War to the dustbin of history. That is why we are presenting to the General Assembly today—on behalf of 85 co-sponsors—a resolution revoking the determination that Zionism is racism. We believe it is time to take this step, thereby recovering for the United Nations its reputation for fairness and impartiality and reaffirming its commitment to the vision of San Francisco.

Mr. President, let me emphasize that this resolution we propose is aimed at no one, at no state, at no region, and at no group. Its sole and simple aim is to right a wrong and to restore the moral authority of this organization. It is not aimed at or linked to the peace process in the Middle East. However, I will say that my government believes that this action can only help, and not hinder, efforts currently underway to bring peace to that region. For 16 years, the existence of the "Zionism-is-racism" determination has stood in the way of those who wish to see the UN play a more significant role in the peace process. It is simply a fact that Resolution 3379 contradicted the spirit of Security Council Resolutions 242 and 338, which are the continuing basis for a peaceful settlement in the Middle East.

Even more significant, however, was the message which Resolution 3379 sent to the people of Israel. It told them that their national aspirations were inspired by racism. It told them that their national existence was illegitimate. It told them that the international community, in all its solemn majesty, had once again subjected the Jewish people to a singular form of persecution.

It is almost a cliche to say that there can be no true peace without confidence—mutual confidence on the part of all sides to a conflict. There can be no peace without the recognition by each side of the other's legitimacy. There can be no true or lasting peace without a spirit of brotherhood.

The resolution we introduce today would send a different message to the people of Israel from the one this body sent in 1975. But, fundamentally, it is not Israel which needs this action; it is the United Nations which requires it. Its passage will vindicate the universal principles upon which the UN was founded

and redeem the hopes which all mankind vested in the United
Nations in 1945.

UN ROLE IN ESTABLISHING
A NEW WORLD ORDER[4]

In recent years, the question of establishing a new international
order has become a topic of widespread discussion. This reflects
the concern people have about the future of the world at a juncture when a new world structure is replacing the old one. It is
noteworthy that although there is a variety of propositions advanced by various sides concerning the establishment of a new
international order, they have one point in common, namely,
most countries hope to see a role of the United Nations in this
process.

Challenges

The world has undergone dramatic changes since the late
1980s. The post-war bipolar system based on the Yalta structure
has collapsed. International relations are undergoing readjust-
ment and the tendency towards multipolarization is gaining momentum. And this has offered opportunities for an enhanced UN
role in establishing a new international order. But at the same
time, the UN is also faced with great challenges.

1. The disintegration of the world pattern characterized by
bipolar confrontation came hand in hand with a detente between
the United States and the Soviet Union. Changes in the balance of
power among major countries and the decline of the Soviet Union
in particular have relatively diminished the ability of the two superpowers to manipulate world affairs. Under such circumstances, changes have also taken place in the relationship among
the five permanent members of the UN Security Council. Thanks
to the co-operation of the non-permanent members of the Security Council and the support of the relevant parties and countries
in the regions concerned, the five permanent members of the UN

[4]Article by Li Luye, Director-General of the China Centre for International
Studies, from *Beijing Review* 34:12–16 S 30–O 6 '91.

Security Council succeeded in urging Iran and Iraq to accept the Security Council resolution on their ceasefire and troop withdrawal, in bringing about the independence of Namibia on the basis of the relevant UN resolutions, and in working out the framework documents on a comprehensive settlement of the Cambodian question. These successes in removing regional hotspots have strengthened the co-ordinative relationship among the permanent members of the Security Council, improved the co-operative relationship between the permanent and non-permanent members, and enhanced the prestige of the UN and its Security Council. Notwithstanding some differences on the Gulf crisis, the Security Council members fully displayed their consensus on stopping the Iraqi invasion and restoring Kuwait's sovereignty. This shows that as the old world pattern is giving way to a new one, it is most likely for the UN to play a greater role in removing international tensions, resolving problems in regional hotspots and promoting world peace. This is what the international community expects most of the United Nations.

However, the Gulf War, the tremendous changes in Eastern Europe and the turbulence in the Soviet Union have tipped the balance of the existing world pattern, bringing about a tendency of a few big powers jointly dominating the world. While these powers stress that the United Nations should be given a "central role," they in fact are placing themselves above the United Nations, giving out orders to the whole world. They adopt an opportunist approach towards the UN, making use of it when it suits them and discarding it when it goes against them. If this tendency is allowed to develop unchecked, the United Nations, although impossible to be completely "hijacked" by a few big powers, cannot bring genuine peace and development to the world. The numerous developing countries will be the worst victim of such a world order dominated by big powers.

Whether the new international order is to be established on the domination by big powers or in observance of the principle of equality of sovereign states as provided for in the United Nations Charter is a major challenge facing the United Nations.

2. During World War II, the allied nations, overlooking their ideological differences, joined hands and won the great victory in safeguarding world peace and opposing aggression. They then reached a consensus on establishing an international order based on the purposes and principles of the United Nations.

However, shortly afterwards, some Western powers waged a

cold war of ideology, pursuing a policy of armed intervention and containment towards the socialist countries, and fought two regional wars in Asia to this end. And before long, the socialist countries were also locked in a struggle between hegemonistic expansionism and anti-expansionism. This shows that there can also be serious confrontations even between countries sharing the same ideology if the strong wantonly bullies the weak. Historical lessons teach us that in international relations all countries, whether they have the same social system or not, should seek common ground while putting aside differences in order to live together in peace. If state-to-state relations are handled along ideological lines and values of one kind are imposed on all the countries, the world will inevitably be plunged into chaos. It is precisely because the two sides accepted and observed the norms of international relations based on the Five Principles of Peaceful Co-existence, especially the principle of non-interference in each other's internal affairs, that relations between China and the third world countries have enjoyed a sustained and steady development. It is also by the same reason that, for a period of time in the past, China and the Western developed countries, including the United States, not only brought their relations back to normal, but also made progress in their bilateral co-operation. This marked the development of healthy tendencies in international relations in the past ten years or more. It promoted world peace and stability, stimulated the relaxation of tensions in the Asian-Pacific region and provided useful experiences for establishing a new international order in the period of transition from the old world pattern to a new one. It also reflected the common aspiration of the overwhelming majority of the countries, especially the developing countries.

However, some countries and influential personages in the West viewed the dramatic changes in Eastern Europe as an "unexpected victory" of the West in the cold war of ideology. It is against such backdrop that there has been a big upsurge of the tendency of big-power interference in others' internal affairs, a tendency that some big Western powers tried hard to impose their values and ideology on other countries. As a result, the normal functioning of the United Nations was seriously disturbed.

The United Nations faces yet another major challenge: whether to refrain, under the principles enshrined in its Charter, from intervening, by whatever reasons or under whatever pretexts, in matters which are essentially within the domestic jurisdiction of its member states, or to push the Western values and ideology and willfully interfere in the internal affairs of the member states?

3. The changes in the world pattern, far from bringing any tangible economic benefit to the third world countries, have resulted in further widening the poor-and-rich gap between them and the developed countries. The North-South question is in essence a question of development. In as early as 1974, the United Nations adopted the Declaration on the Establishment of a New International Economic Order and its Programme of Action. However, over the past decade and more, poverty of the overwhelming majority of the developing countries has not been alleviated but rather aggravated. Such serious imbalance as the rich developed countries getting richer while the poor developing countries getting poorer is one of the root causes of the turbulences and tensions in some regions of the world. In the absence of economic development of the developing countries, there will be no genuine peace and stability in the world. Experiences have proved that a new international order cannot be built on the basis of the old international economic order. This has become a view shared most extensively in the United Nations in the economic field over the post-war decades. However, due to a lack of sincere political will in this regard on the part of a small number of developed countries, the resolution on the establishment of a new international economic order so far remains basically a mere scrap of paper. Over the past few years, the developing countries have strongly demanded for breaking the stalemate, giving a fresh impetus to North-South co-operation and resolving in real earnest the major economic difficulties facing them. The trend towards economic internationalization and regional economic co-operation in the world today reflects growing economic interdependence of the nations of the world and provides new fields and opportunities for solving the North-South question. The United Nations should lose no time to once again place on [its] agenda the settling of the question of North-South imbalance in international economic field as an urgent task.

It is noteworthy, however, that a few developed countries in the West attribute poverty of developing countries to their failure to practise political pluralism, a market economy and privatization after the Western model. Moreover, they take regional turbulence and conflicts caused by poverty and other factors as a major threat to future international security and have readjusted their military deployment accordingly in an attempt to strengthen their capability of armed intervention in case of emergencies. As is known to all, poverty of third world countries has many causes, of which the old international economic order and the economic relationship based on exchange of unequal values between the North and the South, which long placed the developing countries in an unequal and unfair position, is the main one. It will get nowhere to impose a particular Western model of development on the developing countries instead of reforming the old economic order. Nor is armed control a fundamental remedy for regional turbulence and conflict. The best way out is for the Western developed countries to undertake to reform the old economic order and gradually translate their commitment into specific actions. Whether or not the United Nations can make fresh efforts and achieve substantive progress in this regard will also be a major challenge to the organization.

Upholding the UN Charter

China's proposal for the establishment of a new international order on the basis of the Five Principles of Peaceful Co-existence is in keeping with the characteristics of the current transitional period from the old to the new pattern. It is aimed at moving the emerging multipolar-oriented international relationship in a direction favourable to world peace, development and harmonious co-existence of all countries. This not only conforms to the purposes and principles laid down in the UN Charter that should be strictly observed by all states, but also meets the strong common desire of the member states for an enhanced UN role. The Chinese side has no intention to replace the UN Charter with the Five Principles. However, in order to implement, to the letter and spirit, the purposes and principles of the UN under the new circumstances for the benefit of establishing a new fair international order, I believe it is necessary to further underscore the following major points contained in the UN Charter.

1. "The principle of the sovereign equality of all its members" is the first and foremost principle stressed at the beginning of the UN Charter and also a fundamental principle to be adhered to in establishing a new international order. It provides that all members of the UN, big or small, strong or weak, rich or poor, are equal members of the international community enjoying the equal right to the common participation in the discussion and

settlement of world affairs. In international relations, all countries must strictly "respect the sovereignty, territorial integrity and political independence of any state." The UN Security Council is authorized to handle major affairs concerning the maintenance of international peace and security and its five permanent members are conferred the right to exercise the veto when necessary. This only means they assume major responsibilities and obligations and by no means implies that they can arbitrarily abuse such power to impose their own will on the Security Council. The UN and its Security Council should base their authority on equal treatment of all countries and protection of the interests and rights of small and weak nations and must not allow a few big powers to turn them into a tool for seeking selfish interests.

2. "All members shall refrain in their international relations from the threat or use of force against the territorial integrity or political independence of any state." "All members shall settle their international disputes by peaceful means." These are two important principles governing international relations. Only when countries refrain from mutual aggression will it be possible to settle international disputes peacefully, check invasion and maintain world peace. In order to emphasize "peaceful settlement of international disputes," Chapter 6 of the UN Charter is specially devoted to specific provisions in this respect. The UN is very cautious in resorting to mandatory measures and force to suppress acts of aggression undermining world peace and endangering international security. The application of Chapter 7 of the Charter is strictly confined to dealing with acts of aggression that endanger world peace and international security. The Security Council has set strict reviewing procedures in this regard lest it should be abused or misinterpreted. If all member states, the five permanent members of the Security Council in particular, comply with these principles and provisions, and refrain from willfully adopting selective and opportunist approach and double standards, the Security Council will be able to take on the genuine authority in deterring aggression and maintaining peace. There are signs that certain Western powers attempt to introduce ideological issues into the Security Council or to abuse the provisions of Chapter 7 of the Charter in such a way as apply them to the settlement of ideological disputes. We must heighten vigilance against such tendency of blatant violation of the spirit of the UN Charter.

3. "Nothing contained in the present Charter shall authorize

the United Nations to intervene in matters which are essentially within the domestic jurisdiction of any state." This is also an important principle governing international relations. In order to reaffirm and highlight the importance of this principle, the United Nations successively adopted the Declaration Against Intervention and the Declaration on the Principles of International Law which provide in explicit terms that no state has the right to intervene in the internal and external affairs of any other state; no state may use, or encourage the use of, economic, political or any other measures to coerce another state into submission; no state shall organize, finance, instigate, or connive at the overthrow and subversion of the regime of another state with violence, or create civil strife in another state; no state shall, in any form whatsoever, prevent another state from choosing its own political, economic, social and cultural systems.

Notwithstanding the major changes, the world will not be dominated by only one kind of values or ideology. Rather, the trend towards multipolarization will make it more diversified. Today, all countries, particularly the developing countries, are exploring their respective roads of development and carrying out various kinds of reforms. No single model shall be imposed on the different practices of the peoples of all countries. We are faced with a constantly changing world. If one has faith in his own values, he should respect the right of other countries to choose independently their own social, political and economic systems and road of development in light of their national conditions. As is mentioned above, all countries, whether sharing the same ideology or having different ideologies, can live together in peace provided they abide by the principle of non-interference in each other's internal affairs. Otherwise, there will be conflicts and confrontations, and the world will find no peace and tranquillity.

4. "To achieve international co-operation in solving international problems of an economic, social, cultural, or humanitarian character, and in promoting and encouraging respect for human rights and for fundamental freedoms" is also one of the important purposes of the UN. One may recall that most people of the colonies and semi-colonies before World War II were denied the basic human rights and freedom to live as human beings under the colonial rule characterized by jungle law. One can also recall the massive violations of human rights and basic freedoms in Europe and Asia during World War II. Past experiences have fully proved that without national independence and state sover-

eignty, human rights of the weak are totally out of the question. Despite the major changes in the world situation, this truth will remain unchanged so long as power politics still exists. According to the UN instruments concerning human rights, the rights of the peoples of all countries shall be exercised through necessary domestic legislative, judicial and administrative measures. Furthermore, countries can have different guarantee measures in this regard in light of their own realities and are allowed to impose certain restrictions on some aspects. The guarantee of human rights has its universal significance, but, after all, it is a matter to be determined by each individual country in accordance with its own conditions. The deliberations of human rights issues at the UN are conducted by specially organized organs under the relevant rules. There exist longstanding differences between the developing countries and some developed countries on human rights issues debated in the UN. The crux of the issue is whether the human rights question can be exploited to interfere in the internal affairs of a country. In this respect, the true edge is usually not on the side of a few developed countries. As a matter of fact, on such key issues as massive human rights violations, some individual Western powers have adopted an approach of appeasement and connivance which have so far prevented people in certain regions from realizing their basic national rights.

In the field of human rights, there is an increasing awareness of the fact that economic development will inevitably affect the extent to which people can enjoy the various kinds of basic rights. Therefore, the right to development is made an important element of human rights by the UN resolution. Facts show that without economic growth, people will remain in perennial poverty, deprived of the right to basic necessities. On the other hand, the realization of the right to development presupposes the replacement of the old inequitable international economic order with a new international economic order that is fair and rational and based on equality and mutual benefit. In the final analysis, the settlement of the human rights question is closely related to the reform of the old international order and the establishment of a new one.

The establishment of a new international order depends on the participation and promotion of all the sovereign states and cannot be decided by a few big powers. It calls for the broadest possible international co-operation on the basis of the principle of seeking common grounds while putting aside differences instead of inciting new conflicts and confrontations in the international community. Since it involves the basic rights and interests of different types of countries, it is difficult to have a consensus in this regard in a short period of time. Sustained efforts are needed to gradually put it in place. But this in no way diminishes the necessity and urgency of this question, particularly at this transitional period when the old world pattern is giving way to a new one. Whither the world? Whither the United Nations? These questions have become even more prominent. What type of a new international order is to be established will have an important bearing on the success or failure of mankind in the next century with regard to the question of peace and development.

JAPAN, THE UNITED NATIONS, AND HUMAN RIGHTS[5]

Thirty-five years ago the Japanese flag was first raised outside the United Nations' building in New York City, symbolizing Japan's readmission to the international community and its commitment to the principles and obligations contained in the U.N. Charter. In the ensuing period, Japan has become a major economic and a minor military power; its political status in the world body, however, has not grown proportionately.

This gap between potential and actual influence in the U.N. is usually assumed to reflect Japan's fear that a high political profile could cost it access to markets and raw materials. But focusing on Japan's economic concerns overlooks the more fundamental reason for the passivity that so often seems to characterize Tokyo's foreign policy in and out of the world body. At the core of the worldview of Japan's political elite lies a strict interpretation of national sovereignty. Thus, the priority for Japanese officials is to defend internal practice against external pressures rather than actively seek out common interests. This defensive posture is often mistaken for passivity.

The operation of this worldview is no more vividly displayed

[5]Article by John M. Peek, Assistant Professor of Political Science, Centenary College of Louisiana, from *Asian Survey* 32:217–229 Mr '92. Copyright © 1992 by Regents of the University of California. Reprinted with permission.

than in Japan's position on U.N. activities concerning human rights. Briefly stated, Tokyo holds that human rights issues are a domestic matter and, therefore, generally beyond the mandate of the U.N. Accordingly, this article will demonstrate that (1) Japan has been a reluctant participant in the U.N. bodies dealing with human rights issues, and (2) it has generally responded defensively to human rights proposals at variance with Japanese law or practice. It should not be assumed, however, that U.N. activities have had no impact on the promotion and protection of human rights in Japanese society. This article will also attempt to show that the United Nations has played a significant role, arguing that it has served as an informal, third-party ally to Japan's disadvantaged in their struggle to overcome the indifference of the ruling Liberal Democratic Party (LDP) and the insulated Japanese bureaucracy.

A Reluctant Participant

From August 1945 until December 1956, the Japanese government stood on the sidelines as the victors of World War Two structured the postwar world order. Japan had no say in the drafting of the U.N. Charter or the use (and misuse) of the organization in its formative years. In a very real sense, Japan entered the organization in early 1957—as did most Third World nations a decade later—with a perception of the U.N. as the domain of the old colonial powers. Lacking any significant national stake in the U.N.'s existing principles and structures, Japan's early years in the world body were marked by a nearly total absence of initiative, except in its efforts to remove the "enemy clause" from the Charter.

The low priority given to the U.N. by the Japanese government at this time can be seen in the history of the United Nations Bureau (UNB) within the Ministry of Foreign Affairs. The UNB was created more than a year after Japan's admission to the world body, and its original staffing levels were insufficient to deal with the range of issues and programs handled by the U.N. Even now the bureau's staffing is only approaching a level that would allow it to shift from a responsive to an initiative posture. However, its status within the Foreign Ministry continues to be near the bottom of the internal hierarchy, and one advances in the ministry by moving out of the bureau, not into it.

Initially, human rights issues fell under the wide-ranging

mandate of UNB's Political Division. Of the approximately dozen members of this division, only one or two were regularly assigned to human rights questions. By the late 1970s, there was general agreement within the bureau that this arrangement could not continue, and international criticism of Japan's apparent indifference to the plight of Southeast Asian refugees made UNB's reorganization equally important to the LDP. In 1984 the interests of the bureau and the LDP gave birth to the Human Rights and Refugee Division (HRRD) with a staff of ten.

Initially, the HRRD devoted nearly all of its resources to muting criticism of Japan's handling of the "boat people," and a very significant portion of the division's energy is still directed toward this issue. Currently, HRRD is basking in its success at getting Sadako Ogata elected as the U.N. High Commissioner for Refugees and the completion of her first year in the post. Professor Ogata has proven to be a dedicated administrator, but her actions alone are unlikely to improve Japan's international image given its "closed door" immigration policy.

Gradually, the division has come to expend more of its energy on more conventional human rights issues. A major impetus behind this process is the periodic reports that Japan must submit to the U.N. Human Rights Committee (its first in 1980, a second in 1987, and a third in 1991). As we will note below, the committee's criticism of Japan's reports has caused HRRD to view its responsibility with increasing seriousness. Since its creation, the HRRD staff has doubled. This reflects a growing sensitivity of the LDP and the Foreign Ministry to Japan's image abroad. Both wish to counteract the notion that Japan's foreign policy places economic interests above humanitarian concerns. Regardless of its motivational origins, the creation of the division has institutionalized human rights issues as an important focus of the UNB. Already there are rumblings from within HRRD suggesting that the Japanese government should play a more active role in U.N. efforts to promote and protect fundamental human rights. So far these rumblings have received only scant attention outside the bureau.

Inadequate initial staffing of the UNB easily translated into low performance levels in the various bodies of the United Nations. At the time of Japan's admission to the world body, human rights issues were handled primarily by the Third Committee of the General Assembly. A review of Japan's speeches before the Third Committee reveals a level of participation well below that of the other major powers until the 1980s. Its statements were not only infrequent but also generally short and without significant substance. Recently, Japan has become more vocal in terms of the frequency, content, and intensity of its statements but the vast majority of them remain responsive rather than initiative in nature.

Originally, the U.N. Commission on Human Rights (UNCHR) was also expected to play a major role in the promotion and protection of human rights by investigating possible violations and making recommendations to the Social and Economic Council. Early on, however, the commission limited the sources from which information on violations could be obtained and abdicated its authority to request action against the offending state. Not until the mid-1960s would the UNCHR seek to reassert its original potential. Currently, it limits its attention only to "persistent and gross" violations of human rights.

By the time of Japan's admission to the U.N., the commission's activities were already relatively tame. Even so, Japan still chose to forgo the opportunity to be represented on it. While on the one hand, the Japanese government disapproved of empowering UNCHR with the ability to propose sanctions, it feared, on the other hand, being drawn into a public denunciation of the human rights policies of any particular state. Japan's reluctance to participate only intensified in the late 1960s as the commission broke out of its self-imposed restrictions. Even direct appeals by India and others in the early 1970s did not persuade the Japanese government of the need to join UNCHR.

In 1979 Tokyo's attitude toward participation on the commission began to change, and Japan ratified the International Covenants on Political and Civil Rights and on Economic, Social, and Cultural Rights. Now committed to upholding an international regime of human rights, Japan's stake in protecting itself from unwanted or highly politicized criticism by the UNCHR increased markedly. In 1982 Japan sent its first representative to the commission, Sadako Ogata, and two years later its first representative to the Subcommission on Minorities. Even under the dynamic Ogata, Japan's participation on the UNCHR was relatively low key. In 1982 Japan abstained on nearly three-fourths of the nonconsensual resolutions placed before the commission. This was consistent with its recommendations that the UNCHR should use quiet diplomacy and not public condemnation and avoid proposing any specific sanctions to the Economic and Social Council. Subsequently, Japan's involvement in the workings of the commission and the subcommission has changed little. Domestic frustration over the passivity of Japan's representatives to these bodies spilled into the open in 1989 with calls in the national media for the resignation of Japan's UNCHR representative.

Japan's participation on the Commission on the Status of Women (CSW) has also been less than inspiring. Highly vulnerable to domestic and international criticism of the secondary status accorded women in Japanese society, the government sought and gained a seat on the commission in 1960. It can be seen that its primary motive was defensive in nature by the infrequency with which it has supported or ratified the women's rights guidelines put forth by the CSW. Japan has yet to ratify, for example, the critical 1957 Convention on the Nationality of Married Women and the 1962 Convention on the Consent to Marriage, Minimum Age for Marriage, and Registration of Marriage. Until the Japanese government shows a greater willingness to follow the recommendations of the commission, Japan's participation in its activities must remain highly circumscribed.

Still floating around U.N. corridors is a proposal to create a High Commissioner for Human Rights. The proposal was strongly supported by the United States until the 1980s, after which American interest waned. Early on, the Japanese government responded negatively to the proposal, holding that such an office would likely be highly politicized and only add another layer of bureaucracy to an already ineffective system. At the core of Japan's position was its objection to any further encroachment on the internal affairs of sovereign nation-states. In the early 1960s, Japan dropped its open rejection of the proposal under intense pressure from the United States but never publicly indicated a willingness to support it. The Japanese government was thus relieved by the general neglect of the proposal by the Reagan and Bush administrations.

We have seen that Japan maintained a very low profile in U.N. human rights activities from the late 1950s until the mid-1980s. It is, therefore, understandable that Japan would be criticized for its passivity and/or indifference. A more accurate characterization, however, would be that Japan was active in providing an adequate defense against possible criticism of its own domestic human rights record and in reminding other states that human rights issues are essentially internal matters. Little activity beyond that was needed according to the strict "realism" that guided the foreign policy of the LDP and Foreign Ministry. Some movement in the nature of Japan's involvement in human rights in the late 1980s does, however, provide a faint hope that Japan may yet make a limited contribution to the promotion of human rights abroad.

A Defensive Posture

The U.N. Charter lists promotion of respect for human rights among the main functions of the organization. Thus, the Charter assumes the existence of a universal set of rights and suggests the need for some kind of machinery to ensure compliance. The reaction of the Japanese government to the various human rights conventions and covenants passed by the U.N. suggests, however, a quite different perspective. Tokyo has made it quite clear that rights are developed within a particular culture and political system. Accordingly, Japanese officials usually hold that while the U.N. may identify common categories of rights, it may neither set specific international human rights standards nor impose sanctions.

The first major act of the U.N. in the area of human rights was the passage of the Universal Declaration of Human Rights in 1948. Still under U.S. Occupation, the Japanese government played no role in drafting the document and took no formal position on its specific contents. But the government's strong opposition to the human rights reforms imposed by the Occupation during this time period indicates that it probably had strong reservations about the declaration. The government, for instance, argued against Occupation reforms by stating that the centrality of the family needs to take precedence over the individual, rights have to be linked to duties, elimination of ascriptive-based social relationships results in anarchy, and rights cannot be considered absolute when there exists a threat to the public welfare. These arguments were clearly antithetical to the assumptions of the New Dealers who guided the Occupation and drafted the declaration.

The nonbinding nature of the document muted the necessity for Japan—after it joined the U.N.—to stake out a more formal position on it. Moreover, the prospect of turning the declaration into a binding treaty seemed remote in the heyday of the Cold War that followed Japan's admission. Not until 1966 was Tokyo faced with the necessity of publicly having to accept or reject the two covenants produced from the declaration: the International

Covenant on Civil and Political Rights and the International Covenant on Economic, Social, and Cultural Rights. The government decided not to act until further study of the two covenants could be completed.

Domestic critics charged that this policy of additional study reflected a concerted effort to avoid commitment to the concept of universal rights. Concurrently, the critics charged the ruling party with clinging to the dream of dismantling the Occupation reforms and reviving the social system of pre-war Japan. Such a process would be much more difficult if domestic and external opponents could refer to an international human rights document to legitimize their challenge to the ruling party. In addition, the critics pointed to particular articles in the two covenants that threatened the interests of powerful segments of Japanese society as being the real reasons behind Japan's failure to expedite the ratification process. In short, they charged the government with using cultural relativism as a cover for its defense of special interests through the tactics of stonewalling and paralysis by analysis.

The charges leveled by the government's critics seem to be borne out by a number of factors. First, the Japanese government was fully aware of the covenants' contents prior to 1966 and of the implications on Japanese law and practice. Second, even if some additional study was needed, it hardly explains the passage of more than a decade before the government would decide to act. Japan did not sign the two covenants until 1978, and it ratified them in 1979. Third, if its reservations were firmly based in Japanese culture, the government should have been able to act more quickly and forcefully in setting forth its formal reservations before and at the time of ratification. Fourth, most of Japan's formal and informal reservations appear to originate in the political interests of the ruling party and not widely accepted cultural norms.

Since the end of the Occupation, the LDP has been at loggerheads with the labor movement in Japan, especially those unions in the public sector supporting the opposition parties. Consequently, any elements in the covenants that would strengthen the rights of unions were of grave concern to the ruling party. It was, therefore, hardly surprising that the Japanese government issued reservations to Article 8 of the Economic Covenant and Article 22 of the Political Covenant. These reservations in essence denied those in the public sector the right to organize and strike. While not issuing a formal reservation, the government did not

conceal its additional objection to the right of trade unions to join
international federations, also contained in Article 8. The ruling
party has long considered such organizations to be controlled by
communists. Thus, it holds that encouraging domestic unions to
join would only further politicize the already left-leaning union
movement in Japan.

Japan also issued a reservation to a portion of Article 7 of the
Economic Covenant by rejecting the right to remuneration for
public holidays. The government argued that such holidays
should not be considered as state-imposed limitations on the right
to work for which compensation must be provided. Given the
large number of public holidays in Japan, the government's position involves substantial savings in public and private sector wage
payments. This fact is hardly lost on Japan's unions and opposition parties, but their voices of protest have not been acknowledged by the government. Article 7 also contains the right of a
reasonable limitation on the length of the workday and workweek. Given the long-standing feud between the Japanese government and the International Labor Organization over just this
issue, it must be considered another factor in Japan's reluctance
to ratify the Economic Covenant. In 1984 for the first time, the
government called upon the private sector to move gradually toward a five-day workweek. To prevent overtime payments, however, the government indicated its willingness to extend the workday from eight-and-a-half to ten hours. The government set a less
than positive model for a reduced workweek by initially allowing
only a few public employees to take off one Saturday a month. At
the present, nonessential public employees receive every other
Saturday off. Neither the public nor private sector appears to be
in any hurry to comply with the intent of Article 7.

Only slightly less important is the government's unspoken lack
of enthusiasm for Article 7's call for equal remuneration and
promotional opportunities for women. In both the public and
private sectors, it is an open secret that women will be paid less
and classified as working in nonpromotional track positions even
when doing the same work as their male counterparts. Moreover,
it is still widely held among members of the ruling party that a
woman should stop working when she marries or at least at the
birth of her first child. Critics charge that the government's attitude is less a reflection of tradition than the need to create a
reserve of cheap labor.

The government counters criticism by pointing to passage of

the Equal Employment Opportunity Law in 1984. In doing so, it fails to note that the law was strongly opposed by women's groups and all opposition political parties, which objected to the law's use of words such as "employers should strive" rather than "must" and the complete lack of enforcement provisions. Few outside the government believe that the law is consistent with the spirit of the Economic Covenant. The intent of the law seems to have been little more than a symbolic bone tossed to domestic and international critics in anticipation of the upcoming 1985 world conference ending the U.N. Decade for Women.

Article 24 of the Political Covenant dealing with the rights of children also highlights differences between the ruling and opposition parties. Prior to 1985, Japanese nationality could only be passed to a child through the father. As a result, even if the child was born in Japan to a Japanese mother, the child was denied all the rights and entitlements granted to citizens. By the early 1960s, women's groups and opposition parties were issuing strong pleas for the government to change the nationality law. The pleas generally went unanswered until the decision was made to ratify the two covenants. Clearly, the threat to the centrality of the male head of the household weighed heavily on the minds of the ruling party leaders. Opposition to "mixed marriages" most certainly was a contributing factor. The intensity of these feelings can be surmised from the fact that five years would pass from the time of ratification of the Political Covenant to passage of a new nationality law in 1984 allowing for the establishment of Japanese citizenship through the mother.

The intent of Article 6 of the Political Covenant is to limit severely the types of crimes to which the death penalty can be applied, as a first step toward its abolition. The move to limit the application of the death penalty to particularly brutal crimes is acceptable to the Japanese government, but the call for its total elimination is not. The government contends that public opinion in Japan favors retention of the death penalty, but this is questionable given that few Japanese give much credence to the deterrent value of capital punishment or view criminals as unreformable. In fact, the voices being raised in support of eliminating capital punishment appear to be growing more numerous and louder every year.

Japan's final formal reservation is to Article 13. This article calls for the progressive introduction of free education at the high school and college level. The government contends that this is simply impractical financially. Cost may not be the only consideration, however. Currently, the private school system in Japan provides an alternative path for those who do not excel on admission examinations but who do have financial resources. Instituting a free and consequently expanded public educational system would result in the closure of private schools and the alternative path they provide for the sons and daughters of the political and economic elite. How does one maintain the social hierarchy in a system based solely on merit? Perhaps the Japanese government's reservation recognizes that one cannot.

Finally, the Japanese government has issued a de facto reservation to Article 41 of the Political Covenant. This article empowers the newly created Human Rights Committee (HRC) to deal with the claims of human rights violations by one state against another if both parties have issued a separate declaration recognizing this provision. Japan strongly opposes empowering the committee to do anything but review the periodic reports submitted by those states who are party to the Political Covenant. It has yet to consider seriously making the required declaration. The government links its objection to the possible excessive politicization of the HRC's activities. Others suggest that the government is really concerned about sanctioning any international examination of Japan's existing social problems.

Passed along with the two human rights covenants was an optional protocol that allows states to grant individual citizens the right to inform the HRC directly of a possible violation of the covenants by their government. Japan strongly objects to this deviation from the standard practice of limiting the source of grievances to recognized states. This position is, of course, quite consistent with a view that limits the realm of world politics to state-to-state relations. This placement of state over individual rights is also consistent with the LDP's emphasis on cultural relativism. It is, however, of questionable consistency with the intent of the covenants and democratic theory.

Before proceeding it needs to be noted that the strongest reservations on the part of the Japanese government to the covenants appear not to be based on aspects of Japanese culture. Nearly all the formal reservations and most of the informal ones deal not with social but with economic issues. All but a few seem to originate in the LDP's desire to preserve its political power and the economic interests of its core benefactor—big business. Therefore, one is drawn to the conclusion that the efforts of the

Japanese government to postpone ratification of the covenants as long as possible reflects an attempt to deprive the demands of dissident groups of an additional basis of legitimacy.

The Impact of the U.N. on Japan

I have suggested in the above that U.N. activities have played a role in bringing about changes in Japanese law and social practice. I recognize that these external stimulants are often supplemental to domestic pressures, but believe that the impact of U.N. activities has been incorrectly neglected in most scholarship on Japan. I now intend to highlight some examples of these activities that have played in the development of human rights in Japan.

U.N. activities seem to have had the most visible and forceful impact on the women's rights movement in Japan. In the immediate postwar period, one of the top priorities of the movement was to reverse official tolerance of prostitution. In 1957 under moderate domestic pressure, the government finally passed a Prostitution Prevention Law. The decision to take up its passage at this time was more than a little related to events in the United Nations. That same year, the U.N. was to hold a Conference on Slavery and Similar Practices, and the topic of prostitution in Japan was expected to be brought before the conference. To preempt the prospect of international scrutiny, the Japanese government passed the domestic legislation mentioned above and quickly ratified the long-pending, 1949 U.N. Convention for the Suppression of the Traffic in Persons and the Exploitation of the Prostitution of Others.

In the mid-1960s, U.N. activities reflected the intense involvement of Western nations in civil rights issues, thus providing renewed hope to those active in the women's rights movement in Japan. The 1966 passage of the two human rights covenants made it more difficult for the Japanese government to ignore the issue of women's rights and it added credibility to the movement's demands. The 1967 U.N. Declaration on the Elimination of Discrimination Against Women further raised expectations and intensified pressure on the government to address the issue seriously. As was previously indicated, it was during this time that the Japanese government shifted its tactic from denying the existence of a problem to outlasting pressure through claiming the need for further study. This tactic of paralysis by analysis was swept aside in the mid-1970s by a renewed concurrence of domestic and international pressure. The U.N. declaration of 1975 as International Women's Year compelled the LDP to act in order to prevent the further alienation of women voters. As the 1975 world conference on women's issues rolled around, so did the LDP's attention to passage of a limited Childcare Leave Law and the creation in the prime minister's office of the Headquarters for the Planning and Promotion of Policies Relating to Women.

The first year of the U.N. Decade for Women, 1976, would be the same year in which the two human rights covenants would go into effect. Facing the prospect of a further intensification of domestic and international pressure, the LDP indicated its intention to ratify the covenants in the near future. It was at this time that the government began to look seriously at the need to revise equal employment legislation and the nationality law. Concurrently, it carried out the 1975 world conference's call for each country to draft a plan of action. In 1977 the prime minister was presented with the completed National Action Plan on Women's Issues. For the first time, responsibility for progress in the area of women's rights was placed firmly in the prime minister's office.

In 1979 the General Assembly adopted the Convention on the Elimination of All Forms of Discrimination Against Women, and women's groups throughout Japan called for immediate ratification. The government tried to stall. As the Mid-Decade Conference on Women in 1980 neared, the government bent to domestic pressure and, along with the desire to avoid being a target of criticism at the conference, signed the convention. At the conference, Japan in essence pledged to ratify the convention by the end of the Decade for Women. Not long before Japan's delegates began to pack their bags for the trip to the 1985 Conference on Women, the LDP passed the new Nationality Law, an Equal Employment Opportunity Law, and ratified the convention. Again we have a case in which the timing of the passage of domestic human rights legislation is clearly related to events in the United Nations.

Following the 1985 Conference, Japanese officials set about drafting Japan's second National Action Plan. Women's groups in Japan have since attempted to hold the government to its commitments through contacts with relevant ministries and appeals in the media. In 1991, for example, they again pressed the government to increase significantly the number of women on advisory committees in accordance with U.N. standards. Women's groups have also threatened to take their concerns before one or more of the U.N. bodies such as the Human Rights Committee.

Unlike many other U.N. bodies, the HRC has been willing to examine information supplied to it by recognized human rights organizations. The Japan Civil Liberties Union has been at the forefront in directing the committee's attention to human rights problems in this and other areas. The HRC's review of Japan's periodic reports has aided women's groups in keeping the pressure on the government for deeds rather than words. The review of Japan's 1980 report took special note of the lack of tangible results toward meeting the goals set in Japan's first National Action Plan. While Japan's 1987 report contained little more on the issue of women's rights, its representatives did come to the review with extensive information on the role and status of women. The committee expressed its gratitude for the representatives' effort to answer a wide range of questions but still expressed concern over what appeared to be a lack of active governmental involvement in the promotion and protection of women's rights. The members of the Foreign Ministry's Human Rights Division can be expected to be even better prepared for the review of Japan's 1991 report to the HRC. Perhaps their desire for information will help provoke additional activity in other sections of the government. If not, Japan's third report will also likely be followed by a series of negative articles in the domestic and foreign press, to the irritation of the LDP.

The impact of the activities of the committee is, of course, not confined to women's rights issues. There is HRC concern over the apparent lack of governmental efforts to promote and protect the rights of the Ainu, Burakumin, aliens residing in Japan, the mentally ill, students, the elderly, journalists, the disabled, and those suspected of criminal offenses. Partly as a consequence of the committee's criticism, the LDP in 1988 passed a new Mental Health Law and Employment Promotion for the Disabled Law. Nor are women's rights activists the only groups to have appealed to the U.N. as an instrument in their struggle with the Japanese government. In recent years, groups representing foreign workers, the Ainu, and Burakumin have been especially active in attempting to use the United Nations as an alternative channel to the political elite of Japan.

These examples indicate that while U.N. activities alone have not been sufficient to produce social change in Japan, they have often been a necessary factor in prodding the modest social changes that have occurred over the last couple of decades. As a respected third party, the U.N. has provided increased legitimacy to the demands of the disadvantaged in Japanese society, made available public forums not easily controlled by the Japanese government (e.g., special conferences and the Human Rights Committee), created a channel of access to top decision makers by way of the Foreign Ministry, and held the Japanese government somewhat accountable for decisions not to comply with international standards.

In a very real sense, U.N. human rights activities have had as much if not more impact on Japan than Japan has had on the efforts of the organization to promote and protect human rights. It could hardly be otherwise as long as Tokyo continues to operate on the basis of a very limited view of the role of any multilateral organization. Japan's foreign policy will continue to be unilateral and defensive in nature until there is a greater acceptance among Japan's political elite of the practical necessity of creating an international system based on a core set of universal norms. The first step in this process must be a recognition that Japanese claims of being unique are in the long run self-destructive; Japan's future lies in emphasizing human commonalities not differences.

A VIEW FROM RUSSIA: RUSSIA SHOULD SEEK U.N. REPRESENTATION AND PERMANENT SEAT ON SECURITY COUNCIL[6]

What should be done with the UN seat that belonged to the Soviet Union? International scholars, officials at UN headquarters and diplomats are not the only ones racking their brains over this question. The entire system of international relations must now undergo serious changes in connection with the breakup of the USSR.

As everyone knows, the Soviet Union was one of the United Nations' founding members. Ukraine and Belarus are also UN members. As for Russia, which was deprived of explicit attributes of statehood for many years, to this day one can speak of its presence in the organization only in terms of indirect (via the center) UN membership. But the center is gone, or almost gone.

[6]Translation of an article from *Izvestia*, December 16, 1991, by A. Portansky, from *Current Digest of the Soviet Press* 43/50:23–24 '91. Copyright © 1991 by *Current Digest of the Soviet Press*. Reprinted with permission.

Consequently, Russia should seek to obtain full-scale official representation in the UN. In all likelihood, this should happen in the very near future, because only Russia, with the concurrence of the former Union republics, can assume the role of guarantor of the former Union's international commitments.

There Have Never Been Any Commonwealths in the UN

The problem of who will inherit the permanent seat on the UN Security Council that the USSR still holds is much more complex. No one ever imagined the possibility that a state that was a permanent member of the Council could "disappear" or be changed. As long as there was still hope that a union treaty would be signed, it was automatically assumed that the seat on the Security Council would pass to the new federal or confederal state. The recent signing of the agreement to form the Commonwealth of Independent States has drastically reduced the possibility that a confederation, much less a federation, will be formed. Can a commonwealth of states, in this case the CIS, become a permanent member of the Security Council? This question remains very problematic. At any rate, there is no historical precedent for this, although there have been aspirants to such membership—for example, the European Community.

Many officials of the UN Secretariat believe that in this situation, it would be quite possible to transfer the permanent seat on the UN Security Council to Russia as the USSR's likely successor in the international arena and as the republic that possesses the lion's share of the former Union's nuclear potential. To all appearances, such a transfer would satisfy the other permanent members of the Security Council, and the entire procedure could be limited to sending out notes to this effect to UN members, provided that all the republics of the former Union agreed to this. But are all of them prepared to give their consent?

The UN's consideration of the question of who will succeed to permanent membership on the Security Council will, to all appearances, revive an issue that has been raised before—that of reforming the entire UN system. The fact is that in 1946 there were only 51 states in the UN, and 11 of them were represented on the Security Council. Today there are 166 UN member countries, but changes in the numerical size of the Security Council have been negligible: There are 15 members, five of which are permanent members. A few days ago, at the 46th session of the UN General Assembly, a large group of countries raised the question of expanding the size of the Security Council.

Quite a Few Candidates

India's representative recalled that a General Assembly draft resolution on expanding the UN Security Council to 21 members was drawn up in 1979, but that consideration of the matter has constantly been postponed. Former US Secretary of Defense R. McNamara also believes that the Security Council's organizational structure has become obsolete and fails to reflect the current balance of forces in the world. In this sense, Germany and Japan should be permanent members of the Security Council. (Granted, raising the question of their permanent membership in the Security Council would be inappropriate within the framework of the present UN system, which was created by the victors of World War II.)

There have also been calls for giving permanent seats on the Security Council to such countries as India and Brazil, in view of their gross national products and populations. But could a UN so reconstituted effectively perform its most important role—for example, opposing aggression like the Iraqi attack on Kuwait?

For the present, none of the five permanent members of the UN Security Council want to expand its size. As a result, the current General Assembly session adopted a decision to postpone this question until the next session.

If the UN has to undergo changes, it is obviously better that they proceed smoothly and painlessly from the standpoint of the world community, and that the extremely complex processes taking place in our country do not undermine the entire international community system.

THE UN: IMPACT GROWS, COVERAGE LAGS[7]

The United Nations traditionally had a short busy season— the first few weeks of October, when the General Assembly brought presidents and prime ministers to rub elbows in the Dele-

[7]Article by Michael J. Berlin, former U.N. correspondent for the *Washington Post*. From *Washington Journalism Review* 14:36–38 O '92. Copyright © 1992 by *Washington Journalism Review*. Reprinted with permission.

gates Lounge and clog the streets of Manhattan's East Side. The rest of the year often consisted of endless weeks with little or no real news.

All that has changed. Since the Persian Gulf War, there has been no down time. The war was followed by a succession of major stories on its aftermath; the release of most of the hostages in Lebanon; an agreement to end the Cambodian civil war; ongoing U.N. involvement in Afghanistan, Central America, southern Africa and Somalia; and most recently, the U.N. peacekeeping role in Yugoslavia. And because of the United Nations' added responsibilities, institutional events also were more newsworthy. The election of Egypt's Boutros Boutros-Ghali as the new secretary-general, the ongoing U.N. budget crisis and the revocation of the 1975 resolution equating Zionism with racism all got good play.

"The United Nations has become a regular, featured story in all major newspapers in the world today," says a harried Francois Guiliani, Boutros-Ghali's spokesman. "The coverage is extraordinarily heavy."

Phil Arnold, who served until recently as the press counselor at the U.S. Mission, predicts that "more and more assignments will come to the United Nations, more and more interventions around the world will be initiated here. There has been a breakdown of the [U.N. Charter] principle of noninterference in the internal affairs of nations, and issues like refugees, global warming, terrorism, human rights and drugs will be discussed and ironed out here."

But with all that going on, who is covering the United Nations for the American media? The media are running more U.N. stories and playing them more prominently, but much of that comes from wire reporters or packs of journalists who parachute in briefly to skim the hard news. Editors and senior producers are still understaffing this productive and highly visible news source.

When I was sent by the New York Post to cover the United Nations during the 1967 Arab-Israeli war, the institution was staffed by all of the elite American and European media. The Baltimore Sun, Boston Globe, Chicago Tribune, Chicago Sun-Times, Christian Science Monitor, Kansas City Star, Los Angeles Times, Philadelphia Inquirer, St. Louis Post-Dispatch, Washington Post and all the New York metropolitan dailies had correspondents based at U.N. headquarters. The three networks, Time, Newsweek and the wires were there. The New York Times alone had four reporters there: Drew Middleton, Juan de Onis, Kathleen Teltsch and Sam Pope Brewer—all prominent bylines in their time.

It was a plum assignment. This was where the Cold War was being fought. When the superpowers or their clients battled, they squared off in the Security Council or General Assembly. Regional crises were played out there, from the Middle East wars to the decolonization of Africa. The population explosion and the environment became global issues in U.N. meeting rooms.

But in the mid-1970s, as relations between Washington and the United Nations worsened and radical resolutions by U.N. bodies grew further from global realities, American editors soured on the dateline.

Things began looking up in 1987 as the institution dealt with Afghanistan, the Iran-Iraq war and the independence of Namibia. It was the forum in which improved U.S.-Soviet relations could most easily be discerned. Elite foreign news organizations began to return.

Still, when I left in 1988, the New York Times was the only U.S. newspaper to keep a full-time correspondent at U.N. headquarters. The wires—the Associated Press, United Press International, Reuters, Agence France-Press, and the West German news agency, Deutsche Presse Agentur—all had staff there, and there were a few stringers. But that was it.

By now, however, more Europeans have returned with reporters or stringers. British media at the United Nations now include the Independent, the Time, the Guardian, the Financial Times and the BBC. Le Monde has two correspondents. But it is surprising that there are so few American reporters at a place where so much of the new global politics is being played out.

Wire stories from the United Nations are picked up by major dailies, however. The AP logs show that at least nine major newspapers are running U.N. stories on their front pages regularly, a far cry from the poor play the institution got before the gulf war. But most are still using AP or other wires, rather than their own coverage, which would provide depth and analysis as well as access to exclusives, interviews and features.

One U.S. newspaper that has never stopped covering the United Nations is the New York Times. Its current correspondent, Paul Lewis, recalls that shortly after he arrived in 1987, the five permanent members of the Security Council—the United States, the Soviet Union, China, Great Britain and France—

began to work together and in June 1988 the United Nations achieved an end to the Iran-Iraq war.

From that point on, Lewis recalls, "It was just one thing after another. Once you start writing stories [editors] print, they get used to printing stories from the United Nations. It becomes part of their daily life."

In addition to U.N. coverage, Lewis says, the Times uses him to cover other international news in New York. "I do endless interviews with foreign cabinet members coming through before or after Washington visits," he says. "What strikes me is that nobody else has followed in my footsteps. You do see hordes of firemen for the big stories, and specialized people coming here to cover El Salvador negotiations or an environmental story."

For Lewis, the United Nations' underutilized news resources start with the unannounced weekly meetings of the Security Council's five permanent members "to coordinate large areas of their foreign policies. These meetings are secretive, but it comes out, it comes out. And a great deal that happens elsewhere gets *known* here.

"But you have to know the people, have lunch, wander down to the second-floor lounge, see who you bump into, and ask what's on their minds," Lewis continues. "I tell them my rumors, they advance them. The cocktail parties are work. . . . I often come back to the office after parties and change stories for the second edition."

Only a few of the other daily newspapers that consider themselves national or elite have made permanent arrangements to increase coverage.

Among them is Newsday, whose global rover, Pulitzer Prize winner Josh Freidman, had the standing to decide that he wanted to hang out at the United Nations when he wasn't traveling. When he arrived in 1987, he says, his editors told him, "We don't like too many U.N. stories." But now, Friedman says, "I have trouble getting in my foreign trips. So many responsibilities have been relegated to the United Nations by the United States and the Russians that events at the United Nations have to be covered. . . . I don't know why American reporters aren't here with me. I feel I'm shooting fish in a barrel." Friedman left to teach at Columbia's journalism school this fall and Newsday has not yet permanently replaced him.

Another reporter who has chosen to cover the United Nations is Ana Puga, who became the Houston Chronicle's first Washington diplomatic correspondent in 1991. "When I began," she says, "it was impossible to think of covering foreign affairs without covering the United Nations. You can't really cover it by telephone, so I go to New York regularly. I find it more interesting than the State Department, where one line comes down from the top, because at the United Nations there are competing voices, voices you can't hear in D.C., like the Iraqis or the PLO."

A number of specialized magazines and newsletters, especially those covering the oil industry and finance, now call U.N. sources at least once a week to keep up-to-date on developments in the Persian Gulf and elsewhere. Many have sent writers on special projects, according to U.N. spokesman Fred Eckhard. However, the major newsmagazines are not there. Veteran Time magazine correspondent Bonnie Angelo says she covers the institution more often than in the past, tapping "specific good sources," but only by telephone.

Angelo voices a lament common to many reporters who try to sell U.N. stories upstairs. "It's still hard to get editors out of the mindset that prevailed four or five years ago," she says, when many believed that what happened at the United Nations wasn't important.

"It has been a really bad dateline," says Boston Globe Foreign Editor John Yemma. The Washington Post's assistant managing editor for foreign news, Michael Getler, concurs: "It's a cliché that the United Nations was predictable for so long that the dateline was a symbol of editorial duty fulfilled. . . . Too often [the news] was unreal and . . . had a sameness about it."

The United Nations' old image still haunts it in the broadcast world. Two of the five television networks have upgraded coverage from zero to stationing a producer—but not a television correspondent—at the First Avenue skyscraper.

A major task for ABC's Tom Osborne and NBC's Bob Toombs is to schedule guests for talk and news shows. Osborne also does reporting for ABC Radio and produces spots about once a week for the evening news. CNN is credited by a number of reporters with inspiring coverage of the beat during the Iraq-Kuwait crisis, when editors around the country watched newsroom monitors showing Jeanne Moos and her cameras camped out in U.N. corridors awash with news sources (including the only Iraqis available). Since the end of the gulf war, CNN sends crews and correspondents over less often. CBS and PBS have virtually no staff presence. New York television stations, however, got in the habit of spot news coverage during the war and continue to send crews for breaking stories.

The most significant U.S. radio coverage is done by National Public Radio, which is able to have reporter Jim Zarroli and stringer Linda Fasulo at U.N. headquarters thanks in part to an annual grant from the Ford Foundation.

Zarroli says the United Nations has drawbacks for radio reporters because so much of the information comes from sources who won't allow themselves to be taped. "You have three minutes of your own voice, with 'officials say' as the only attribution," he explains. "And what you get is the big picture. There's no way to humanize U.N. stories, even on the immunization of children."

Currently 2,400 news industry staffers from 74 countries have permanent accreditation at the United Nations, an increase of 43 percent from pre-gulf war figures. Of them, 1,350 are from U.S. news organizations, but most are broadcast technicians. No more than 200 are print or broadcast reporters, which is not significantly more than in previous years. In addition to those with permanent media accreditation, some 7,000 news staffers visited U.N. headquarters for a day or more in 1991, boosting the total number of news industry visitors to 49 percent more than in 1989. But again, only a small proportion of these visitors were reporters.

Many news organizations with national aspirations, such as the Boston Globe, Chicago Tribune and Philadelphia Inquirer, still rely on wire copy for most of their U.N. coverage. Others, such as the Washington Post, use stringers, forays by reporters from their New York or Washington bureaus or telephone calls. Like Angelo of Time, a number of editors and Washington reporters believe the telephone is an acceptable alternative to on-site coverage.

Yet covering the United Nations is more like covering the U.S. Senate than the Washington diplomatic beat. It's difficult to develop sources from afar, and when it counts, the ones in the know are likely to be inaccessible by phone. Legwork is the only sure thing.

Obviously, a beat of this type cannot sustain itself on pack-journalism spot news and serendipitous exclusives. "You can have only so many wars," says one U.N. official. But the United Nations is an ideal listening post, where a variety of diplomatic news can be obtained from a plethora or sources, and perspectives extend beyond the foreign policy interests and domestic political assumptions of the United States. Newsday's Freidman says his

U.N. contacts helped get him stories abroad. "Because I was here I got into Iran" after the gulf war, he says.

The United Nations' greatest value for foreign-news editors may well be that it is outside the Washington Beltway, physically and metaphysically. This has two potential benefits.

One is that analytical coverage of traditional breaking stories—what should the world do about Yugoslavia?—can reflect political perspectives beyond the conventional wisdom in Washington.

The other is that U.N.-based reporters can take a fresh look at world news. David Anable, who covered the United Nations for the Christian Science Monitor, later became the paper's managing editor, and now runs the journalism school at Boston University, says that the United Nations is an ideal place "to dig out the big issues of the next century." To do that, he says, it is necessary to "break out of the American domination of the definition of the global agenda."

Despite all these good reasons for upgrading coverage of the United Nations, there are a number of practical drawbacks.

U.N. bodies often operate with total disregard for deadlines. News such as the selection of a secretary-general breaks without warning. Votes are delayed until midnight or later (sometimes because one player wants to minimize media attention). There is no strong centralized authority that places a high priority on media. Boutros-Ghali, like his predecessors, is a diplomat rather than a politician, and has little time for the resident press corps. One U.N. information official concedes that "the United Nations still does not use media effectively."

The U.S. Mission also is limited by State Department and White House restrictions on its relationship with the press. Other missions—those of Great Britain, France or Japan—brief their national journalists more frequently and reveal more inside information. But little of it is earthshaking.

A more serious obstacle to U.N. coverage is its cost. Getler estimates it would cost the Washington Post $100,000 to cover the beat with a staff reporter. For television it might be twice that. "In the old days," says Arnold, the former U.S. Mission press counselor, "the New York Times sent a man to Prague and nothing happened for five years, but when it did he knew what it was all about. But the economics of the news business are different now. Yes, they're missing something. In the last 18 months U.N. coverage would have been worth it. But for the preceding 18 months, no."

In Boston, Chicago, Philadelphia and Washington and at the Wall Street Journal, editors say they know they're missing things by relying on wires for U.N. coverage, but it's a question of priorities. "If I had the money available, I'd rather use it abroad," says Foreign Editor Fran Dauth, who supervises six foreign correspondents for the Inquirer. "The United Nations would *not* come to mind. . . . The system we have [using wires and an occasional story by the New York or Washington bureau] is adequate, not good."

For many who would like U.N. coverage without a full-time staffer there, assigning a New York or Washington reporter to occasional visits appears to be the logical alternative. But even if such forays could generate better coverage than the wires provide, this arrangement generally faces bureaucratic obstacles that limit effectiveness. These reporters are usually paid by national desks, while their U.N. copy goes to the foreign desk. And both desks want to manage the reporters.

One solution might be to have the national and foreign desks split the cost of a New York-based U.N. correspondent. Another might be to have a foreign correspondent, based at the United Nations, also cover Canada or the Caribbean. The Washington Post did this in the early 1970s. Alternatively, the Newsday system, under which a foreign rover is based at U.N. headquarters and reports to the foreign desk, might provide more overall coverage for the same cost.

For mid-range newspapers, the usual solution, when the wires are not deep enough and the cost is too high for a staffer, is to hire a stringer to provide analysis and a few exclusives. The problem at the United Nations, however, as several reporters and editors concede, is that the beat got so arid in the many years of news drought that the pool of U.N. stringers dried up. Perhaps the foreign editors of two or three non-competing papers could recruit a U.N. super-stringer and let the stringer's expertise develop gradually.

Although the U.N. beat has been reborn, media staffing is lagging behind the news. But it is no longer appropriate for news organizations to content themselves with surface coverage of U.N. events. In an era when the United States remains the only superpower, it is all the more incumbent on editors and senior producers to seek out alternative perspectives on international affairs. Covering the United Nations with a beat reporter is the obvious way to do it.

POLLS RATE THE UN[8]

Results of public opinion polls released on 4 April [1990] by Under-Secretary-General for Public Information Thérèse P. Sévigny showed that a majority of people in Australia, Canada, Mexico, South Africa and the 12 member countries of the European Community believe that the UN's performance is good rather than poor.

UN Secretary-General Javier Pérez de Cuéllar commented that the polls' results were "very encouraging". The general public now recognized that the UN is succeeding as an institution for the resolution of conflict and the promotion of peace in the world, he stated.

The polls were conducted in the second half of 1989 on behalf of the Department of Public Information (DPI).

People thought well of the performance of the UN in all countries polled. Around half of all people surveyed in Australia, Canada, Mexico and the European Community as a whole said the UN was doing a good job, while no more than 25 per cent in any country felt it was doing a poor job. Those findings were consistent with a poll conducted in the United States at the beginning of 1989, which also showed more Americans felt the UN was doing a good job.

That was a significant improvement over 1985, when polls conducted in Australia, Canada, the United States and six European countries showed less support for the view that the UN is doing a good job. The only exception to the positive results for the UN was in South Africa, where 39 per cent of whites living in urban areas said the UN was doing a poor job, as compared to 23 per cent who felt it was doing a good job.

The publication of these polls came during a period which has seen major achievements for the UN, particularly in the peace-keeping and peace-making fields. Reasons given by persons of the view that the UN is doing a good job largely reflected their perception of the Organization's achievements in those areas. Those of the opposite view believed there were too many national interests at play for the UN to reach agreement and be effective.

[8]Article from the *UN Chronicle* 27:40 Je '90.

Environmental protection was the most popular UN issue. Human rights, drug abuse, international peace and security, children and crime prevention were also considered important. Television and newspapers were the main sources of information about the UN in all countries polled. Radio, magazines and books were other sources.

IV. THE UNITED NATIONS AND ITS CRITICS

EDITOR'S INTRODUCTION

"Get the U.S. out of the U.N. and the U.N. out of the U.S." was a 1960s rallying cry of the far right-wing John Birch Society. While conservative criticism of the U.N. has diminished in recent years, it certainly has not disappeared, as the first two selections show. In "Closing Time for the U.N.?" *National Review* contributing editor Brian Crozier proposes dissolving the United Nations and establishing an Association of Free Nations. In the next article, Ernest van den Haag, Distinguished Scholar at the conservative Heritage Foundation also offers a pessimistic assessment of the world body in *Social Education* magazine.

Even some commentators on the liberal end of the political spectrum are gloomy, but for different reasons. "Why the Right Loves the U.N.", by British journalist Ian Williams, writing in *The Nation,* claims that conservatives are funding some right-wing organizations aimed at creating a world organization that is more ideologically compatible with their views. In the following report, Costa Rican journalist Mia Taylor Valdes accuses the U.N. of hypocrisy for condemning left-wing Cuba's human rights record while ignoring serious rights violations in right-wing Guatemala. Finally, Indian journalist Bhaskar P. Menon presents arguments in defense of the United Nations against the accusations of its critics.

CLOSING TIME FOR THE U.N.?[1]

The gulf war showed what the United Nations can do if skillfully handled. The aftermath of the battle showed what the UN

[1]Article by Brian Crozier, contributing editor, from *National Review* 43:44–45 My 13 '91. Copyright © 1991 by *National Review,* Inc. Reprinted with permission.

can't do, and why the time is ripe for a fundamental change. Such as putting something else in its place.

Having done his Hannibal act, with stunning success, General Norman Schwarzkopf wanted to win the war as well as the latter-day battle of Cannae. The issues are clear enough. Do the Allies merely defeat Hitler in battle? Or do they push on, as agreed at Yalta, and oblige him to take his own life in the Berlin bunker? Does the United States help the Hungarians in 1956, or does it encourage them to rise, then sit by while the Red Army massacres them?

In other words, do we "liberate" Kuwait, then sit and watch while Saddam Hussein's forces massacre the Kurds? Or do we rid the world of an evil and bloodstained tyrant?

Understandably, President Bush wanted UN sanction for armed action against Saddam's regime. He obtained it, with great skill and perseverance ["Handling the United Nations," April 1]. Bush knew he could get a Security Council consensus for the liberation of Kuwait. He also knew that he couldn't hope for Big Five assent to a combined action to bring down the Iraqi dictator. China, with memories of the Tiananmen and Tibet suppressions still very much alive, would have vetoed any such move. So would the Soviet Union, in the wake of armed repression in Tbilisi and with unrest in Lithuania and elsewhere.

In major crises, the UN has "worked" in its peacekeeping role only in anomalous circumstances. In 1950, the Security Council united for action when the Korean War began, because the Soviet Union was boycotting it. This time, it united for action because Mikhail Gorbachev had been awarded the Nobel Peace Prize and is in the market for Western money. Even so, he tried for a peace of non-humiliation for the man the Soviets had helped so much: Saddam Hussein.

Flawed from Birth

There is absolutely no guarantee that in future conflicts the UN will repeat the isolated successes of 1950 and 1990. In fact, the UN is a legalistic absurdity, deeply flawed from birth.

The accident of history that made the USSR the West's glorious ally also made it a permanent member of the UN Security Council, with power of veto over actions of which it disapproved. Furthermore, since the UN was the creation of the victorious Allies, the emerging major democracies, Germany and Japan, were automatically excluded from the role to which their economic power and military potential have long entitled them.

There were other *ad initio* flaws. One of the five permanent members was to be China, but the assumption that it would be Nationalist China was dashed by Mao Tse-tung's victory over Chiang Kai-shek. The Nixon-Kissinger initiative of 1972 rectified the anomaly without curing the fault.

The argument, sometimes heard, that at least the UN General Assembly provides a platform where the disputatious may let off steam invites an answer: steam at that price comes too expensive, easily undersold by the steam New Yorkers can readily buy from Con Ed.

In 1969, writing in the shocked aftermath of Brezhnev's occupation of Czechoslovakia (which, incidentally, I had forecast), I first proposed a working alternative to the United Nations. I called it the Association of Nations. Today, in the light of the collapse of Communism in Eastern Europe, I offer a revival of the idea, with a small change of name: the Association of Free Nations (AFN).

In this context, "small" does not mean "minor." What is needed is an international body with an inner council of states that are free in the American, British, or German sense, with freely elected assemblies, freedom of speech, free economies, and the rule of law (the adverb "relatively" being understood in each stipulation). Not a military alliance, but a body concerned primarily to consider international crises of aggression and armed conflict, and take concerted action.

To write in these terms is not to be starry-eyed about our democracies, all of which are imperfect, each in its own way. But one major point shines out: democracies, it seems, don't go to war against each other. War between those traditional enemies, France and Germany, seems unthinkable so long as each is a democracy. And democratic Japan is hardly likely to do another Pearl Harbor.

An international body dedicated to the maintenance of peace must, by definition, exclude the predatory states. So what about the greatest predator of all: the Soviet Union?

To pose the question is to invite the reservation: wait and see. Wait and see whether the Soviet Union survives its current crisis, whether it turns itself into a kind of United States of Eurasia, whether Lenin's party (and Gorbachev's) stays in the Kremlin or yields to an elected alternative. Wait and see whether Moscow continues to keep a Communist regime in power in Afghanistan and to aid a Communist regime in Angola. So many waits, so many sees.

Initially, then, the AFN's inner council would exclude the USSR; it would consist of the U.S., Japan, Germany, France, Britain, Italy, and (possibly) Spain: free nations with economic substance and actual or potential military muscle. Free and non-predatory countries such as Canada, Australia, Benelux, and the Scandinavians would automatically qualify for full membership.

Associate membership would be open to countries that are not free and democratic, but do not attack their neighbors. On this basis, even a very unfree country, such as Saudi Arabia, could be admitted. There would be marginal cases, such as South Africa and Argentina. South Africa: not yet a democracy but heading that way. Non-predatory? In my view its involvements of some time ago in Namibia and Angola were ultimately defensive. Argentina? Quite recently democratic, but an invader not many years ago. *Candidate* membership could cover such marginal cases.

Apart from the Soviet Union, the biggest marginal case of all would be China. Countries that export terrorism, such as Libya and Syria, would be out in the cold, qualifying not for membership but for remedial action by the AFN. Totally disqualified would be Iraq, Cuba, and probably Vietnam.

Discarding the existing UN would be tricky but by no means impossible. As the Charter stands, it is not open to any nation or group of nations to dissolve the United Nations. There is, however, nothing to prevent any nation from abrogating its membership. Expelling predatory states would cause unnecessary problems. It would be far simpler for the putative members of the AFN Council to quit, along with those qualifying for full membership. The associate and candidate members would soon follow, leaving the unvirtuous to ponder the merits of aggression and isolation.

The Balance Sheet

Am I serious? What a frivolous question! The benefits of an Association of Free Nations would be immense, the drawbacks minimal. At times of crisis, the inner council would be free to act, in most cases without fear of a hostile veto, since those likely to cause crises would be out in the cold. Predator nations would be isolated, and the pressure on them to mend their ways would increase. The old UN would be consigned to where it has long belonged: that mythical place that Khrushchev and other Communists used to call the garbage heap of history.

What I am proposing is a challenge to Western statesmanship. And there, I suppose, I have struck a snag. Statesmanship, just now, is in short supply.

IS THE UNITED NATIONS USEFUL?[2]

Although refusing to join at the last moment, the United States was instrumental in creating the League of Nations after World War I. After World War II, the United States insisted on creating the United Nations and became a leading member. The two organizations had different structures but an identical paramount aim: the prevention of war. They also suffered from the same fatal flaw, which made their failure ineluctable and their creation an exercise in self-deception.

The United Nations is a misleadingly named association of territorial nation-states. Each is sovereign, i.e., independent of any superior authority on earth in fashioning its laws, including whether and when to be at peace or at war with other nation-states. The definition of sovereignty by Jean Bodin in the 16th century, *potestas legibus absoluta* (power unfettered by law), is as realistic today as it was then. Sovereign countries are not accountable to anyone. Their relations with one another are not governed by enforceable laws and norms.

To be sure, nations usually follow established customs in their relations with one another. Minor conflicts normally are settled by negotiation, or, if this fails, by decision of an agency such as the International Court of Justice (which sits in The Hague in the Netherlands). Nations also make treaties with one another including peace and nonaggression treaties. Treaties, customs, and other arrangements (e.g., the diplomatic immunity accorded ambassadors or the treatment of prisoners of war) are usually made in good faith: the parties intend to stick to what they arrange be-

[2]Article by Ernest van den Haag, Distinguished Scholar at the Heritage Foundation, from *Social Education* 53:289–290 S '89. Copyright © 1989 by National Council for the Social Studies. Reprinted with permission.

cause it is advantageous to all. After all, that is why the arrangements came into being in the first place.

However, treaties are adhered to only as long as they are convenient to the parties. They are ignored when violation is in the short- or long-run interest of the violator, as perceived by one or more of the parties. Treaties cannot be enforced. When you arrange a date, you usually intend to keep it. However, if you stand up your date, little can be done about it. The arrangement cannot be enforced. So it is with international treaties.

International "Laws"

It is deceptive to call international laws "laws," inasmuch as what are called laws *within* each sovereign country are *enforceable* rules. The wronged party can compel the noncompliant party to appear in court (an impossibility in international law); a domestic court can order the parties to do what it decides and can punish wrongdoers, enforcing its decisions by means of the police. The police can impose court decisions on wrongdoers as long as a state functions.

Nothing of the sort can be done about the relations among sovereign countries. There is no power separate from and superior to a sovereign nation that can compel it to follow any treaty, rule, or decision it does not want to accept—unless it be another nation's willingness to go to war against it. Nations defeated in war can be forced to do the victor's will. But the UN was meant to avoid, not to sponsor war. It has no independent army.

The UN can make decisions and pass resolutions—it keeps busy doing so—but it cannot enforce either. So too with the International Court of Justice. When the Iranian government decided to disregard custom, treaties, and international "law" and destroy the United States embassy, steal its documents, and imprison its diplomats, Americans were indignant. Diplomatic immunity had been flagrantly violated. But international "law" was not and could not be enforced.

Since World War II, there have been about 150 wars, some minor like that between India and Pakistan; or Britain, France, and Israel vs. Egypt; or the invasion of Hungary and Czechoslovakia. Some were not so minor—Korea, Vietnam, Iran and Iraq, and the Soviet invasion of Afghanistan. The list is long. The UN was never able to prevent or end any war, although its bureaucrats often pretended influence they did not have.

Consider the war in Korea, actually fought by Americans and South Koreans with a few allies, against North Koreans and the Chinese. The United States fought this war under the UN banner, but the banner is all the UN contributed—and that was only because the Soviet delegation had not been alert. The war ended with no peace treaty but with a fairly solid truce when it became clear to the parties that nothing much could be gained by continuing to fight.

The war in Vietnam ended when the United States realized that it could not win without committing far more resources than it wished to commit. The UN had no influence in starting or ending either war. The "Cuban missile crisis" was resolved without anyone's mentioning the UN. The Iran/Iraq war ended when Iran realized that it could not conquer Iraq and vice versa. To be sure, the UN passed many resolutions to end the war. They were ignored. Once the parties decided to stop fighting, they used the UN resolutions and conference facilities to arrange a precarious truce. Neither the facilities nor the resolutions were essential to or even significant in ending the war!

Once the Soviet Union decided that its invasion of Afghanistan was too costly and unrewarding militarily and politically, it used UN facilities to arrange its withdrawal. But peace, if it comes, does not come because of any UN activity. Peace comes when fighting nations (or one of them) see no point in continuing. War and peace and international relations generally are shaped not by international organizations or laws, but by power—by power independent of law (*potestas legibus absoluta*).

A country pursues its interests by organized violence when war seems rewarding. The Turks invade Cyprus when they feel that the Greeks and Cypriots will not yield to negotiations but will be unable to resist invasion. Having achieved independence of part of the island from Greek domination, they consent to a truce. The truce lines may be patrolled by third parties—say, Irish or Danish troops—and, if there is an international organization such as the UN, it will lend the uniforms and banners and make the arrangements.

Supranational Organization

It is a wishful and rather silly mistake to confuse an *international* organization, such as the UN, with a *supranational* one. An international organization has no power over its members. It is not independent of and above parties in conflict, for it consists of those parties, their allies, and some neutrals. There is nothing it can do (other than pass resolutions) if members want to go to war. If the United States and the Soviet Union were to go to war, what could the UN do other than sit by?

A supernational organization would, by definition, be independent of the parties as a domestic court is. The parties would have to give up their sovereignty, if they wished the supernational authority to decide conflicts among them and to impose its decisions by force if necessary.

But it is hard to see how a supernational organization could come into existence. Conceivably there will be fewer and bigger states in the future, but I doubt whether they will want to give up their independence. As long as there are independent and armed nations, the possibility of conflict (and, ultimately of war) exists. Diplomacy can sometimes settle conflicts and avoid war, but diplomacy existed before the UN and does not depend upon it.

If the UN cannot prevent war, is there any way of doing so? If a government is much stronger than prospective enemies, there will be no war: nobody attacks in the certainty of being defeated. Hence, *si vis pacem, para bellum* (if you want peace, prepare for war) works. One can, by means of armament and alliance, try to discourage aggression. Unilateral disarmament, however, promises victory to an attacker and thereby invites attack.

Armament is not a cause of war. Rather, war, the fear of it, or the intention to wage it is the cause of armament. There is no possibility of guaranteeing, with or without the United Nations, that war will not happen. We can often postpone it, as physicians postpone death, by curing particular illnesses. But physicians cannot ultimately eliminate death. Nor can diplomats and armaments eliminate war. People do not picket hospitals on the ground that they are merely postponing death rather than eliminating it; yet they picket defense departments for merely postponing war. Perhaps the reason is that war seems to be under human control, whereas death is a natural event.

Organizations such as the UN serve two purposes:

(1) They make it possible for some people to believe that the impossible—eliminating war—is possible. This may lead them to oppose armaments and may generally have bad effects, as self-deceptions often do.

(2) When a government realizes that it has to do something it would rather not do, e.g., yield on an important matter or admit

defeat, it may use the UN to hide what is really happening, thereby keeping its prestige and making it easier to disguise the unavoidable, and thus to make it more acceptable. This may be useful at times.

Whether the very limited usefulness of the UN warrants its great expense is another matter. Further, the UN has become counterproductive in some ways. In the Near East and in South Africa, the majority of the General Assembly has more often been interested in feeding the fire by inflammatory speeches than in extinguishing it. Not that it matters: power decides, not words.

Anti-American Propaganda

Some UN agencies have spent money profligately on high, untaxed salaries for bureaucrats, on busywork, and—not least—on anti-American propaganda. The majority of UN members are anti-American largely because (1) they resent our power and prosperity and (2) they are governed by Marxist governments that resent capitalism. UNESCO (which we finally left) was outstanding in using our money to propagandize against us and spending it in wasteful ways; but other agencies were not far behind. We pay officially a quarter and, in practice, more of the UN expense used for anti-American propaganda. The UN bureaucracy is inflated and largely useless. To be sure, some agencies, e.g., the World Health Organization, are useful. But there have been many useful international agencies—e.g., the International Postal Union—long before the UN; there is no need to connect them with the UN. On the contrary, doing so usually leads to politicization and waste.

The idea that the UN serves as a useful meeting place is doubtful. What are embassies for, and telephones, and planes by which government diplomats visit one another and can have as much contact as they wish?

When the UN was founded, Cordell Hull, Roosevelt's Secretary of State, exulted: "No spheres of influence, no alliances . . . will be necessary now that there is an international organization." Abba Eban, Israel's ambassador to the UN, later commented: "This is . . . the most absurd utterance ever made since the invention of language." But many Americans still believe that the UN can somehow replace foreign policy with international power. Nothing can. As for the UN, it has proved useless, if not harmful. Nothing would be lost if it were given up.

WHY THE RIGHT LOVES THE U.N.[3]

The right has spent many years attacking the United Nations. Indeed, for years the Heritage Foundation had a special section with no other task than to calumniate the U.N. and all its works. Now, in the Bushian new world order, conservatives see hitherto hidden attractions in the organization. But be assured. "No. The Heritage Foundation hasn't changed its position on the U.N. Absolutely not. There's been a change in the U.N.," says Burton Yale Pines, vice president of the Heritage Foundation and longtime head of its U.N.-baiting U.N. Assessment Project.

"Everything the new Secretary General has done—the appointment of Governor Thornburgh as Under Secretary General, and the composition of the East European delegations—means that the U.N. is no longer a forum for world Bolshevism and anti-Americanism," Pines told me. Dick Thornburgh is a "thoroughly competent supervisor and administrator who will make the organization more responsive to reality." Pines's—and Heritage's—plaudits confirm the worst fears of many at the U.N.: that Thornburgh's role is not just to cut the organization to the smaller *size* the United States wants but also to carve it into the *shape* the American right wants.

Secretary General Boutros Boutros-Ghali's ratification of Bush's patronage appointment of the man Pennsylvania disappointed was followed by Boutros-Ghali's appointment of Joseph Verner Reed to an unspecified portfolio. Once described as "a 14-karat nitwit" by Senator Thomas Eagleton, Reed, a former Chase Manhattan vice president, was made Ambassador to Morocco by Reagan in 1981, and now has the job of organizing the U.N.'s fiftieth-anniversary celebrations.

Reed has also joined Burton Pines on the executive committee of the Institute of East-West Dynamics, which in its own way encapsulates the new relationship between the U.N. and Washington. A nonprofit organization set up to promote profit, it offers training in free-market economic principles to the "economies in transition" in Eastern Europe. The institute seems to have secured an initial $250,000 grant from the United Nations Devel-

[3]Article by Ian Williams, a British journalist, from *Nation* 254:478–482 Ap 13 '92. Copyright © 1992 by The Nation Company, Inc. Reprinted with permission.

opment Program [U.N.D.P.], having been referred there by the State Department.

U.N.D.P. is the world's biggest multilateral development grant aid agency, and one can see that it may be doing good work from this description in *Barron's* magazine by Christopher Whalen: "The so-called United Nations Development Programme seeks 'development approaches that are ecologically sound, self-sustaining and equitable in their distribution of resources and opportunities,' meaning socialist by design and directed from the top down." Whalen, who works for The Whalen Company, a consulting firm, added, "A large number of senior UN officials are European Socialists, who still believe, despite the overwhelming weight of evidence to the contrary, that centralized economic control is getting a bum rap."

Whalen's blast might seem a bit ungrateful, given that his father, Richard Whalen, the head of The Whalen Company, is on the board of advisers of the Institute of East-West Dynamics. Father and son are listed as "public policy experts" by the Heritage Foundation.

The current sweetheart relationship between Heritage and the U.N. began last October, when a group of conservative Congressmen wrote to John Bolton, Assistant Secretary of State for International Organization Affairs, pointing out what sterling work the Institute of East-West Dynamics was doing: "This private voluntary organization, with which you are familiar, is, in our opinion, at least as worthy a recipient of such funds as any other such U.N.-affiliated organizations." They asked him to grant the institute $2 million.

Bolton, an Ed Meese disciple who led the campaign to withdraw U.S. membership in UNESCO [United Nations Educational, Scientific, and Cultural Organization], had no problem with the request. He approached U.N.D.P. in late November and suggested that it pay the institute the $2 million. A week later he congratulated U.N.D.P.'s administrator William Draper 3d for making the "initial contribution" of $250,000 to the institute, adding that "I trust UNDP will make the funds available to the Institute as soon as possible so as not to delay the implementation of this worthwhile endeavor."

Draper is a clubbable conservative, a friend of George Bush and generally well regarded in U.N.D.P. Both he and U.N.D.P. were put in a difficult position by the letter. U.N.D.P. is funded by voluntary contributions, and 10 percent of its cash comes from the U.S. government—through Bolton. A U.N.D.P. spokesperson confirmed that the request had been made, but said that the quarter-million "for management training programs in Eastern Europe had not yet been approved. It is going through the regular appraisal process." That institute director Reed makes no secret of his desire to inherit Draper's job as head of U.N.D.P. may help lubricate the appraisal machinery.

The key figure in all this is the president of the Institute of East-West Dynamics, Pedro Sanjuan, an American who has just retired as Director of Political Affairs for the U.N. A former director of the conservative American Enterprise Institute's Hemispheric Center, Sanjuan was appointed Assistant Secretary of State for Insular Affairs by Reagan, after which he was given a job at the U.N. during Jeane Kirkpatrick's memorable time as U.S. ambassador. The connecting theme in Sanjuan's appointments to the board of the institute seems to be membership in the community of conservative American veterans of undeclared wars in Central America.

Sanjuan had a remarkably low profile at the U.N. for such a senior position. Many senior U.N. staff members assumed that his function was to "shadow" his Soviet nominal superior. One insider says "he spent a lot of time in Washington, allegedly putting out fires with the Heritage Foundation, for [former Secretary General] Pérez de Cuéllar," adding, however, "it's funny, he always seemed to have a can of kerosene and a box of matches when he went." Sanjuan fulfills the almost obligatory qualification of disparaging U.N.D.P., which, he says in a recent article for the International Freedom Foundation journal *laissez-faire*, "seems to be falling prey to the predominance of ideology over pragmatism." Sanjuan, a charming and plausible person, steered a resolution through the General Assembly of the U.N. last October that endorsed the work of the Institute of East-West Dynamics. He persuaded the Eastern Europeans to propose it, and it passed without a vote. "We thought the institute would get us more money," an Eastern European diplomat told me.

As the institute's own policy material suggests, this was a "first at the U.N." Normally a different procedure is followed in affiliating nongovernmental organizations. The General Assembly resolutions short-circuited that procedure by calling on the Secretary General "to take appropriate measures in order to provide for cooperation between the Institute and the competent United Nations bodies." The General Assembly resolution claimed that the institute "has developed a comprehensive program of instruction for universities and international organizations to train managers and other professional persons" and "will also run parallel training program for parliamentarians." A press release heralded it as the "beginning of a new era of cooperation between the UN and market-oriented institutions, including foundations, corporations and other Western organizations." It pointed out that the institute was "authorized to accept voluntary contributions from UN member states"—so much for the Eastern Europeans' hopes it would give *them* money.

Although the resolution went through with no opposition, Ron Spiers, an American who was a U.N. Under Secretary General, resigned from the institute's advisory board in protest at this unprecedented use of the General Assembly to approve such an organization. Members of the U.S. mission were also unhappy about it, but told concerned U.N. staff members that they were operating under instructions from Washington—presumably Bolton. Other U.N. employees did not learn of the resolution until the day before it passed. One senior official said, "The lawyers didn't like it, but the permanent five agreed to go along with it, so it went through. But a lot of people were angry about it."

So what was the rush? Well, at the end of February Pedro Sanjuan retired from the U.N.—and for many months the address and phone number for the Institute of East-West Dynamics has been his home in Westchester County, New York. When the organization is up and running he expects to be paid $85,000 a year for his services.

Sanjuan is at pains to explain that the board of the institute is "bipartisan," which he seems to use in the peculiar American sense that blesses a group of conservatives who agree on everything but are prepared to accept patronage impartially from either Democratic or Republican incumbents. For example, the chairman of the institute is the Democrat Angier Biddle Duke, who was U.S. Ambassador to El Salvador at a time when the United States was not noted for its restraining influence on the death squads. Duke was a member of PRODEMCA, which, *The Washington Post* reported in 1986, funded *contra*-associated groups in Nicaragua and helped pay for ads supporting Reagan's bid to fund military and "nonlethal" aid to the *contras*.

Another executive committee member, Peter Hannaford, has what many might see as a rather idiosyncratic commitment to democracy. His P.R. firm, The Hannaford Company, served as the initial headquarters for Ronald Reagan's presidential ambitions, and it represented the military rulers of Guatemala and Argentina during the years when death-squad killings were at their height. The Hannaford Company gave credit to Argentina's junta for "one of the most remarkable economic recoveries in modern history."

Also on the advisory board is Duncan Sellars, chairman of the International Freedom Foundation [I.F.F.] and former executive director of the Conservative Caucus. One of the I.F.F.'s less endearing traits is its uncritical support of the white South African government.

Sellars told *The Nation*, "The institute will fill a gap the U.N. has not filled hitherto. It will teach market methods, market economics. It's good to see groups like Pedro's channeling the U.N. in the right direction, especially if it takes funds that would otherwise be used to support traditional U.N.D.P. policies. U.N.D.P. does promote the 'third way,' mixed economies. I don't think Pedro would, and I certainly wouldn't countenance that. The institute will balance that 'third way' approach."

While the institute has many plans, one has to look hard to see any concrete achievements, until recently. On March 8, [1992,] the institute, with its new badge of respectability, co-sponsored with the Heritage Foundation a conference at the U.N. to advise the new Baltic delegations on how they could best use the U.N. Billed as speakers were Duke, Sanjuan and Burton Yale Pines.

A session on how to use the media was addressed by Amity Shlaes, who wrote an article last October in *The Wall Street Journal* attacking U.N.D.P. because its budget "largely ignores East Europe's economic progress." She ended her speech by quoting Christopher Gacek, who at the time watched the U.N. for the Heritage Foundation but is currently with the American Enterprise Institute: "The danger now is that the U.N. is a rudderless place, and that it will remain rudderless." Gacek is also on the advisory board of the Institute of East-West Dynamics.

The institute exemplifies the conservative network's effect on the U.N., but the main thrust of "reform" in the United Nations is being carried out under the guise of increasing efficiency—a function given expressly to Dick Thornburgh. To promote such "efficiency," bodies like the Center for Trans-National Corporations are being effectively neutralized, and under Thornburgh it is unlikely that other initiatives for conservatives' pet hates, such as debt forgiveness for the Third World, will receive much support.

The process is a win-win proposition for the American right. They will either gain control of the organization and use it to push their particular view of the world, or they will make U.S. control so obvious they diminish whatever prestige the U.N. and its agencies have, making it ineffective as a platform for the concerns of the rest of the world. Either way, the prospect of a United Nations of America is one that can appeal only to a narrow section of American, let alone world, politics. As the now-retired Ron Spiers says, "You have to have diversity. If the U.N. is seen as too Western, it's going to lose its authority."

Boutros-Ghali, living in hope that Washington will pay its half-billion-dollar debt to the organization, is trapped. If the U.N. is to have a meaningful role in the new world order, it needs U.S. support, certainly until Europe and Japan decide to match their political clout to their economic strength. But what profit is the U.N. if it loses its soul to the American far right, which has consistently opposed everything the organization stands for?

DOUBLE STANDARD FOR
HUMAN RIGHTS[4]

For six weeks every year, the United Nations Human Rights Commission assembles to hear chilling accounts of torture, disappearance, and murder in countries around the world. Then it pronounces its judgments and recommendations. But political factors often overshadow humanitarian considerations in the world's highest forum on human rights. Two judgments by the 1992 Commission illustrate this problem.

This year, Cuba was placed under item twelve of the Commission's agenda, a category reserved for the world's worst violators. The U.N. envoy who had been monitoring the island's situation was promoted to *rapporteur,* signifying a level of scrutiny only merited by extremely serious cases.

Guatemala, on the other hand, received a less severe judgment. Despite urgent pleas from human-rights monitoring orga-

[4]Article by Mia Taylor Valdes, a Costa Rican journalist, from *The Progressive* 56:20–21 Ag '92. Copyright © 1992 by The Progressive Magazine. Reprinted with permission.

nizations for giving the country item-twelve status and intensifying U.N. supervision, the Commission decided to keep Guatemala under item nineteen, a much more benign category that provides "consultative services" to help governments improve human-rights records.

While the Commission cannot enforce its decisions, a condemnation can shame a country into curbing its most blatant abuses. And the Commission's decision can influence the amount of financial aid countries receive from international lenders—which increasingly condition loans on humanitarian records.

The Commission's decisions are not taken lightly. Expensive, high-pressure lobbying of Commission delegates starts months before the annual meeting. Countries in a particular region often agree to vote to protect each other from condemnation. (The African bloc, for example, has made it practically impossible for the Commission to condemn human-rights abuses on that continent, except in South Africa.)

In considering Cuba's case, the Commission heard reports from international monitoring groups as well as Cuban exile organizations. Fidel Castro refused to allow the Commission-appointed human-rights monitor, Rafael Rivas Posada, into Cuba, claiming his appointment was politically motivated. So Rivas was forced to collect testimony from Cuban exiles who monitor human-rights abuses from abroad.

Ambassador Nikolaus Scherk, the Austrian delegate, summarized for the Commission the "serious violations" documented in Cuba in 1991: "denial of freedom of expression and association, persecution against dissidents and opponents of the regime, including threats, summary judicial proceedings, and abuses against the prison population."

Humanitarian groups are disturbed by the persecution of human-rights activists within Cuba. Even Cuba's staunchest supporters were offended by a notorious incident earlier this year, in which a mob dragged poet/activist Maria Elena Cruz Varela from her home and forced her to eat the paper on which she had written a protest poem. Cruz is now serving a two-year prison sentence for signing a petition calling for free elections and amnesty of political prisoners.

But if Cuba's case is disturbing, Guatemala's record is appalling. The Human Rights Commission report for that Central American country concurs with the Guatemalan government's own human-rights attorney general, who documented more than

6,000 cases of serious human-rights violations in 1991. They include assassinations, disappearances, torture, death threats, and murders of street children. Stating that "Guatemalan society is characterized by a state of terror," Christian Tomuschat, the U.N.-appointed investigator, reported that political murders "are an almost daily occurrence."

Tomuschat's investigation echoes the conclusions of most independent human-rights groups monitoring Guatemala. They report a level of human-rights abuses seldom equaled in modern society. Even the U.S. State Department in its 1991 Human Rights Report calls Guatemala "the worst human-rights violator in this hemisphere."

Yet the United States voted not to condemn Guatemala at the United Nations, while working frantically to line up votes for a condemnation of Cuba.

A number of factors helped the United States achieve its goal. "Until very recently, Cuba could depend on the solid support of the Communist bloc and the Latin American bloc," said a State Department official. This year, four Eastern European nations set a new precedent by voting against their former ally. Russia, Hungary, Bulgaria, and Czechoslovakia—all harboring bitter memories of Communist repression and a desperate need for foreign aid—joined the United States in voting for condemnation of Cuba.

The Latin American bloc also cracked this year when Argentina, Chile, Uruguay, and Costa Rica voted against Cuba. Otto Reich, co-chair of the U.S. mission to the U.N. Commission, acknowledged that President Bush strongly lobbied Latin American presidents for their support on the Cuba vote at their February drug summit in San Antonio.

When the time came to vote on Guatemala, the United States and the Latin American bloc stood firm in their support of the government. The Guatemalan government expressed "great satisfaction" over the vote.

Declaring that the Commission's judgment had nothing to do with reality, leader of popular groups were disheartened. "What more can we do to show the world what is going on in Guatemala?" asks Myrna Anaya, general co-ordinator of the Central American Human Rights Commission.

"The United States uses a double standard at the Commission to further its global strategy," says Oswaldo Enriquez of the Guatemalan Human Rights Commission.

In the case of China, another Marxist government with a much worse human-rights record than Cuba's, the United States used blatant delaying tactics at this year's meeting to derail a vote that might have condemned a valuable trading partner.

"The U.N. Commission has so much potential to help countries like Guatemala achieve justice," says Anaya. "But its ideals are being subverted by U.S. political aims. It is losing its credibility."

THE UNITED NATIONS AND ITS CRITICS[5]

It is prudent to begin an article on the United Nations and its critics by explaining what the organization is. Most people seem to think it is no more than an idealistic venture at world peace, and even those who tend to support the organization have been made dubious by the entirely negative campaign of distortion and falsehood of such critics as the Washington-based Heritage Foundation. Despite its recent peacemaking achievements in Afghanistan and in the Iran-Iraq war, people in general are apt to put down the United Nations as a talking shop, a place where world leaders come to strut and fret in the international limelight. Although there is an undeniable element of theater in the public proceedings of the United Nations, it is and has been much more. The achievements of the organization are historically important and it has been far more successful than people generally believe.

Perhaps the best way to explain the organization is to put it in historical perspective. When we do that, it becomes immediately apparent that it was not created by utopian idealists. The United Nations was founded in the closing days of the most destructive war in world history, hardly a crucible of idealism, and the people involved in its creation—Roosevelt and Stalin, Churchill and Chiang Kai-shek among others—were not known for their naïveté. The negotiators who worked out the charter of the United Nations at the San Francisco Conference in 1945 left no doubt

[5]Article by Bhaskar P. Menon, Indian journalist working for the U.N., from *Social Education* 53:291–294 S '89. Copyright © 1989 by National Council for the Social Studies. Reprinted with permission.

that they were creating an organizational response to the wide-ranging needs of the modern world.

Historical Underpinning

To understand the nature of these needs, we have to look back to the beginnings of the scientific and industrial revolutions in Europe, the great transforming movements that made it possible and necessary to develop international relations beyond systems based on feudal alliances. Scientists were the first internationalists in the modern sense of the word, for their work required common standards that cut across all national, linguistic, and cultural barriers. The technological revolution widened the pull of internationalism. The telegraph, for instance, imposed standardized equipment and a common code for its operators as it spanned the multilingual map of Europe. The development of railways and steamships eased travel, made mail service cheap, and allowed the trade of staples in addition to traditional luxuries. The growth of these broad interactions among countries made it necessary to set common standards and coordinate activity across borders, and the earliest international organizations were founded to do that. The International Telegraphic Union, which is now the oldest member of the United Nations system (renamed the International Telecommunications Union) belongs to that first generation of organizations. The World Meteorological Organization and the Universal Postal Union also date from that period.

The scientific and industrial revolutions in Europe set in motion a series of economic, social, and political changes that shaped the evolution of international organizations. Two processes of change, both rooted in the industrialization of European societies, are of essential importance. One was the political emergence of industrial workers in every modernizing society of Europe, a class of people uprooted from the land and feudal ties, making increasingly powerful demands for social change. The other was the demand for raw materials and markets generated by the newly industrializing economies, and the unrestrained competition for colonies to which this led. The former process, despite determined resistance from the old order, altered the dynamics of all societies in which it occurred, and in one, Czarist Russia, it precipitated the Marxist revolution. The latter process led, in a period when it was still possible to think of war as "diplomacy by other means," to World War I. In belated response to these events, governments joined to create the League of Nations, incorporating in it the International Labor Organization (ILO).

The major difference between the first-generation international organizations and the League was that, unlike its technically oriented predecessors, the League was politically driven. The broadness of its mandate on the one hand and the special capacity of the ILO to deal with an important socioeconomic issue on the other represented radical innovations. Though the League failed, the ILO survived, and it is today a United Nations specialized agency, continuing the steady, valuable work of improving labor conditions and extending human rights values into labor law around the world.

Building on the Lessons of the League: The Security Council

The failure of the League had a direct effect on the United Nations, for many of the people involved in creating the organizations were the same. They tried in creating the United Nations to avoid the pitfalls that had spelled disaster for the earlier experiment. For instance, they sought to buttress the executive ability of the United Nations in maintaining world peace by arranging for a Security Council in which the five "Big Powers" of the time would act in concert, and only they would have the right to veto action. (The League Council had acted by consensus, in effect giving every member a veto.) The assumption was that Britain, China, France, the Soviet Union, and the United States, allies against Nazi Germany, would continue to act together in the Security Council.

This, of course, did not happen; before the ink on the charter was dry, the cold war, then still undeclared, had begun. Critics of the United Nations have, from the beginning, had much to say about the "ineffectiveness of the Security Council." But built as it was, straddling the largest fault line in the world's political crust, how could it have been otherwise?

If the Security Council could not advance into the brave new world of big-power cooperation, neither could the world slide back entirely into the politics of the past; the atomic explosions over Hiroshima and Nagasaki within weeks of the signing of the UN charter suddenly altered all strategic assumptions. World war assumed a new "unthinkable" dimension. Driven by the blind fears of the cold war, an arms race began that put at risk the very existence of life on earth.

All this is not to agree with critics who say that the Security Council has been completely ineffective. In fact, reviewing the last four decades, it is amazing how often, despite its crippled political condition, the council has served as the court of last resort, the place where international conflicts go when all other solutions have failed and armies are on the march. At such critical times as the Berlin blockade in 1949 or the Cuban missile crisis in 1962, the Security Council has served to defuse tensions and head off nuclear confrontation. On other occasions, as in Cyprus, the Middle East, the Congo, and most recently in the Iran-Iraq war, it has been able to introduce peacekeeping forces into situations of conflict, separating adversaries and giving time for negotiations. Helping in this process has been the office of the Secretary-General of the United Nations, which has evolved during the last four decades a quiet competence to deal with the thorniest of issues. The agreement to resolve the situation in Afghanistan, worked out during laborious years of negotiation under the auspices of the Secretary-General, is only the latest and most visible achievement of the office.

Admittedly, the Security Council has never been able to enforce peace, as intended in the charter; but the United Nations can hardly be blamed for a situation in which the "big powers," fighting proxy wars, have been unwilling to act together to end them. The current improvement in East-West relations has had a direct effect on the functioning of the organization, making its proceedings more collegial than ever before. It is not coincidental that the situations in Afghanistan and in Namibia seem on their way to resolution, and prospects for winding down several other regional conflicts seem good.

Attention to Economic and Social Affairs

The founders of the United Nations also gave it, in contrast to the League, a wide mandate in economic and social affairs. The UN became the center of a system of specialized agencies that included not only the older organizations dealing with the mail, telecommunications, meteorology, and labor but new ones dealing with food and agriculture, health, education, science and culture, and money and finance. With a coordinating Economic and Social Council reporting to the General Assembly, the system overall was designed to be capable of flexible response to a wide range of economic and social contingencies. The United Nations itself was given a mandate that was without precedent in the history of international affairs: the promotion of human rights.

In giving such capability to the United Nations system, its founders were again guided by the experience of the League. The earlier organization had floundered in part because its members had been guided by the most narrow sense of self-advantage in international economic relations.

Seeking to maximize exports and minimize imports (under the assumption that the greater a country's positive balance of trade, the more powerful it was), they had merely succeeded in creating such volatile conditions in world markets that international trade began to shrink and finally collapsed.

Without external markets, major industrial producers had to cut back, throwing millions out of work and thus further reducing economic demand. That traumatic process, remembered now as the "Great Depression," created social conditions that encouraged political extremism.

The resurgence of Germany under fascist rule and Hitler's militarist attempts to set right the perceived wrongs of history put the world irretrievably on the road to World War II.

The Allies fought World War II in the name of freedom and national self-determination. Although the imperial powers of Europe did not particularly want to extend these rights to their African and Asian colonies, their dependence on colonial manpower and matériel made it necessary at least to make promises.

As it turned out, in the face of determined nationalist movements, the promises had to be kept. India, a founding member of the United Nations despite its status then as a British colony, became free in 1947. Other territories in Asia and Africa followed, the rapidity of the process belying all expectations. This changed the composition of the United Nations, converting it within two decades from an almost all-white club obedient to the major Western powers to an organization in which newly independent African and Asian countries began to chalk out "nonaligned" agenda. For many Western critics, this was unacceptable. The socialist countries in the United Nations, always a small minority, saw an easy political opportunity in the situation and sided with the Afro-Asian group, further alienating Western opinion.

One of the effects of the numerical dominance of the "developing countries" in the United Nations was that the organization turned much more firmly to support economic and social development. This involved considerable institutional growth, a process that has been a favorite target of critics. The organization's "burgeoning bureaucracy" and its "bloated budgets" are almost folklore in some countries. On examination, the growth of the UN system is clearly seen to be driven by need and, in the context of the problems at hand, quite modest. In the early years, the General Assembly created UNICEF, the UN Children's Fund, and the UNHCR, the office of the High Commissioner for Refugees. Both initially focused on the situations in Europe resulting from World War II, but soon widened the scope of their activities to cover endemic conditions in poorer countries. UNICEF and UNHCR, as well as the World Food Program (set up in 1963 as a conduit of world food surpluses to the needy), have enjoyed wide Western support. Others have been more or less problematic.

In 1964, the General Assembly convened the first UN Conference on Trade and Development (UNCTAD), which it later institutionalized. UNCTAD has been a favorite target of right-wing Western critics because it has been perceived as addressing the problems besetting world trade from the perspective of developing countries.

Its Keynesian prescriptions to stabilize world commodity markets (on which most developing countries depend for their income) have been characterized as "anti–free market," though similar measures have been taken in many Western countries including the United States (for agricultural products).

In 1965, against considerable Western resistance, the General Assembly created the UN Development Program (UNDP). It has grown, with solid support from the very countries that initially resisted, to become the world's largest source of *grant* technical assistance (the World Bank provides more as a *lender*). The UN Institute for Training and Research, a think tank established the same year, has been less of a success. With a small staff and a bare-bones work program, it manages to squeak from budget year to budget year. The UN Industrial Development Organization, founded in 1966, has been converted from a New York–based General Assembly program to the more independent status of a specialized agency headquartered in Vienna, but it too limps along without adequate financing. In contrast, the UN Fund for Population Activities established in 1969 has seldom suffered for lack of contributions, even after the Right-to-Life movement succeeded in knocking out official United States funding in recent years. Institutional growth continued in the 1970s with the establishment of the UN Disaster Relief Operation in Geneva and the

UN Environment Program in Nairobi (both in 1972), the UN Centre on Transnational Corporations in New York and the World Food Council in Rome (both 1974), the United Nations University in Tokyo (1975) and the Centre for Human Settlements in Nairobi in 1978.

The decade of the 1970s was also marked by a new assertiveness of developing countries at the United Nations. This too evoked vociferous criticism from many Western critics. Particular venom was directed at the call for a New International Economic Order (NIEO) in 1974. Coming on the heels of the OPEC action in 1973 in raising oil prices, the NIEO resolution (as it soon came to be called at the UN), seemed to many to be a call to transfer wealth from the rich countries to the poor.

In reality, the call was no more than a plea for negotiated and rational change in world economic affairs, the need for which was underlined repeatedly during the decade of the 1960s as the United Nations organized a series of world conferences on major global problems—environment, population, food, water, energy, raw materials, employment, land reform, science and technology, industrialization and trade. Each of these conferences produced strategies and plans of action, some of which are being implemented with considerable effect. On others, action has been slow.

The overall call for a renegotiation of the world's economic structures, however, has been, as the saying goes in New York, pecked to death by ducks. The demise of NIEO is viewed with approval by many critics of the United Nations, but they seem to ignore the fact that, if some of the major issues raised under the rubric of the NIEO had been negotiated effectively, the world economy would not now be threatened with mountainous debt, widening trade imbalances, and continuing monetary instability.

Even more controversial than the call for reordering the world economy was the call for a new International Information Order. In essence, the call was to give more voice internationally to developing countries, to end the domination of global news flows by a handful of agencies in a few countries.

Although few could quarrel with the aim of free and more balanced flow of information, many Western journalists took alarm at the prospect of governments getting into the business of regulating the international flow of news. UNESCO [United Nations Educational, Scientific and Cultural Organization], where this debate centered, came under increasing attack, and to express their disquiet, the United States and Britain withdrew from that agency.

The Financial Crisis of the 1980s

By the 1980s, dissatisfaction with the working of the United Nations was widespread. Few governments, North, South, East, or West, were happy with the way things had gone. Each group of countries had discovered in turn the limits to which the organization could be used as an instrument of parochial policy. Increasingly, they seemed to be ignoring the hard lessons of history and attempting to deal with the complexities of the modern world with unilateral policies of coercion and force.

In 1982, the year Javier Perez de Cuellar [took office as Secretary-General], he warned in his annual report to governments that the world was on the verge of "a new international anarchy." In 1985, the 40th anniversary year of the United Nations, the General Assembly took stock of the situation and called for wide-ranging reforms.

During this period, some critics of the UN, especially the Heritage Foundation, carried on a well-financed and unscrupulous propaganda campaign. They accused the organization of being a nest of spies, of being anti–free market, of being biased, wasteful, inefficient and a stalking-horse for every kind of disreputable foreigner, from garden-variety rapists to political terrorists. Initiatives in the United States Congress led to several pieces of legislation that required withholding US funds from the United Nations, and as these were implemented, the organization slipped rapidly into the red.

The amount of money involved is not, by the standards of governments, very large. The regular budget of the United Nations—the funds governments are mandated to pay—is about $800 million a year. This is, to put it in perspective, less than what New York City spends on its Fire Department; it is less than the world spends in 12 hours on arms. The clamor some critics make about the 25 percent (some $200 million) United States contribution to the UN budget is entirely disproportionate, especially when we consider that the UN community spends about four times that amount in New York City.

The Solid Achievements

When we consider what the United Nations has achieved in its 43 years of existence, the noise over its budget seems even more unnecessary. In addition to its widely known activities to further the welfare of children and to protect such vulnerable groups as refugees, the organization has been instrumental in engineering a quiet revolution of historic significance in several other arenas. It has, for instance, codified more international law than in all past history. It has extended international law into outer space, negotiated a comprehensive law of the sea, and is the main architect today of international environmental law.

In human rights, the UN is responsible for three critically important achievements.

First, it put human rights high on the international agenda. The Universal Declaration on Human Rights was adopted by the General Assembly three years after it began work. In doing this, the United Nations was making history, for no government before then would even admit human rights as legitimate for discussion at an international level. When, for instance, the Japanese proposed that the Covenant of the League of Nations include an article prohibiting discrimination on the basis of race or nationality, it got no support. Racial discrimination was a widely accepted practice then, and few thought it a matter of pressing concern for governments.

The *second* major achievement of the UN is in translating the Universal Declaration into binding international covenants. Not only are the majority of the world's countries now parties to these covenants, but many have incorporated these rights into their own laws. It is undoubtedly true that in many countries the actual observance of these rights lags far behind their legal acceptance. This is where the *third* achievement is significant. The monitoring mechanisms established under the major covenants on human rights require governments to report periodically on prevailing situations. The organization also provides a range of "advisory services" (including expert advisers, scholarships, training courses, and seminars) calculated to empower people to protect their human rights.

Although the UN cannot enforce human rights observance in any country, it has set international standards and created a climate in which no government, with the exception of South Africa, admits to large-scale violations. Undoubtedly, such violations occur, but it must be considered a historic step forward that an international conscience now exists on the matter, and offending governments are put in a position of having to disguise realities the world considers reprehensible.

In the case of South Africa and its system of *apartheid,* the United Nations has helped keep the issue before the international community for four decades and it continues to be an important focal point of efforts at peacefully resolving an acute and explosive situation.

In economic and social development, action to save the human environment, taking stock of the planet's resources and problems, and proposing solutions, the United Nations has a solid record of achievement.

During a period of tumultuous change in global political and economic relationships, the organization has provided a frame of stability, a crucially important forum. It has not only succeeded in keeping open the lines of communication between East and West, North and South, but it has managed to build, against all odds, the foundations of law and practice essential for a peaceful world order.

BIBLIOGRAPHY

An asterisk (*) preceding a reference indicates that the material or part of it has been reprinted in this book.

BOOKS AND PAMPHLETS

Baehr, Peter & Gordenker, Leon. The Untied Nations in the 1990s. St. Martin's Press. '92.

Berridge, Geoff. Return to the UN: UN diplomacy in regional conflicts. St. Martin's Press. '91.

Blue helmets: a review of United Nations peace-keeping. UN. '90.

Boudreau, Tom. Sheathing the sword: the UN Secretary-General and the prevention of international conflict. Greenwood Press. '91.

Commemoration of the fortieth anniversary of the United Nations. UN. '85.

Ekins, Paul. A new world order: grassroots movements for global change. Routledge. '92.

Finger, Seymour Maxwell & Saltzman, Arnold A. Bending with the winds: Kurt Waldheim and the United Nations. Praeger. '90.

Finkelstein, Lawrence S., ed. Politics in the United Nations system. Duke University Press. '88.

Gerson, Allan. The Kirkpatrick mission: diplomacy without apology: America at the United Nations, 1981–1985. Free Press. '91.

Gibson, John S. International organizations, constitutional law, and human rights. Praeger. '91.

A Global agenda: issues before the 46th General Assembly of the United Nations. University Press of America. '91.

Harrelson, Max. Fires all around the horizon: the U.N.'s uphill battle to preserve the peace. Greenwood. '89.

Hazzard, Shirley. Countenance of truth: the United Nations and the Waldheim case. Viking. '90.

Hilderbrand, Robert C. Dumbarton Oaks: the origins of the United Nations & the search for postwar security. University of North Carolina Press. '90.

Keeping faith with the United Nations. UN. '87.

Luard, Evan. A history of the United Nations. St. Martin's. '89.

Muller, Joachim W. The reform of the United Nations. Oceana. '92.

Norton, Augustus R. & Weiss, Thomas George. UN peacekeepers: soldiers with a difference. Foreign Policy Association. '90.

Report to Congress on voting practices in the United Nations. U.S. Department of State. '91.

Schoenberg, Harris O. A mandate for terror: the United Nations and the P.L.O. Shapolsky. '89.

Sherry, George L. The United Nations reborn: conflict control in the post-cold war world. Council on Foreign Relations. '90.

Siekmann, Robert C. National contingents in United Nations peacekeeping forces. Kluwer. '91.

Skogmo, Bjorn. UNIFIL: International peacekeeping in Lebanon, 1978–1988. Lynne Rienner. '88.

Taylor, Paul & Groom, A. J., eds. International institutions at work. St. Martin's. '88.

United Nations and a just world order. Volume 3. Westview. '91.

United Nations. Dept. for Disarmament Affairs. Study on the role of the United Nations in the field of verification. UN. '91.

United States/Congress/House/Committee on Armed Services. Crisis in the Persian Gulf: sanctions, diplomacy, and war: hearings before the Committee on Armed Services. 101st Congress. 2nd session. U.S. G.P.O. '91.

United States/Congress/House/Committee on Foreign Affairs/Subcommittee on Europe and the Middle East. U.N. role in the Persian Gulf and Iraqi compliance with U.N. resolutions. 102nd Congress. 1st session. U.S. G.P.O. '92.

———. U.N. Security Council resolutions on Iraq: compliance and implementation. U.S. G.P.O. '92.

United States/Congress/House/Committee on Foreign Affairs/Subcommittee on Human Rights and International Organizations. Recent developments in the United Nations system. 101st Congress. 2nd session. U.S. G.P.O. '90.

Vincent, Jack E. Support patterns at the United Nations. University Press of America. '91.

Wells, Robert N. Jr., ed. Peace by pieces—United Nations agencies & their roles: a reader & selective bibliography. Scarecrow. '91.

Yoder, Amos. Evolution of the U.N. system. Taylor & Francis. '89.

ADDITIONAL PERIODICAL ARTICLES WITH ABSTRACTS

For those who wish to read more widely on the subject of the United Nations, this section contains abstracts of additional articles that bear on the topic. Readers who require a comprehensive list of materials are advised to consult the *Reader's Guide to Periodical Literature* and other Wilson indexes.

Beyond the chartered path. Ruth Pearson. *The Bulletin of the Atomic Scientists* 47:8–10 D '91

The UN is facing new opportunities and new dangers in the wake of the Soviet Union's demise. The end of the cold war has prompted former enemies to become friends, enabled the UN to take collective action in the Persian Gulf War, and allowed the world to focus increased attention on human rights. The countries of the former Eastern bloc are in the midst of a difficult transition, however, as exemplified by the civil strife in Yugoslavia. Moreover, industrialized and developing countries continue to disagree on a variety of international issues, including various proposals for structural reorganization at the UN. The next UN secretary-general will need great diplomatic skill to deal with these and other problems.

And now—the U.N. century. William Epstein. *The Bulletin of the Atomic Scientists* 48:22–3 My '92

Part of a special section on the future of nuclear weapons. Circumstances are favorable for eliminating the threat of nuclear weapons. The most immediate threat–the proliferation of nuclear weapons and missiles— must be dealt with by strengthening the nuclear Non-Proliferation Treaty (NPT), which expires in 1995. To ensure the NPT's renewal, the 5 nuclear powers should agree to a total ban on testing and producing new or modernized nuclear weapons, formally undertake to reduce and eliminate their nuclear arsenals, and pledge to defend any nonnuclear country that is threatened with or subjected to a nuclear attack. Another approach to eliminating nuclear weapons is to revive the Baruch Plan, which was rejected in 1945. The plan called for creating a UN international atomic development authority under the control of the Security Council, which would have custody of a few nuclear weapons for deterrence, and preventing individual states from owning nuclear weapons.

The owe-as-you-go plan. Vicki Kemper. *Common Cause Magazine* 17:6–7 My/Je '91

The United States owes the UN millions of dollars. In the early 1980s, the United States started withholding some UN dues for political reasons, and Congress voted in 1985 to withhold 20 percent of the U.S. payment until the UN altered its budgeting and staffing policies. Although the UN's stock has appreciated considerably since then, the United States currently owes the UN almost $300 million in back dues plus another $271 million in 1991 dues. In contrast, Iraq's account is paid in full, and the Soviet Union's debt equals about 1 percent of America's. The Bush administration has promised to wipe out America's UN deficit, and Congress decided in 1990 to pay the country's UN dues for that year in full plus 20 percent of the U.S. debt.

Bush's ambivalence. David Callahan. *Commonweal* 119:9–10 Mr 13 '92

President Bush's new attentiveness to the UN should be encouraged, but he and the U.S. foreign policy establishment must first learn to place their trust in the politics of cooperation and the rule of law. Until now, Bush's foreign policy has been shaped by a desire to retain global primacy and the freedom of action that comes with such a position. During the Persian Gulf crisis, Washington, not the UN Security Council, took the lead in condemning Iraq, and Washington, not the council, ran the resulting war. As a result, Operation Desert Shield and Operation Desert Storm can hardly be cited as ideal examples of collective security. Nevertheless, the Bush administration has helped fuel great momentum in favor of cooperation and international law, particularly now that the cold war is over. Washington must realize that both U.S. security and U.S. prosperity are best guaranteed in the long run within a genuine partnership of countries.

NGOs and the United Nations system. *Environment* 34:16 Je '92

The UN is encouraging non-governmental organizations (NGOs), with which the UN has a long tradition of cooperation, to participate in the 1992 UN Conference on Environment and Development, which will be held in Rio de Janeiro. The focus of NGO activity at the conference will be the 1992 Global Forum, a series of simultaneous, independent events featuring the International NGO Forum; the Inter-Sectoral Dialogue; the Parliamentary Earth Summit; events that will focus on the world's indigenous peoples; meetings and workshops on women's issues; events focusing on children and young people; and an International Forum of Arts, Culture, and Environment. Participation in the Global Forum and the UN's system of formal relations with NGOs are discussed.

A new role for the U.N. Konstantin Kolenda. *The Humanist* 51:42+ Jl/Ag '91

The UN must act as an arbiter for the newly resurgent ethnic and nationalistic disputes that are threatening to erupt into violence. At a time when it seemed possible to hope for global peace, tensions between the nuclear powers have been replaced by bitter and explosive local wars. History shows that it is possible for different ethnic groups to live harmoniously while preserving their unique heritages. The UN could help foster such harmony by serving as an impartial third party, hearing and arbitrating conflicts between a country's feuding ethnic groups.

Stepping into the fray. Hilary Mackenzie. *Maclean's* 105:18–20 Ap 20 '92

The UN is increasing its worldwide activism. By the end of May, the UN will have 44,000 troops deployed worldwide, up from 11,500 in February. It has initiated 10 peacekeeping missions since 1988, compared with 13 in the previous 40 years. The increased UN presence has prompted some Third World countries to complain that the agency might unnecessarily intervene in their affairs on such pretenses as stopping human rights abuses or hunting terrorists. Because of increased mission costs, which will hit an annual $3.2 billion by April 1993, the UN may have to stall new deployments and scale back existing ones, such as the mission in Cyprus. To bolster funds, Russia has proposed a plan to allow multinational corporations to fund missions. Some diplomats have suggested a 1 percent levy on arms sales and a tax on international airline tickets.

On the firing line [Canadians part of UN peacekeeping operations; special section; with editorial comment by Kevin Doyle]. *Maclean's* 105:4, 24–6+ My 4 '92

A special section examines Yugoslavia's civil war. Since June 1991, Yugoslavia has been witness to a civil war that has claimed an estimated 10,000 lives and is threatening to spread beyond the federation's borders. The fighting began when the Yugoslavian republics of Slovenia and Croatia declared independence, prompting Serbia, the federation's largest republic and staunchest defender, to send armed forces into Croatia in support of that republic's ethnic Serbian minority. In April, the UN dispatched a peacekeeping force of 14,000, of whom 1,200 are Canadians. The writer describes the devastation he observed when he accompanied Canadian soldiers on patrol along Croatia's battlefront. Related articles discuss Yugoslavia's history of ethnic tension and the spread of the civil war to the republic of Bosnia and Hercegovina.

A potential landmark for female human rights. Gayle Kirshenbaum. *Ms.* 2:13 S/O '91

Experts have proposed the first UN Convention Against Sexual Exploitation, a measure that seems a necessary response to massive increases in global prostitution and efforts to promote prostitution as a legitimate profession and desirable lifestyle. The initiative is framed around the rights of women in prostitution and would broaden all women's rights. A report of an international meeting of experts, held by the Coalition Against Trafficking in Women (a UN non-governmental organization) and the Unesco Division of Human Rights and Peace indicates that there is currently no international instrument that explicitly stipulates it is a human right to be free of sexual exploitation. The proposal rejects regulation and decriminalization as well as criminalization of prostitution, and it penalizes the customers and pimps, not the women. The points of the convention proposal are listed.

Hello, Ghali. *The Nation* 253:763–4 D 16 '91

The UN Security Council has chosen Boutros Boutros Ghali, Egypt's foreign minister, to be the new UN secretary-general. Boutros Ghali was selected because he is from the Southern Hemisphere, a qualification apparently demanded by France and China. There was also strong sentiment among the nonaligned countries that an African should hold the post. Boutros Ghali's primary area of expertise is Africa, where he has helped mediate conflicts in the western Sahara and Liberia on behalf of the Organization of African Unity. He supports the privatization wing of Egypt's ruling National Democratic Party and serves as the deputy secretary of the Socialist International. Now 68 and in poor health, he is expected to serve only 1 term.

Watching rights. Aryeh Neier. *The Nation* 254:775 Je 8 '92

The UN's efforts in war-ravaged Cambodia have been extensive and commendable. Under the agreement signed in October 1991 by the government of Cambodia and the 3 military factions combating it, a UN Transitional Authority in Cambodia (UNTAC) has been established under the direction of senior UN diplomat Yasushi Akashi of Japan. Akashi's responsibilities include the repatriation and resettlement of 375,000 refugees living in border camps, the demobilization and disarmament of 70 percent of the 200,000 troops from all combatant forces and a comparable number of militiamen, and the drafting of the law under which free and fair national elections, the first in Cambodia's history, are to take place by May 1993. Although UNTAC has made some mistakes, its mission is generally being carried out well and has a chance of success. If the UN can breathe new life into Cambodia, the world will turn to it to help other devastated countries.

Russia slips into the Soviet seat. Gertrude Samuels. *The New Leader* 75:5–7 F 10–24 '92

Russia took over the Soviet Union's seat in the 15-nation UN Security Council without debate or a vote. The move was set in motion when Russian president Boris Yeltsin sent a letter to the UN last December 24 stating that Russia would occupy the Soviet Union's council seat. The action was approved by the shaky Commonwealth of Independent States' 10 other republics and came after the General Assembly had finished its work for the year and dispersed. Knowledgeable observers say that, for the foreseeable future, Russia can be expected to maintain the relatively low key, cooperative posture assumed by Mikhail Gorbachev before his ouster. Still, a random sampling of diplomats reveals that some are reacting to the move with mixed emotions, and others with a tinge of bitterness. The reactions of UN diplomats from Poland, Nigeria, Canada, Saudi Arabia, Czechoslovakia, and Israel to the Russian role in the UN are discussed.

Territorial integrity is not sacred. *New Perspectives Quarterly* 8:24–7 Fall '91

Part of an issue on nationalism and global integration. In an interview, Brian Urquhart, scholar-in-residence at the Ford Foundation and, from 1974 to 1986, undersecretary-general of the UN, discusses how the UN will face the growing conflict between national sovereignty and interdependence: The basic question about national sovereignty is how the world is going to reach a working agreement balancing national sovereignty, which is the foundation of the UN, and international responsibility, which is the UN's mission. For humanitarian and environmental reasons, the ground rules must be rewritten. The only way to accomplish this is through the promulgation of universally applied and enforceable international law. The upcoming Brazil Conference on Environment and Development will be a critical test of how much sovereignty nations and governments are willing to cede for the common good of the planet.

In a new era and groping. John Newhouse. *The New Yorker* 67:90–104 D 16 '91

Although the end of the cold war has enabled the UN to take a larger and more useful role in world affairs than ever before, the organization faces an array of problems that could limit its effectiveness. The 5 permanent members of the Security Council—the United States, Britain, France, China, and the Soviet Union—rarely exercise their veto power anymore, but working by consensus doesn't necessarily make difficult tasks easier, as the recently concluded process of choosing a new secretary-general attests. Eventually, the job was awarded to Egyptian deputy prime minister for foreign affairs Boutros Boutros Ghali, who has vowed to institute the wide range of reforms that the Security Council's members advocate. In addition to daunting budgetary difficulties, Boutros Ghali must cope with questions concerning the expansion of the council, the revision of the UN charter, and the role of the United States in the UN.

A man for all nations. Bonnie Angelo. *Time* 138:28 D 2 '91

Boutros Boutros Ghali is the first African to be appointed UN secretary-general. The election of the Egyptian diplomat marked a victory for the UN's African bloc. Boutros Ghali brings strong qualifications to the world forum's helm. The Egyptian deputy prime minister is an expert in international law and has a record filled with degrees, decorations, and scholarly writings in 3 languages. He helped negotiate the Camp David peace process, and he was involved in the mediation of many quarrels among African countries.

Challenge for the new boss. Bonnie Angelo. *Time* 139:28–30 F 3 '92

The UN's new secretary-general, Boutros Boutros Ghali, must reform the organization's bloated bureaucracy. Despite its vast assets, the UN is overstaffed, underfunded, and mismanaged, and its endeavors are often badly conceived or hobbled by petty politics. Many of the UN's problems stem from its elaborate and entrenched system of patronage. Of the organization's many specialized agencies, some have proved to be embarrassing, and others have outlived their usefulness. There does appear to be a movement toward reform, however. Thirty concerned ambassadors have presented a blueprint for reform to the new secretary-general, who has since pledged to eliminate whatever is wasteful or obsolete.

The U.N. marches in. Jill Smolowe. *Time* 139:32–3 Mr 23 '92

UN peacekeeping forces, in their most ambitious undertaking to date, have been assigned to bring peace and stability to Cambodia and Yugoslavia. UN forces are supposed to disarm and disband combatants, prepare for the return of hundreds of thousands of refugees, and see that political negotiations can be conducted in Yugoslavia and democratic elections can take place in Cambodia. The operations will cost more than 3 times the amount that the UN spent on global peacekeeping in 1991. Nevertheless, UN diplomats hold that the price of peace, while steep, is less costly in the long run than letting war rage. The tasks ahead for UN troops in Yugoslavia, where hostilities continue to flare between the Serbs and Croatians despite a formal cease-fire, and in Cambodia, where the troops of Hun Sen's government and 3 rebel factions must be dispersed, are discussed. The annual costs of the 9 ongoing UN peacekeeping assignments and of the new missions are listed.

Peacekeeping loves company. Strobe Talbott. *Time* 139:54 My 18 '92

The Pentagon is planning to shift its focus from fighting World War III to dealing with major regional conflicts. Military planners are trying to keep their options open so that the United States can act on its own to conduct a campaign such as the invasion of Panama, but whenever possible, the Pentagon would prefer that U.S. forces lead UN troops in a campaign like the Persian Gulf War. However, there is a trickier third contingency—that U.S. forces might participate in a multinational UN peacekeeping mission led by a non-American general. That prospect makes some Pentagon officials uneasy, but Gen. Colin Powell, the chairman of the Joint Chiefs of Staff, is much less grudging about multilateral operations in general and the UN in particular.

Human Rights Commission approves principles to protect rights of mentally ill. *UN Chronicle* 28:36–9 Je '91

The UN Commission on Human Rights adopted 82 resolutions and 8 decisions during its 47th session, which took place in Geneva between January 28 and March 8, 1991. The commission endorsed a draft set of principles for the protection of the mentally ill and for the improvement of mental health care. It also asked the General Assembly to declare a Third Decade to Combat Racism and Racial Discrimination, to begin in 1993. Other commission decisions and statements dealt with human rights and the environment, the export of hazardous wastes to Africa, the rights of children and migrant women, contemporary forms of slavery, the rights of minorities and indigenous people, unacknowledged detention, judicial impartiality, and human rights situations in 13 specific countries.

Preparing the world for disaster. UN Chronicle 28:40–55 Je '91

A special section focuses on international disaster relief and prevention. Such natural disasters as locust plagues, earthquakes, cyclones, wildfires, avalanches, tornadoes, volcanic eruptions, and floods claim more than 1 million lives each decade. These events can collapse buildings, contaminate air and food supplies, and devastate water supplies and waste removal systems, leading to disease, malnutrition, and population displacement. Most natural disasters cannot be prevented, but advance preparation can limit their impact. To promote such mitigation efforts, the UN General Assembly declared the 1990s the International Decade for Natural Disaster Reduction. Articles cover activities related to this decade, the Office of the UN Disaster Relief Co-ordinator, the impact of Hurricane Hugo, and scientific techniques for disaster prediction, risk evaluation, and damage assessment.

And the debate continues. *UN Chronicle* 28:59 S '91

During its 45th session, the UN General Assembly considered a number of proposals to restructure the Economic and Social Council. Delegates from five Scandinavian countries suggested that in some cases, the assembly should authorize the council to make final decisions on reports from subsidiary bodies. The 12 countries of the European Community recommended that some of the council's subsidiary bodies be merged, abolished, modified, or expertized. The Group of 77 asked that the council's membership be readjusted in 1992 to ensure equitable geographical representation.

Dag Hammarskjold: virtuoso of multilateral diplomacy. *UN Chronicle* 28:74–5 S '91

Dag Hammarskjold, the second secretary-general of the UN, was an exceptional international leader by any standard. The son of a Swedish family with a long tradition of public service, Hammarskjold earned a Master's degree in political economy from Uppsala University in 1930 and a Ph.D. in economics from the University of Stockholm in 1934. Between 1936 and 1953, he served his country as undersecretary of finance, chairman of the national bank's board of governors, undersecretary in the foreign office, and vice-minister of foreign affairs. While serving as UN secretary-general from 1953 to 1961, he displayed great skill at mastering specific issues and policies and at dealing with prominent world leaders. He died in an airplane crash in 1961 while traveling to the Congo on a peace mission.

Fresh hope in South-east Asia. *UN Chronicle* 28:53–4 S '91

Part of a special section on the world refugee crisis. The Comprehensive Plan of Action for Indochinese refugees, adopted in June 1989, establishes a legal framework to address the problem of refugees and asylum seekers from Vietnam and Laos. Over the past 15 years, 2 million people have left Indochina. The number of people leaving under the Orderly Departure Programme has risen steadily in recent years, while the number of refugees arriving by boat has diminished. Thousands of Vietnamese and Laotians have returned to their homelands, where the governments have promised amnesty and assistance to returnees, and the prospect of peace in Cambodia has prompted the UN High Commissioner for Refugees to intensify its preparations for repatriating Cambodian refugees. Approximately 500,000 Indochinese remain in camps throughout Southeast Asia, however.

Interpreters: life inside the glass booth. Elsa B. Endrst. *UN Chronicle* 28:72–3 S '91

The UN Interpretation Service employs 142 linguists from 22 countries to interpret multilingual deliberations at UN headquarters in New York and elsewhere around the world. Working in soundproof glass booths, they orally translate speeches as they are being delivered. The translators work in teams of 2, taking turns at the microphone that usually last 30 minutes each. According to Monique Corvington, the chief of the Interpretation Service, the job requires a thirst for knowledge, an ability to concentrate, and a thorough knowledge of at least 3 of the UN's working languages—Arabic, Chinese, English, French, Russian, and Spanish. Cultural differences, proverbs, idiomatic expressions, the emergence of new words and terms, and the wide range of subjects discussed all add challenges to the interpreters' work.

Women refugees: the caretakers adrift. *UN Chronicle* 28:51–2 S '91

Part of a special section on the world refugee crisis. Of the world's 15 million refugees, 75 percent are women and children. According to refugee officials, women asylum seekers require special attention because of the threat of sexual abuse and battery, economic exploitation, and discrimination. Many women refugees are single mothers who are faced with the task of feeding and caring for their children as well as themselves, and many have difficulty finding gainful employment because they are illiterate, unskilled, and destitute. Programs to assist women refugees must integrate women into every step of the asylum process while taking concrete steps to lessen the threat and impact of violence. The UN High Commissioner for Refugees and other refugee assistance organizations are working closely with such UN bodies as the UN Development Program, the UN Population Fund, and the UN Children's Fund to help women refugees become self sufficient.

Committee evaluates African recovery and sets New Agenda.
UN Chronicle 28:62–3 D '91

The UN General Assembly's Ad Hoc Committee of the Whole has formulated a plan for economic recovery and development in Africa. The UN New Agenda for the Development of Africa in the 1990s was adopted by consensus at the ad hoc committee's September 3–14 meeting and recommended for approval by the assembly. In its assessment of the previous 5-year plan, the committee noted that targets for growth, food security, human investment, and debt reduction had been missed and that many countries and the continent as a whole had experienced declines in these areas. The new agenda calls for innovative schemes to reduce the external debts of African countries, a feasibility study on the establishment of an African diversification fund, and political and economic reforms within African countries.

Boutros Boutros-Ghali of Egypt becomes sixth UN Secretary-General. *UN Chronicle* 29:2–5 Mr '92

Boutros Boutros Ghali, an Egyptian scholar and statesman, took office as the sixth UN secretary-general in January. Born in Cairo in 1922, Boutros Ghali has taught international law and international relations at the University of Cairo. As a member of the Egyptian diplomatic corps, he played a major role in the Egyptian-Israeli negotiations that produced the Camp David Accords in 1979. His candidacy was supported by the Organization of African Unity, which noted that no African had yet served as UN secretary-general. In his induction speech, he declared that his priorities would be to strengthen the UN's peacemaking and peacekeeping roles, narrow the economic gap between North and South, bolster fundamental freedoms and democratic institutions, and streamline the UN's administrative operations.

Democratic ships of state sailing through dangerous waters. *UN Chronicle* 29:43–9 Mr '92

Part of a special section on the 46th session of the UN General Assembly. Latin American and Caribbean speakers applauded the end of the cold war and the triumph of democracy but observed that political progress in their own region had not cured poverty and underdevelopment. They noted that despite progress toward ending warfare and the establishment of bilateral and multilateral political and economic ties, democratic regimes in Latin America might face trouble if they cannot meet popular demands for economic prosperity and social well being. In particular, they called for debt forgiveness and new assistance for development. Other issues of concern to the delegates included drug abuse, the Uruguay Round of international trade negotiations, and the environmental problems that will be discussed at the UN Conference on Environment and Development in Rio de Janeiro in June.

Goodbye to Perez de Cuellar: a most productive decade at the UN. *UN Chronicle* 29:6–8 Mr '92

During his 10 years as secretary-general, Peruvian diplomat Javier Perez de Cuellar led the UN to an unprecedented role in world affairs. Last fall, he noted that the thaw in the cold war and the major powers' new willingness to participate in UN activities had enabled the organization to move from the edge of international affairs to near the center. During his tenure, the UN played a role in the end of the Iran-Iraq War, the withdrawal of Soviet forces from Afghanistan, the emergence of Namibia as an independent country, the signing of peace accords for Cambodia, the release of most of the Western hostages in Lebanon, and an agreement on a peace plan for El Salvador. Perez de Cuellar has warned that the UN faces other complex challenges, including ethnic strife, political and economic inequality, disregard for human rights, and threats to the global environment.

Out of the shadows. *UN Chronicle* 29:88 Mr '92

A UN expert group has proposed a draft Declaration on Violence Against Women that will be considered by the UN Commission on the Status of Women in 1992. In a number of resolutions adopted during its 46th session, the General Assembly addressed the effects of poverty, underdevelopment, and ill health on women and women's contributions to environmental protection, population control, and sustainable development.

Zionism no longer equated with racism: Resolution 3379 rescinded! *UN Chronicle* 29:67 Mr '92

On December 16, 1991, the UN General Assembly repealed Resolution 3379, which declared that Zionism is a form of racism and racial discrimination. That resolution, adopted in November 1975, is only the second UN edict ever rescinded. The vote to abrogate Resolution 3379 was 111–25, with 13 countries abstaining. U.S. deputy secretary of state Lawrence Eagleburger, a prime mover in the repeal campaign, called the resolution a cold war relic and predicted that its repeal would assist efforts to bring peace to the Middle East. Khalil Makkawi of Lebanon, speaking for the Arab Group, warned that the repeal would set a dangerous precedent for the authority of other UN resolutions and would hamper the Middle East peace process by inflaming extremists on both sides.

Fact sheet: UN Security Council Resolutions 706 and 712 on Iraq. *US Department of State Dispatch* 2:697 S 23 '91

UN Security Council Resolutions 706 and 712 are summarized. Resolution 706 provides for a limited, one-time sale of oil from Iraq for the purpose of funding the purchase of humanitarian items needed by the people of Iraq and for Iraqi reparations of war damages. This resolution is implemented by Resolution 712.

Fact sheet: UN peace-keeping operations. *US Department of State Dispatch* 2:722 S 30 '91

Data are presented on UN peacekeeping operations in Kashmir, Palestine, Cyprus, the Golan Heights, Lebanon, Central America, the demilitarized zone between Iraq and Kuwait, the Western Sahara, El Salvador, and Angola.

The U.N.—a force at last. Richard Z. Chesnoff. *U.S. News & World Report* 112:12–13 F 10 '92

Once dismissed as a debating society, the UN is taking on renewed relevance. Through the UN, the world moved almost as one against Iraq's aggression. Since the Persian Gulf War, the UN has continued to stand up to Iraq, challenged Libyan terrorism, and agreed to send a peacekeeping force to Yugoslavia. Currently, the UN is stewarding the end of El Salvador's civil war, organizing a referendum in Morocco, and administering Cambodia. With the crumbling of the old world order and the reshuffling of the superpowers, the UN is gaining more prominence, but potential triumphs could be blocked by finances. The UN is in the red, costs are mounting, and global recession is inhibiting international willingness to give money. Meanwhile, smaller members are pushing for more clout, and new secretary-general Boutros Boutros Ghali is reportedly planning a shakeup to keep the UN on its new course.

The new world chaos. Robin Knight. *U.S. News & World Report* 112:10–11 My 4 '92

The UN is having a difficult time finding the money to carry out its mission. Today, UN officials are struggling to broker cease-fires in Afghanistan and Somalia, implement a reconstruction project in Cambodia, oversee Angola's cease-fire, check on Saddam Hussein's military ambitions, and address problems in Yugoslavia. Meanwhile, the United States and its allies are having trouble funding the UN because of deficits, the recession, and falling public support for foreign entanglements. Dozens of nations are behind in their UN dues, including the United States, which owes $555 million.

Architects of democracy. Susan V. Lawrence. *U.S. News & World Report* 112:54–5 My 18 '92

In Cambodia, the UN is undertaking its most ambitious and expensive operation ever. The $2.3 billion mission seeks to ensure the end of 22 years of civil war, prepare the devastated society for its first democratic elections, and build political institutions that will endure after international monitors are removed. The efforts have been hindered, however, by the murderous Khmer Rouge, which has barred UN forces from some areas and resisted UN attempts to map mine fields. As a result, the UN has not been able to enforce the cease-fire, and it has not completed the task of finding sites for camps where the 200,000 troops of Cambodia's 4 armies are to start reporting in June.

United Nations and the future of global peace. Ronald E. Powaski. *USA Today* (Periodical) 120:19–20 N '91

The peacekeeping capabilities of the UN should be strengthened. The UN has enjoyed more success in ending wars than in preventing conflicts, mostly because its peacekeeping forces are small, lightly armed, and usually dispatched to monitor cease-fires after a conflict has ended. The UN needs more substantial military might at its disposal if it is to prevent wars. To this end, some countries advocate the creation of a permanent UN peacekeeping force. The UN also needs to improve its ability to resolve conflicts before they reach the crisis stage. Among other things, the UN should cooperate more closely with regional defense organizations and send fact finding missions to potential trouble spots. Other measures that would boost the UN's peacekeeping capabilities include utilizing the World Court more fully and ensuring that the UN receives adequate financing.

Consent within nations, cooperation between nations. Douglas Hurd. *Vital Speeches of the Day* 58:16–18 O 1 [O 15] '91

The U.K. secretary of state for foreign and commonwealth affairs addresses the 46th session of the UN General Assembly in New York City: The principle of empire is collapsing. The empire put together by the Russian czars, which Lenin and Stalin transformed into a Communist empire, has been destroyed, and a new system that tries to accommodate the principle of national identity is struggling to be born. Though nationalism is a legitimate expression of a people's aspirations, it can be sterile if it fails to respect the rights of individuals and minorities, and it can be dangerous if nation-states don't work together for collective security and collective prosperity. The goals of consent within countries and cooperation between nations are within reach, however, and the British government will work within the UN to help them be grasped.

Solidarity. François Mitterrand. *Vital Speeches of the Day* 58:292–3 Mr 1 '92

In an address before the UN Security Council in New York, French president Francois Mitterrand proposes steps toward achieving collective military and economic security in the world. He calls for the creation of new instruments of global action, such as a chemical weapons ban and an arms-free zone; a renewed human rights role for Unesco; a commitment to reducing military spending in order to aid development; and the creation of new approaches to aiding those countries that have been unable to make real progress toward development.

An old structure in a new world. S. Nihal Singh. *World Press Review* 38:20–1 D '91

An article excerpted from the Hindustan Times of New Delhi. Democracy may have replaced communism in Eastern and Central Europe and in the Soviet Union, but it has not taken hold in the UN. The original goal of the UN charter—to have the 5 permanent members of the Security Council police the world—appears to be coming to fruition now that the UN is no longer an ideological battleground for the United States and the Soviet Union. The so-called Big Five—Britain, China, France, the United States, and the Soviet Union—do not reflect the power equations of today's world, namely the stature of Germany and Japan and the massive expansion in UN membership. Instead, the UN has become an instrument of U.S. policy, as the Security Council's conduct during the Persian Gulf War demonstrated. This U.S. dominance makes it unlikely that the council will be expanded or that General Assembly will be given greater powers.

The new boss will work for the third world. Dieter Buhl and Fredy Gstelger. *World Press Review* 39:22–3 F '92

An article excerpted from Die Zeit of Hamburg. In an interview, UN secretary-general Boutros Boutros Ghali discusses what he hopes to accomplish in the world through his new position, how well the UN has served thus far in mediating international relations, the effect of the end of the cold war on the UN's influence in the world, his fear that European and other countries in the North are becoming too involved in their own problems to help countries in the South, the UN's role in bringing peace to the Middle East, and whether Europeans should take a greater role in the Mideast peace process. He notes that an international organization such as the UN is critical for reminding the rest of the world of the needs of the Third World. He also points out that he is less interested in obtain-

ing financial or technical assistance for the South than he is in having the
North pay attention, on a political level, to events that take place there.

A poor record on human rights. Catharine Lumby. *World Press Review* 39:35 Ap '92

An article excerpted from the Sydney Morning Herald. The UN has
never acted on its mandate to promote and protect human rights. Today,
there are more than 15 million refugees worldwide, a figure that has
doubled in the past 10 years. During the same period, resources available
to the UN high commissioner for refugees have barely been increased. A
radical reassessment of UN policy is needed to determine the grounds for
which international intervention is appropriate. One sign of progress is a
recent UN resolution guaranteeing humanitarian intervention in refugee
crises. Other reforms under consideration include giving the UN Security
Council authority to order arms embargoes and other sanctions, the use
of UN-sanctioned crisis prevention forces, and a stronger UN role in
preventive diplomacy.